100 Years of Permanent Revolution

T0329621

100 Years of Permanent Revolution

Results and Prospects

Edited by
BILL DUNN and HUGO RADICE

Pluto Press

First published 2006 by Pluto Press
345 Archway Road, London N6 5AA
and 839 Greene Street, Ann Arbor, MI 48106

www.plutobooks.com

British Library Cataloguing in Publication Data
A catalogue record for this book is available from the British Library

ISBN 978 0 7453 2521 7 paperback
ISBN 978 0 7453 2522 4 hardback
ISBN 978 1 8496 4320 7 PDF

Library of Congress Cataloging in Publication Data applied for

10   9   8   7   6   5   4   3   2   1

Designed and produced for Pluto Press by
Chase Publishing Services Ltd, Fortescue, Sidmouth, EX10 9QG, England
Typeset from disk by Stanford DTP Services, Northampton, England
Printed and bound by CPI Group (UK) Ltd, Croydon, CR0 4YY

Contents

1

Permanent Revolution: Results and Prospects 100 Years On[1]

Hugo Radice and Bill Dunn

The year 2006 marks the centenary of the publication of Trotsky's *Results and Prospects*. This short essay gave the first considered articulation of his theory of permanent revolution. In a sense, it therefore represents the founding document or original sin of 'Trotskyism'. The elaboration and defence of its perspective would remain a primary feature of Trotsky's political life (Deutscher 1954).

The basic ideas are straightforward. We will elaborate briefly below, while several of the subsequent chapters illuminate particular aspects in more detail. In short, Trotsky rejected a 'stages' theory of revolution – that Russia would have to wait until capitalism was fully developed before socialism could be put on the agenda. Any Russian revolution had to be understood not in isolation, but as a world event both in its causes and its consequences. Despite its absolute 'backwardness', competition with the West, and penetration of capital from the West, produced vast concentrations of workers capable of challenging Tsarist power. Russia alone lacked the material basis for establishing socialism, but the seizure of power by a workers' government could lead an international revolutionary process. On a world scale, the development of capitalism already provided ample economic foundations for socialism.

The last 100 years have not produced the envisaged international revolution. Meanwhile several attempts to build socialisms on a national basis have produced monstrous dictatorships. These also provided easy targets for the defenders of capitalism and the status quo. With the collapse of the Soviet Union, for many the Marxist project is redundant and its continued articulation at best quaint. Yet reading Trotsky today one is struck by his potential relevance. The contemporary talk of 'globalisation' again insists, with Trotsky, that we have to understand the world in its interconnections.

1. Thanks to Carmen Couceiro Vicos for her comments on an earlier version of this chapter.

National economies are not separate and independent either from each other or from a global capitalist system. Still we experience poverty and 'backwardness' alongside extremes of wealth and the latest technology. Again, we still grapple with the problems of the causes and consequences of that world system's unevenness and with the relations between economic and political action. These are longstanding questions of social science, but they are being played out with renewed urgency in the anti-globalisation or anti-capitalist movement.

The reputation of Trotsky's theory has varied with that of its author. Perhaps most commonly it has suffered the worst of fates: neglect. Initially printed in small numbers and quickly suppressed, even many leading Russian Marxists, including Lenin, had not read *Results and Prospects* before the successful revolution of 1917. Afterwards, for a while, the coincidence of Trotsky's thinking with that of the Bolsheviks, whom he joined in 1917, and his own leading role in the revolution and early Soviet republic, made his works essential reading. *Results and Prospects* was republished in Moscow, and translated and used by the sympathising communist parties around the world. It was accepted as a prophetic account of the development of the Russian Revolution. Moreover, its analysis also informed strategy beyond Russia, particularly in other poorer countries. However, the revolutionary wave which swept Europe, and on which workers' power in Russia depended according to Trotsky's theory, soon waned. Stalin's triumph again marginalised Trotsky and his supporters. The theory's denial of the possibility of successfully establishing socialism in one country rendered it incompatible with the new aims of the Soviet leadership.

Thereafter, *Results and Prospects* and the theory of Permanent Revolution have lived something of a twilight existence. Trotsky's explicit self-defence, published as *Permanent Revolution*, was printed in runs not much larger than *Results and Prospects*. It was repudiated by the political mainstreams both East and West – it was anathema equally to apologists of capitalism and to those of 'actually existing socialism'. Meanwhile, the sheer weight of vilification understandably put some of Trotsky's supporters on the defensive, and may thereby have contributed to some formulaic interpretations rather than critical reflection and strategic application.

As a result, if this volume hopes to rescue the theory from wholly inappropriate neglect or opprobrium, it does so in a spirit of sympathetic but critical appraisal. Trotsky was not infallible, and his work is open to various interpretations, but he produced original and important contributions to Marxist theory, which are still well worth revisiting.

Subsequent chapters will situate Trotsky's theory within a wider tradition of Marxist and other socialist writing, discuss some of the problems and reconsider its contemporary relevance. The book is overtly partial in two senses. It does not claim to offer a comprehensive or definitive survey, and cannot hope to consider all the historical experiences or places where it might be used today. We particularly regret that it was not possible to include more Southern perspectives. Furthermore, all the authors are broadly sympathetic to Trotsky's project – some are members of avowedly Trotskyist organisations – but all try to examine his contribution in a constructive way, avoiding either demonology or hagiography. Many of the pieces look beyond *Results and Prospects* and examine the world according to its spirit rather than its letter. We hope that together they will help to rehabilitate an important contribution to Marxist theory which, whatever flaws it may have, can continue to stimulate and inform a wide range of contemporary debates.

In the rest of this introduction, rather than outline the subsequent chapters, which are short enough to speak for themselves, we briefly sketch Trotsky's argument and outline its significance. The reader should be warned, of course, that questions of interpretation and application remain hotly disputed.

'Permanent Revolution', as Trotsky acknowledges, was a rather 'high-flown expression [which] defines the thought that the Russian revolution, although directly concerned with bourgeois aims, could not stop short at those aims' (1971:8). The term appears to have been coined by Marx, writing about the 1848 revolutions. Although his usage differs somewhat from that of Trotsky, for both authors it conveys more the idea of continuing or uninterrupted rather than perpetual or never-ending revolution (Draper 1978:201).

Marx did at one point consider the possibility that Russia might skip capitalism and move towards socialism based on communal peasant traditions (Marx 1970). However, for the most part, particularly after Marx's death, orthodoxy saw development as a gradual evolution, with more backward countries mimicking the progress of the more advanced. Unlike various earlier utopian proposals, historical materialism maintained that capitalist industrial development was a necessary precursor of socialism. It created the material basis for an advanced classless society and a working class, united by their common propertylessness, and in practice brought together in ever-larger firms and workplaces, which could achieve this. The success of the most economically advanced countries would force others to follow a similar economic course and their political development would accordingly have to go through a similar phase of 'bourgeois' democracy before socialism became a realistic prospect. Countries that had not yet had bourgeois revolutions along the lines of the great French Revolution needed to do so to begin the process of capitalist accumulation, itself a necessary precondition for socialism.

In Russia this position was exemplified in the Menshevik programme of support for an anticipated bourgeois or capitalist revolution. Russian Marxism had split in 1903, initially over organisational questions. Soon, however, political differences developed, with the Mensheviks becoming the more moderate wing, the Bolsheviks the more radical. Initially, however, particularly in the heady revolutionary months of 1905, the separation and this distinction were far from clear-cut. Nevertheless, broadly speaking, for the Mensheviks, workers could not be expected to play an independent role, but should rather support the bourgeoisie against Tsarism. Any prospects for workers' power in Russia lay in the distant future. The best Marxists could do was to encourage capitalist development and liberal democracy. To expect more was 'utopian', the antithesis of 'scientific socialism'.

The Bolsheviks had a slightly more complex position. They agreed with the fundamental proposition that Russian development along bourgeois democratic lines was necessary. However, they believed the Russian capitalist class to be too politically weak, too dependent on Tsarism, to effect such a transformation. Instead, an alliance of workers and peasants could achieve the democratic revolution and crush reaction. This would involve confiscating large landed estates and introducing pro-labour reforms such as the eight-hour day. But it could not go much further than this; Russia was still a backward agrarian country requiring a prolonged period of capitalist development before it became ripe for a genuinely socialist transformation.

Trotsky argues something more subtle. In particular, Russian 'results and prospects' in the light of the 1905 revolution were not simply a Russian phenomenon but were conditioned by Russia's relations with the rest of the world.

Although the particular argument is original, Trotsky articulates a version of Marxism which can be traced to Marx's own writings, and elements of which can be found amongst his more sophisticated followers. Trotsky himself had begun to develop his ideas in collaboration with fellow emigre Alexander Parvus in Germany in the years before 1905. He also cites approvingly and develops ideas from Karl Kautsky, the leading theoretician of the German Social Democratic Party (SPD). But Trotsky's perspective is also crucially shaped by the experiences of the 1905 revolution in Russia. Here, suddenly, in this backward country, were not only mass strikes but also a new form of alternative government, the workers' council or soviet. These were bodies of deputies, directly elected and immediately accountable to the workers who elected them. Trotsky himself had become the chairman of the key St Petersburg Soviet of Workers' Deputies during the final days of the revolution.

Written during the revolution and while Trotsky was awaiting trial in its immediate aftermath, *Results and Prospects* was an attempt to combine the lessons of the experiences of that revolution with a Marxist analysis of Russian and world capitalist development. It was this combination of the peculiar and the general, an analysis of the specifics of the Russian Revolution but within the wider global context, that provided the basic prerequisite for an adequate evaluation of strategy and tactics for Russian Marxists.

In 1906 Trotsky argued that Russia was indeed in most respects a backward, mainly agrarian society, less than 50 years from the emancipation from serfdom. The vast majority of the population were peasants rather than proletarians. The state was an absolutist monarchy, whose concessions to constitutional rule were few and ephemeral. There was relatively little capitalist economic development and no 'bourgeois' democracy. But it was not simply backward.

However, history does not march forward with each country following a common blueprint and progressing through discrete stages. Rather it is profoundly uneven – it occurs differently in different places, with the more 'backward' influenced by what has gone before elsewhere. This also means that different developmental 'levels' or 'stages' may be combined, found together at the same time in the same country.

Therefore, the conditions of the classically 'bourgeois' French Revolution were not recreated in 1848 and were still less likely to recur in twentieth-century Russia. In France in 1789 'the bourgeoisie, consistently in all its factions, regarded itself as the leader of the nation, rallied the masses to the struggle, gave them slogans and dictated their fighting tactics' (Trotsky 1962: 185). No class capable of playing this role existed in Russia, where capitalism was too cowardly, being either 'an offspring of the State' (1962:173) or 'to a considerable extent of foreign origin' (1962:181). The urban petty-bourgeois *sans-culottes*, so crucial in France, simply did not exist. Trotsky therefore condemned as the method of Mensheviks and 'educated philistines' the reduction of social analysis to 'crude historical analogies' (1962:161). We should not expect the actors to play out the parts assigned to them by previous revolutions (although in identifying Stalin's rise to power as the Russian 'Thermidor' it could be argued that Trotsky himself did not always heed his own advice).

However, this does not simply lead to pessimism about the prospects for revolutionary transformation. Russian development could not simply be understood as peculiar and uneven. It was also combined in two senses. Firstly, in its integration into the world economy, which had a number of important aspects. In particular, the Tsarist state devoted a huge proportion of its resources to competing militarily with more advanced capitalist powers. On the one hand, this exacerbated the general backwardness, taking surpluses that might otherwise have been invested more productively. On the other hand, it brought into Russia first the products and then the machines of Western capitalism. Industrial output, and particularly productivity levels, were still low by Western standards, but these rocketed in the last years of the mid nineteenth century, particularly in military-related areas like railway building, iron production and oil. Thus initially through the intermediary of the state and later in the form of direct investments, Western capital shaped Russian political economy.

Rather than a gradual development through petty-commodity production, with workers in small-scale manufacturing, in Russia 'the proletariat immediately found itself concentrated in tremendous masses, while between the masses and the autocracy there stood a capitalist bourgeoisie, very small in numbers, isolated from the "people", half-foreign, without historical traditions, and inspired only by the greed for gain' (Trotsky 1962:183). So while the bourgeoisie was reckoned unwilling and unfit to make a revolution, the working class was much more concentrated than Russia's overall level of 'backwardness' would suggest. Already by the turn of the century, the proportion of Russian workers in 'large enterprises', those of more than 500 or 1,000 employees, was much higher than it was, for example, in Germany or Belgium (Trotsky 1971). The potential this gave workers was recognised by the Bolsheviks. But for them, because workers remained a small minority within a backward country lacking the material basis for the construction of socialism, they would have to rein in their demands, to pursue only a certain minimum programme of reform.

For Trotsky, in contrast, Russian development was also combined in a second sense. Rather than being discrete, stages of Russian development were combined. A society in many ways still feudal also experienced some of the most advanced forms of capitalism and with them the potential to move beyond them. Accordingly, the proletariat 'must adopt the tactics of *permanent revolution*, i.e., must destroy the barriers between the minimum and maximum programme of Social Democracy' (Trotsky 1962:163). Russian workers could not be expected to stop short at bourgeois democratic demands. The 1905 revolution had already raised the possibility of Soviet power, of workers combining the bourgeois and socialist revolutions. This did not abandon historical materialism, and in particular the insistence on an adequate material basis for socialism. The bourgeoisie ruled in all capitalist countries and while it would be 'false, dead, scholastic' to describe all countries taken separately as ripe for socialism the 'world economy in its entirety [wa]s indubitably ripe' (Trotsky 1962:130).

Trotsky's understanding of the revolution was substantially borne out in 1917, when Lenin and the Bolsheviks came to offer a similar prognosis and lead the October Revolution. This did indeed also provide a massive impulse to other revolutionary movements, particularly in Europe, and for the next few years the prospect of international workers' revolution seemed very real. Ultimately, of course, the revolutions elsewhere failed and Russia remained isolated. A very different form of society emerged in the USSR from that which its founders had envisaged.

In *Results and Prospects*, Trotsky's emphasis was very much on Russia. In the late 1920s he generalised his theory in *Permanent Revolution*, now also looking particularly at the experiences in China. There, the bourgeoisie again failed to lead a democratic national revolution, while despite the absolute backwardness of the country, a mass workers' movement had threatened a much more radical transformation. However, unlike 1917 in Russia, the Chinese Communist Party under Soviet instruction had joined and then been massacred by the 'bourgeois' nationalist Guomindang of Chiang Kaishek. For Trotsky this was a reversion to, and underlined the failures of, the earlier Menshevik strategy. Not only in Russia, but also in other poorer countries like China, the bourgeoisie was now too cowardly, too closely linked to existing states and international imperialist relations to lead a democratic revolution. Conversely, the Chinese experience showed that in other countries too the intrusion of global capitalism had again created a working class which had the potential to lead a revolution.

This generalisation of the theory was less conspicuously successful as general prognosis. The twentieth century witnessed numerous revolutions. Often workers did play a crucial role. Elsewhere peasant movements were led by communists while still other revolutions described themselves as socialist of one form or another, either before or after winning power. However, some rather optimistic readings of various Third World regimes notwithstanding, nowhere was there a sustained repetition of soviet forms of government. Revolutions remained national and limited rather than international and permanent and with them, for most observers, rested the fate (and indeed the very meaning) of socialism.

Small, if numerous, groups of supporters kept Trotsky's theory alive. Their defence of the faith provided a vital organisational as well as theoretical link with his revolutionary project. However, the isolation and frequent need to defend Trotsky from various calumnies and incomprehension involved problems of its own. Trotsky warned precisely against the repetition of formulae as 'supra-historical dogma, with no attempt to analyse the living historical experiences' (1962: 3). Sometimes Trotsky was read as providing a general repudiation of the possibility of 'bourgeois' or 'national' revolution in the developing world – and of the simultaneous possibility of workers' revolution *everywhere*. At the same time, Trotsky's creative approach to political analysis prefigured several of the more innovative later contributions by Marxists such as Gramsci and Lukács, with their emphasis on the need to understand the complexities of class formation and the role of class consciousness and ideas in shaping revolts from below.

We should therefore emphasise that Trotsky describes the *tactics* of permanent revolution. In places there is undoubtedly hyperbole, which might indicate an inevitable trajectory, but this suggests something more cautious. While it is only in 1917 that Trotsky accepts Lenin's organising model, he was, from the beginning, advocating party policy, tactics, a means of achieving a particular, optimal outcome. He was therefore not insisting either that proletarian dictatorship will necessarily happen or that no other outcome is possible, rather that the democratic revolution will be carried through to its 'victorious end' only if the proletariat leads the masses. If this does not happen 'the struggle for national liberation will produce only very partial results, results directed entirely against the working masses' (1962:132). This 'entirely' might be a little too strong but it suggests something closer to the experiences of the twentieth century than some readings of Trotsky would indicate.

However flawed it might be as direct prophecy Trotsky's theory contrasts with the determinist caricature of Marxism and represents an important attempt to articulate dynamic processes of interaction between structural economic changes (themselves often contradictory) and political and social struggles. The prospects of socialism cannot be 'read off' from data such as the absolute number or proportion of workers in a particular country. But at the same time, we cannot ignore such 'objective' conditions or the external constraints put upon the workers' movement. Nowhere is this more clearly borne out at present than in the new ferment of progressive political movements in Latin America. There, the embedding of post-colonial capitalism in 'combined and uneven' global neoliberalism is exposing the limitations of an exported European model of social democracy in the disappointments of Lula's presidency in Brazil, while at the same time generating new forms in the Zapatista rebellion in Mexico, or in Venezuela under Chavez.

Read critically, Trotsky's insights of 1906 can still inform our understanding of the world and our struggles to change it. They can provide the basis for a rejuvenated, anti-determinist Marxism, which can understand better not only the tumultuous last 100 years but also contemporary results and prospects. We hope this small volume contributes to that process.

REFERENCES

Deutscher, I. (1954) *The Prophet Armed* (New York: Oxford University Press).
Draper, H. (1978) *Karl Marx's Theory of Revolution*, ii: *The Politics of Social Classes* (New York: Monthly Review).
Marx, K. (1970) [1881]) 'First draft of the reply to V.I.Zasulich's letter', in K. Marx and F. Engels, *Selected Works*, iii (Moscow, Progress Publishers).
Trotsky, L. (1962 [1930/1906]) *Permanent Revolution* and *Results and Prospects* (London: New Park).
—— (1971 [1922]) *1905* (Harmondsworth: Penguin).

2
From Uneven to Combined Development

Neil Davidson

Results and Prospects introduced Trotsky's two most original contributions to Marxist theory, although it was only later that they received the names under which they have passed into history: the strategy of 'permanent revolution' and – in a much more embryonic way – the theory of 'uneven and combined development'. Both terms are equally important, yet they have not received comparable levels of scrutiny. Perhaps the most accurate and detailed exposition ever made of permanent revolution devotes precisely three out of 231 pages to the subject whose political implications it seeks to discuss (Löwy 1981:52, 89–90). Those works that do attempt to discuss it tend to do so only in relation to 'the advantages of backwardness' and 'the disadvantages of priority' (Anderson 1974:236; Brett 1985:58–9; Deutscher 1971:55; Novack 1980). These are important themes, but they fall within the province of uneven development as such, and they are by no means unique to Trotsky. Indeed, the position was standard in Stalinist textbooks for several decades after the Second World War (Kuusinen 1961:386). It is rare for the distinction to be highlighted (Mandel 1995:1). Trotsky certainly took uneven development as his starting point, as he pointed out when discussing the order of the words in the title of his own theory, but it is precisely the second aspect which distinguishes Trotsky's theory from that of his predecessors and contemporaries (Trotsky 1979: 858). In order to demonstrate the innovation that combined development represents in social theory, it may be useful to briefly trace the prior development of uneven development.

THE ENLIGHTENMENT

Enlightenment thinkers developed a theory of staged development through a series of four increasingly complex modes of subsistence. In the initial formulations at least, most peoples or nations could be expected to traverse these stages, albeit at different historical times, until they finally reached the fourth or commercial stage. There were, however, two exceptions to the universalism of Enlightenment thought on this question.

One was concerned with the socio-economic distinctions between different geographical areas. Eastern societies (principally Turkey, Persia, India and China) were classified by Montesquieu as 'Asiatic' or 'Oriental' Despotisms, terms that implied two characteristics. On the one hand, they referred to the political regime, which bore an uncomfortable resemblance to European absolutism. On the other, they referred to those aspects of the socio-economic order distinct from the West: the absence of hereditary nobility, a legal system subject to the will of the ruler, state ownership of land and, more generally, an overall stagnation made all the more obvious when contrasted with the dynamism of the new capitalist system. It was Smith who decisively shifted Enlightenment views of the East in the latter direction, arguing that the political differences between East and West were based on underlying economic differences. If the West was characterised by private property, manufactures and foreign trade, then the East (which for Smith was typified by China) was characterised by state property, agriculture and a localised internal market.

The other exception was concerned with biological distinctions between different human groups, or 'races'. Enlightenment thinkers were deeply divided on this issue. One trend, represented by Millar, Diderot and Herder, broke with the racist ideology that had been used to justify the conquest of Native Americans and enslavement of Africans by both the absolutist and early capitalist empires after 1492. Another, expressed by Hume, Montesquieu and Kant, doubted whether people with black skins could even be regarded as fully human. But the universality of the first aspect of Enlightenment thought, and consequently the optimism which it displayed down to the French Revolution, could not survive the experience of colonialism and the racism which the possession of colonies engendered. At any rate, not without turning Enlightenment values against the system which required colonies in the first place.

A small minority of Enlightenment thinkers not only allowed exceptions to staged development but, on the other side, nations and peoples compressing or bypassing certain stages. In many cases these alternatives appeared in the margins of work by individuals who otherwise adhered to the classic stages theory of development by successive modes of subsistence. The first example occurred, appropriately enough, in relation to Russia. During the reign of Peter the Great (1672–1725), Russia was forced by pressure from the more advanced absolutisms of Western Europe, particularly that of Sweden, to develop naval and military forces of comparable strength. This led in turn to the need for an indigenous manufacturing sector capable at least of producing ships and cannon. In the short term, Peter imported not only the technology and technicians, but also intellectuals who could advise him on the type of educational system capable of training Russians in engineering and other skills. Many of these were Germans who may have seen in the Tsar a monarch of the type necessary to unite the divided German-speaking principalities. One of these hired savants was Leibniz. He wrote to Peter in 1712, claiming that from a position of backwardness, even blankness ('tabula rasa'), Russia could borrow what it needed from Europe and Asia, but discard in the process what was unnecessary or contingent. This may be the first reference to what would eventually be called uneven development, although it would find no echo for nearly 40 years. Then, during the 1750s, Turgot opined that France, 'whom Spain and England have already outstripped in the glory of poetry', might benefit from her current economic position behind England: 'France, whose genius finishes forming itself only when the philosophical spirit begins to spread, will owe perhaps to this very backwardness the exactitude, the method, and the austere taste of her writers' (Turgot 1973:58). But the suggestion was made only in passing and in relation to culture, not society.

Ironically, it was in Scotland, where the four-stage theory was first formulated, that the alternative was elaborated in the greatest detail. Having helped to establish the organic metaphor of development (childhood, maturity, and decline) in theory the reformers simultaneously set about subverting it in practice. In the successful attempts to overleap several of the stages which England had passed through in moving from the Age of Agriculture to the Age of Commerce, we see for perhaps the first time the brute fact of unevenness being the basis for a developmental strategy (for examples, see Davidson 2005:33–6). But even the astonishing speed of Scottish development could not overcome the legacy of feudal backwardness overnight. For over half a century, therefore, Scotland was the site – perhaps the first site – of what Trotsky would call *combined* development. It did not last. By the second decade of the nineteenth century writers were reflecting, with some astonishment, how far they had progressed in a matter of decades (Anonymous 1815:537; Scott 1972:492). Because Scotland could draw on what England had already accomplished, it was able to make up the same ground in a much shorter period of time. But it was so overwhelmingly successful in doing so that – with the exception of the Highlands – the socio-economic differences between Scotland and England had been overcome by 1815 and the political differences by 1832. No other country would ever complete the transition from feudal agriculture to capitalist industrialisation so quickly or completely. The moment was too brief, the result so uniquely decisive, for any theoretical generalisation from this experience to be possible.

MARX AND ENGELS

There are several differences between the Enlightenment concept of a mode of subsistence and the concept of a mode of production introduced by Marx and Engels. For our purposes the most important is that Marx and Engels were not proposing a universal succession of stages. Those modes of production that they listed in various places were chronological only in two senses. One is that, as Eric Hobsbawm puts it, 'each of these systems is in crucial respects further removed from the primitive state of man' (Hobsbawm 1965:38). The other is that it indicates the order in which these modes of production arose historically; it does not suggest that every social formation is fated to pass under the dominance of each of them in succession. In fact, Marx and Engels seem to have regarded only one transition as universal, that from primitive communism to different types of class society (Asiatic, slave, tributary and feudal). Beyond that, they seem to have regarded the transition from feudalism to capitalism as a possible outcome which was in fact occurring during their lifetime, which in turn opened up the possibility for another, final transition from capitalism to socialism. But neither of these two transitions was automatic or inevitable.

What level of capitalist development was necessary for socialism? At one point in *The German Ideology* (unfinished and unpublished during their lifetimes) Marx and Engels seem to suggest that the forces of production would need to exist at a globally even level of development before socialism was possible (Marx and Engels 1975–2004a:49, 51). During the later 1840s their attention became focussed on Europe and its colonial-settler extensions in North America, which they saw as decisive and where the situation was relatively straightforward. Capitalism was the dominant mode of production only in parts of Western Europe and the eastern seaboard of the United States of America, and industrialisation was still more narrowly focussed. Elsewhere the bourgeoisie were still politically and socially subordinate to the Old Regime. The task for communists was therefore to encourage the revolutions which would overthrow the feudal absolutist states, remove the structural obstacles to capitalist development and thus create the material basis for the international working class that would make socialism a possibility. During the 1840s they assumed that only a short period of time would be necessary for capitalism to develop to the point where the socialist revolution was possible. However, as early as 1858 Marx wrote to Engels admitting that capitalism had a much longer future ahead of it than either man had thought possible in 1848, and that consequently socialism might be a more distant prospect than they had initially hoped (Marx to Engels, 1975–2004:346–7; see also Engels, 1975–2004b:513).

In the meantime, what were the implications of what Marx called 'this little corner of the earth' bringing the rest of the world under colonial domination? In the Preface to *Capital* he wrote that: 'The country that is more developed industrially only shows, to the less developed, the image of its own future' (Marx 1976: 91). He was not suggesting that all countries would take the same length of time to reach the future as the original metropolitan powers, nor that arriving there would have the same implications for late developers, but neither was he suggesting that they could bypass sections of the road. Marx and Engels seem to have taken the view that it was necessary for the European bourgeoisie to introduce capitalism into Asia and Africa because the nature of these societies acted as a block to its indigenous development. Neither man had any illusions about the means by which that bourgeoisie would accomplish this revolution (Marx 1974: 323).

Were Marx and Engels right that India, China and the other colonial and semi-colonial countries could only be dragged from their stagnation by colonial conquest? They certainly exaggerated the lack of socio-economic development prior to colonisation, particularly with relation to India. In this respect they retained the Enlightenment view of the East as immobile and subject to Asiatic Despotism. It is possible that, with sufficient time and freedom from external interference, at least some of these countries might have seen the indigenous emergence of capitalism. But given the existence of the capitalist powers, and their need to secure territories for raw materials, markets and investments, they were not to be given that time or that freedom. What might have been possible had India and the rest been situated in a dimension unreachable by the British navy is a question for science fiction, not historical materialism. Once colonisation had taken place, Marx and Engels needed to take an attitude towards it. Their assumption was that, whatever atrocities the colonial powers committed on the way, they would ultimately develop the countries over which they ruled to the point where they would produce their own gravedigger as they had in the existing capitalist countries. This was their real error. The colonial powers had no intentions of hastening their own demise by developing the economies of the subject peoples, at least not in any systematic way. The implications of this for revolution in the colonial and semi-colonial world only become apparent after the deaths of Marx and Engels.

Only once did either Marx or Engels suggest that capitalist development could be circumvented altogether. This was not in relation to the colonial world, however, but to Russia, the most backward of the European Great Powers. In 1877 Marx argued that Russia did not need to undergo capitalist development but could move directly to socialism through the institution of the peasant commune or *mir*. If not, then Russia would be condemned to suffer all that the peasant populations of the West had suffered. In response, Marx makes two points. First, although the Russian peasant commune may provide the launching pad for the advance to communism in Russia, the advance of capitalism is already undermining the possibility of that happening. Second, even if the latter development does come to fruition, it will not replicate exactly the earlier process in Western Europe (Marx 1975–2004b:199, 200. See also Marx to Zasulich, 1975–2004:72). Under what conditions might the peasant commune play the role that Marx has suggested for it? These were outlined the following year in a preface, published under the names of both men, for the second Russian edition of the *Manifesto*. Here, revolution in Russia may act as the spark, but success is still dependent on the victory of the proletariat in the West (Marx and Engels 1975–2004b:42). That the victory of a revolutionary movement in the West could establish a socialist context for Russian development and thus allow Russia to avoid the fate of capitalism was in their view a possibility, but by no means a certainty. By the early 1890s it had become clear which direction events had taken and Engels changed his position accordingly. In his last writings, he drew up a balance sheet that is clearly loaded against those who still expected the peasant commune to act as the social basis of the Russian Revolution. In the absence of revolution in the West, and the beginning of capitalist development in Russia, the opportunity to bypass bourgeois society had passed (Engels to Danielson, 1975–2004:214; Engels 1975–2004a:423, 424, 431). Beyond the Russian question, only two anticipations of uneven development appear in the work of Marx and Engels.

The first consists of a cluster of references to a particular form of unevenness arising from colonial settlement. In *The German Ideology*, they reflected on how these settlements could be established on the basis of a purer, more advanced version of the dominant mode of production than in the societies the settlers left behind. On the one hand, where the settled territory was uninhabited: 'Thus they begin with the most advanced individuals of the old countries, and, therefore, with the correspondingly most advanced form of intercourse, even before this form of intercourse has been able to establish itself in the old countries.' On the other hand, where the colonised territory was inhabited by peoples at a much lower level of development: 'A similar relation issues from conquest, when a form of intercourse which has evolved on another soil is brought over complete to the conquered country: whereas in its home it was still encumbered with interests and relations left over from earlier periods, here it can and must be established completely and without hindrance, if only to assure the conqueror's lasting power, when they received the most perfect form of feudal organisation' (Marx and Engels 1975–2004a:83). The examples on which they tended to draw later in their careers were from the feudal period (Marx 1973:490; Engels to Schmidt 1975–2004:565). They do not seem to have specifically considered that capitalism might also develop in this way.

The second is a single passage in a review of Frederick List written during 1845. List had argued that Germany should seek to follow the same path of economic development as England (List 1904:156). Marx, on the other hand, rejected the idea that every nation had to repeat the same experience and argues instead that it might be possible for nations to draw on what other nations had accomplished in the specific areas where they were most advanced (Marx 1975–2004a:281). There is the embryo of an idea here, but it never achieved its full term – unsurprisingly, since it would be contrary to Marx's and Engels' own methods to suppose that their thought could run ahead of actual developments. By the time of the foundation of the Second International in 1889, those developments had begun to unfold.

THE SECOND INTERNATIONAL

The second generation of Marxists took as their text on development a passage from the same work by Marx in which he identified the different epochs of human history, the 'Preface to *A Contribution To The Critique Of Political Economy*': 'No social order is ever destroyed before all the productive forces for which it is sufficient have been developed, and new and superior relations of production never replace older ones before the material conditions for their existence have matured within the framework of the old society' (Marx 1975:425–6). Marx by no means regarded the role of socialists as playing a waiting game until the conditions were universally 'mature', yet this was the lesson which theoretical leaders of the Second International drew.

The nation in which this position was articulated and upheld more rigorously than any other was, appropriately enough, Russia, in whose future Marx and Engels had briefly glimpsed a possible alternative, before dismissing it. The key figure on the Russian Marxist left was Georgi Plekhanov. Given the opposition which Plekhanov showed for the Russian Revolution towards the end of his life, it is important not to read back later positions onto those of an earlier period, for Plekhanov was perhaps the most sophisticated thinker of his entire generational cohort. His recognition of the necessity for capitalism in Russia was accompanied by an insistence that the working class which it was bringing into being had to struggle against the new bourgeoisie as hard as it did against the feudal–absolutist state against which both classes were ostensibly opposed. Indeed, he was initially prepared to echo Marx's more unorthodox pronouncements concerning the prospects for Russian development (Plekhanov 1961a:79). But this element of his thought was quickly submerged by the need to emphasise the necessity of capitalist development against the Populists. The ultimate outcome of the revolution in Russia, given the preponderance of land-hungry peasantry, could only be the more extensive implantation of capitalist economy in the countryside, not the agrarian communism predicted by the Populists (Plekhanov 1961b:364–6). If this was true for Russia, then it was even more so for those states, like China, which were further east in geographical terms and further behind in developmental terms:

The West European revolution will be mighty, but not almighty. To have a decisive influence on other countries, the socialist countries of the West will need some kind of vehicle for that influence. 'International exchange' is a powerful vehicle, but it is not almighty either. (Plekhanov 1961b:357–8)

This is a more pessimistic perspective conclusion than that of Engels. It is important to note that, for Plekhanov at least, this was not a racist or paternalist discourse. He maintained essentially the same position in relation to the history of Western Europe: 'Everywhere there has been imitation; but the imitator is separated from his model by all the distance which exists between the society which gave him, the *imitator*, birth and the society in which the *model* lived.' Plekhanov correctly notes that Locke was the greatest influence on French philosophers of the eighteenth century: 'Yet, between Locke and his French pupils there is precisely that same distance, which separated English society at the time of the "Glorious Revolution" from French society as it was several decades before the "Great Rebellion" of the French people.' His conclusion?

Thus the influence of the literature of one country on the literature of another is directly proportional to the similarity of the social relations of those countries. It does not exist at all when that similarity is near to zero. (Plekhanov 1961c:704, 705)

In cruder hands than those of Plekhanov, the perspective simply became one of a socialist West continuing colonialism until the 'backward races' had developed sufficiently to rule themselves. The debate on colonial policy that took place at the Stuttgart Conference of the Second International in 1907 raised some of these issues in stark relief. A Dutch delegate, Hendrick von Kol, supported by Eduard Bernstein among others, argued unashamedly that the colonies were necessary for the continuation of modern industry and as a place of emigration from 'overpopulated' Europe. In the end an anti-imperialist position was adopted by the conference, but opposition to von Kol and his supporters, while stressing that Marx did not propose a universal linear path of development, had little positive to say in respect of how the colonial world could contribute to the struggle for socialism. Marchlewski argued on relativist grounds that non-Western societies also possessed important cultures; Kautsky argued that free trade would allow development to take place; but these positions either celebrated the culture of a pre-colonial past or saw socialism as a prospect for the long-term future (Riddell 1984:9–15). What of the present?

The previous year, Kautsky had identified the disproportionately advanced role which Russian workers were playing in the revolution of 1905, despite the paradoxical backwardness of Russian capital (Kautsky 2003:16). But here, as in the work of Marx and Engels – and his contemporaries like Luxemburg and Mehering – Russia is seen as an exception in Europe, not a model for Asia or Africa. What Trotsky would later call 'the peculiarities of Russia's development' had been noted by other Marxists, notably in 1896 by Labriola (1909:240), who was a major influence on Trotsky's thought (Trotsky 1975:123–4, 133) In other words, several writers had noted and commented on the peculiar militancy of the Russian working class, just as several more had noted the variety of different forms characteristic of the Russian economy. No-one, however, had drawn the connection between them.

The problem lay in the conception of unevenness which emerged from the centre and left of the Second International. This was, to begin with, a major achievement which Lenin was mainly responsible for consolidating into a unified theory. In *Imperialism* (1975) he wrote: 'The uneven and spasmodic development of individual enterprises, individual branches of industry and individual countries is inevitable under the capitalist system.' Uneven development had two aspects. The first is inter-imperialist rivalry, the way in which the relative position of the dominant national capitals changed within the overall ordering of the system, as Germany had overtaken Britain and Japan overtaken Russia. The second was the relationship of dominance by the more developed imperialist states over two other types, 'the colonies themselves' and 'the diverse forms of dependent countries which politically are formally independent but in fact, are enmeshed in the net of financial and diplomatic dependence,...typical of the epoch'. Lenin is thinking of states like Argentina and Portugal in the latter category (Lenin 1975:679, 697–8, 723–4). The central point here is that very few states are capable of joining the ranks of the imperialist powers; their existence acts as a block to the less developed repeating the experience of Scotland in the eighteenth century or (to use Lenin's own examples) of the United States, Germany and Japan in the nineteenth.

What is of interest here is the process by which the few states which achieved Great Power status in the nineteenth century had done so, for it suggests a third aspect of unevenness. Ironically, it was no Marxist but the Russian Populist Herzen in the 1850s who became the first thinker since the Scottish Enlightenment to notice a decisive fact about late development: 'Human development is a form of chronological unfairness, since late comers are able to profit by the labours of their predecessors without paying the same price' (Berlin 1960: p. xx). But for Herzen (and contemporaries like Chernychevsky) this meant that Russia could avoid the traumas of the capitalist transition completely. It was only in the early years of the twentieth century that the insight was properly theorised in a more realistic basis.

Trotsky, writing in 1907–09, was only the first of a group of Marxist thinkers, including Hilferding in *Finance Capital* (1981) and Gramsci in 'The Revolution Against "Capital"' (1977), who noted the way in which more backward states did not recapitulate the entire history of capitalist development again, but began at most advanced forms of technology and the labour process (Trotsky 1973:68; Hilferding 1981:322; Gramsci 1977:36). The insight was not restricted to Marxists. In 1915 the radical American economist Thorstein Veblen claimed – with some exaggeration – that in both economic and political terms Germany in 1870 had been 250 years behind England. By the time of the First World War Germany had overcome this lag, but only in some respects. Veblen argued that, as in the case of Japan, these technologies which arrived 'ready-made' would not necessarily overcome ideological or political backwardness, with which they could coexist for a period at least (Veblen 1939:65–6, 85–6). As we shall see, Trotsky's position was subtly different from this.

By the First World War then, a group of politically diverse thinkers had arrived at broadly similar conclusions about how capitalism had developed since the first epoch of bourgeois revolutions from above had ended in 1871. Specifically, they recognised that there were advantages in starting from a relatively backward position. It was possible to begin industrialisation with the most advanced forms of technology and industrial organisation, rather than work through all the stages of development that their predecessors had experienced. Indeed, it was impossible for them to avoid doing so if they wished to enter the competitive struggle between national capitals with any hope of success.

TROTSKY

We can now return to Trotsky and to the new element which he introduced into the debate. In *Results and Prospects* Trotsky acknowledged the influence of Kautsky on his argument that the working class would be the dominant force in the Russian Revolution, and that the peasantry would only play a subordinate role. Where he went beyond Kautsky – and indeed everyone else who took this position – was in suggesting that the Russian Revolution could lead, not only to the overthrow of absolutism, but to socialism, provided it was joined by the revolutionary movement in the advanced West (Trotsky 1969:65–6, 105–6). What was missing from Trotsky's account at this stage is any explanation for the greater militancy of the Russian working class. The advanced nature of Russian industry, to which he devoted more attention in *1905*, did not in itself provide an explanation. To do so he had to transcend the theory of uneven development, a process he did not complete until the early 1930s. As a result, Russia ceased to be the most backward region of the capitalist world (and consequently an exception) and became the most advanced region of the backward world (and consequently a model). In a sense, until *The History of the Russian Revolution*, permanent revolution was a strategy lacking a complete theoretical basis, which Trotsky now provided.

The most famous (and most often quoted) passage in the *History* remains within the existing framework of uneven development: 'The privilege of historic backwardness – and such a privilege exists – permits, or rather compels, the adoption of whatever is ready in advance of any specified date, skipping a whole series of intermediate stages' (Trotsky 1977:27). This was the privilege enjoyed by Scotland, Germany, Japan and the few other countries that had 'caught up and overtaken' the early developers. But what of those which were unable to adopt all characteristics of the advanced? Where the differences between a backward social order and that of the colonial settlers were too vast to be overcome, the former would simply be overwhelmed and, as in North America and Australasia, virtually exterminated. The real issue concerned those societies like Russia (and further back, China or India), which were sufficiently developed in feudal or tributary terms for capitalism to become established, but insufficiently developed to produce the full range of economic, social and political institutions characteristic of the established capitalist states – in many cases, because they had been forcibly prevented by imperialism from doing so. It is only in relation to these countries that Trotsky finally moves beyond uneven development: 'From the universal law of unevenness thus derives another law which for want of a better name, we may call the law of combined development

– by which we mean a drawing together of the different stages of the journey, a combining of separate steps, an amalgam of archaic with more contemporary forms' (Trotsky 1977:27–8). The implications are threefold.

First, Trotsky was not saying that forms characteristic of different stages of development simply coexist alongside each other in striking or dramatic contrasts, although that could be true. Nor was he just emphasising the existence of transitional modes of production, such as those analysed by Lenin in *The Development of Capitalism in Russia*, although he recognised that these could exist. It was rather that the archaic and the modern had melded or fused in all aspects of these social formations, from the organisation of arms production to the structure of religious observance, in entirely new and unstable ways. It is tempting to describe these as mutations, except that the inadequacy of the language led Trotsky to reject the metaphors drawn from human biology in which stages of development had been described from the Enlightenment to the Third International in its Stalinist phase: 'The absorptive and flexible psyche, as a necessary condition for historical progress, confers on the so-called social "organisms", as distinguished from the real, that is, biological organisms, an exceptional variability of internal structure' (Trotsky 1972:251).

Second, the tensions inherent in these new formations gave rise to conflicts unknown in earlier historical periods. On the one hand: 'The [backward] nation...not infrequently debases the achievements borrowed from outside in the process of adapting them to its own more primitive culture' (Trotsky 1977:27). Tsarism established factories using manufacturing technology characteristic of monopoly capitalism in order to produce arms with which to defend a state characteristic of feudal absolutism. On the other hand, by doing so they bring into being a class more skilled, more politically conscious than that faced by any previous absolutist or early capitalist state (Trotsky 1977:55). Veblen and all subsequent non-Marxist theories of the advantages of backwardness (Gerschenkron, and others) assumed that technological transfers had a limited, or at least delayed, impact on other aspects of social life. Against this, Trotsky argued that these transfers could in fact quicken the pace of change more generally, so that they attained higher levels of development than in their established rivals. As an example of this he drew attention to the greater implantation of Marxist theory among the working classes of Russia and, later, China than in that of Britain.

Third, combined development is a process necessarily confined to individual states. Uneven development occurs at the international level, but it is meaningless to talk about combined development in this respect. The significance of the process is precisely the tensions and conflicts to which it gives rise within the territorial boundaries of particular states, not least because the state itself is a combined formation.

We can now summarise the argument. The theory of uneven development was a major theoretical breakthrough in two respects, by identifying both the relative changes in position between the advanced capitalist powers and the structural inequalities between these powers and the colonial and neo-colonial world which they dominated. It further showed, with regard to the first set of relationships, how in the competitive struggle, national capitals could attain temporary economic advantage, but that their rivals could appropriate the technologies, skills or organisations which had given this lead in their completed form, without having to repeat the entire developmental process. This applied in the case of those undertaking capitalist industrialisation and those already engaged in industrial competition. What the theory omitted, particularly as it became codified under Stalinism, was how this process applied in the case of the colonial and neo-colonial world. Indeed, it was assumed that it was irrelevant: unevenness was seen as a dynamic process *within* the advanced capitalist world, but essentially as static *between* the advanced capitalist world and the colonial or neo-colonial world. The theory of uneven *and* combined development explained what occurs when the same 'overleaping' process takes place in the colonial or neo-colonial world, where it is impossible to fully 'catch up' with, let alone 'overtake' the developed West, but to do so instead in a fragmentary or partial way. But the resulting combined forms, because of their inbuilt social instability, paradoxically made revolutionary outbreaks more likely than in the developed world, with its greater levels of stability and reformist traditions. In other words, combined and uneven development made it possible for a strategy of permanent revolution to be pursued.

There is a particular irony in the fact that Trotsky, who emphasised more than any of his contemporaries the reality of the world economy, was also the thinker who refocused attention from 'the international' in general to its impact on individual nation states. He never faltered in his belief that the socialist revolution could only ever be accomplished on a global basis, but was equally forceful in arguing that the strategies adopted by revolutionaries outside the developed West had to be based on an assessment of the extent of combined development and the specific forms which it took.

REFERENCES

Anderson, P. (1974) *Lineages of the Absolutist State* (London: New Left Books).

Anonymous (1815) 'A Supplement, Containing an Account of the Present State of Agriculture, and the Improvements Recently Introduced', in Lord Kames, *The Gentleman Farmer: Being an Attempt to Improve Agriculture by Subjecting It to the Test of Rational Principles*, 6th edn., (Edinburgh: Bell & Bradfute).

Berlin, I. (1960) 'Introduction', in F. Venturi, *Roots of a Revolution: a History of the Popular and Socialist Movements in Nineteenth Century Russia*, translated from the Italian by F. Haskell (London: Weidenfeld & Nicolson).

Brett, E. A. (1985) *The World Economy Since the War: the Politics of Uneven Development* (London: Macmillan).

Davidson, N. (2005) 'The Scottish Path to Capitalist Agriculture 3: the Enlightenment as the Theory and Practice of Improvement', *Journal of Agrarian Change*, 5/1, (January).

Deutscher, I. (1971 [1957]) 'Four Decades of the Revolution', in *Ironies of History* (Berkeley: Ramparts Press).

Engels, F. (1975–2004a) 'Afterword (1894) [to *On Social Relations In Russia*]', in *Collected Works*, xxvii (London: Lawrence & Wishart).

—— (1975–2004b [1895]), 'Introduction [to Karl Marx's, *The Class Struggle in France 1848 to 1850*]', in *Collected Works*, xxvii (London: Lawrence & Wishart).

—— to Danielson (1975–2004 [17 October 1893]), in *Collected Works*, i (London: Lawrence & Wishart).

—— to Schmidt (1975–2004 [12 March 1895]) in *Collected Works*, i (London: Lawrence & Wishart).

Gramsci, A. (1977 [1917]) 'The Revolution Against *Capital*', in *Selections from the Political Writings*, edited and translated by Q. Hoare and G. Nowell-Smith (London: Lawrence & Wishart).

Hilferding, R. (1981 [1911]) *Finance Capital*, edited with an introduction by T. Bottomore from translations by M. Watnick and S. Gordon (London: Routledge).

Hobsbawm, E. J. (1965) 'Introduction', in K. Marx, *Pre-Capitalist Economic Formations* (New York: International Publications).

Kautsky, K. (2003 [1906]), 'The American Worker', *Historical Materialism*, 11/4.

Kuusinen, O. (ed.), (1961) *Fundamentals of Marxism–Leninism* (London: Lawrence & Wishart).

Labriola, A. (1909 [1896]) 'Historical Materialism', in *Essays on the Materialistic Conception of History*, translated by C. H. Kerr (Chicago: Charles H. Kerr).

Lenin, V. (1975 [1916]) *Imperialism, the Highest Stage of Capitalism*, in *Selected Works*, i (Moscow: Progress Publishers).

List, F. (1904 [1841]) *The National System of Political Economy*, translated by S. S. Lloyd with an introduction by J. Shield Nicholson, new edition (London: Longmans, Green).

Löwy, M. (1981) *The Politics of Combined and Uneven Development: the Theory of Permanent Revolution* (London: Verso).

Mandel, E. (1995) *Trotsky as Alternative* (London and New York: Verso).

Marx, K. (1973 [1857–58]) *Grundrisse* (Harmondsworth: *New Left Review*/ Penguin Books).

—— (1974 [1854]) 'The Future Consequences of the British Rule in India', in *Political Writings*, ii, *Surveys From Exile*, edited and introduced by D. Fernbach (Harmondsworth: *New Left Review*/Penguin Books).

—— (1975 [1859]) 'Preface to *A Contribution to the Critique of Political Economy*', in *Early Writings*, introduced by L. Colletti (Harmondsworth: *New Left Review*/Penguin Books).

—— (1975–2004a [1845]) 'Draft of an Article on Frederick List's Book, *Das Nationale System Der Politischen Oekkonomie*', in *Collected Works*, iv (London: Lawrence & Wishart).

—— (1975–2004b [1877]) '[Letter to *Otechesivenniye Zapiski*]', in *Collected Works*, xxiv (London: Lawrence & Wishart).

—— (1976 [1867]) *Capital*, i (Harmondsworth: *New Left Review*/Penguin Books).

—— to Engels (1975–2004 [8 October 1858]), in *Collected Works*, xl (London: Lawrence & Wishart).

—— to Zasulich (1975–2004 [8 March 1881]), in *Collected Works*, xlvi (London: Lawrence & Wishart).

—— and Engels F. (1975–2004a [1844–5]) *The German Ideology*, in *Collected Works*, vi (London: Lawrence & Wishart).

—— —— (1975–2004b [1878]) 'Preface to the Second Russian Edition of *The Manifesto of the Communist Party*', in *Collected Works*, xxiv (London: Lawrence & Wishart).

Novack, G. 1980 [1957] 'Uneven and Combined Development in History', in *Understanding History: Marxist Essays* (New York: Pathfinder Press).

Plekhanov, G. (1961a [1883]) 'Socialism and the Political Struggle', in *Selected Philosophical Works*, i (Moscow: Progress Publishers).

—— (1961b [1884]) 'Our Differences', in *Selected Philosophical Works*, i (Moscow: Progress Publishers).

—— (1961c [1895]) 'The Development of the Monist View of History', in *Selected Philosophical Works*, i (Moscow: Progress Publishers).

Riddell, J. (ed.) (1984 [1907]) 'Congress Debate on Colonial Policy', in *Lenin's Struggle for a Revolutionary International: Documents, 1907–1916* (New York: Pathfinder Press).

Scott, W. (1972 [1814]) *Waverley: or, 'Tis Sixty Years Since*, edited by A. Hook, (Harmondsworth: Penguin Books).

Trotsky, L. (1969 [1906]) 'Results and Prospects' in Trotsky, L. *The Permanent Revolution* and *Results and Prospects* (New York: Pathfinder).

—— (1972 [1932]) 'In Defence of the Russian Revolution', in *Leon Trotsky Speaks* (New York: Pathfinder Press).

—— (1973 [1907–09]) *1905* (Harmondsworth: Penguin Books).

—— (1975 [1929]) *My Life: an Attempt at an Autobiography* (Harmondsworth: Penguin Books).

—— (1977 [1932–33]) *The History of the Russian Revolution*, translated by M. Eastman (London: Pluto Press).

—— (1979 [1934–40]) 'A Serious Work on Russian Revolutionary History', in *Writings of Leon Trotsky Supplement (1934–40)*, edited by G. Breitman (New York: Pathfinder Press).

Turgot, A.-R. (1973 [1750]) 'A Philosophical Review of the Successive Advances of the Human Mind', in *Turgot on Progress, Sociology and Economics*, edited by R. L. Meek (Cambridge: Cambridge University Press).

Veblen, T. (1939 [1916]) *Imperial Germany and the Industrial Revolution*, with an introduction by J. Dorfman (New York: Viking Press).

3

The Marxism of *Results and Prospects*

Michael Löwy

THE HISTORICAL CONTEXT

Trotsky's theory of permanent revolution, as sketched for the first time in his essay *Results and Prospects* (1962), was one of the most astonishing political breakthroughs in Marxist thinking at the beginning of the twentieth century. By rejecting the idea of separate historical stages – the first one being a 'bourgeois democratic' one – in the future Russian Revolution, and raising the possibility of transforming the democratic into a proletarian/socialist revolution in a 'permanent' (i.e. uninterrupted) process, it not only predicted the general strategy of the October Revolution, but also provided key insights into the other revolutionary processes which would take place later on, in China, Indochina, Cuba, etc. Of course, it is not without its problems and shortcomings, but it was incomparably more relevant to the real revolutionary processes in the periphery of the capitalist system than anything produced by 'orthodox Marxism' from the death of Engels until 1917.

In fact, the idea of permanent revolution appeared already in Marx and Engels, notably in their *Address of the Central Committee to the Communist League*, written in March 1850, while the German Revolution of 1848–50 – in an absolutist and backward country – still seemed to unfold. Against the unholy alliance of the liberal bourgeoisie and absolutism, they championed the common action of the workers with the democratic parties of the petty bourgeoisie. But they insisted on the need for an independent proletarian perspective:

while the democratic petty bourgeoisie want to bring the revolution to an end as quickly as possible…it is our interest and our task to make the revolution permanent until all the more or less propertied classes have been driven from their ruling positions, until the proletariat has conquered state power and until the association of the proletarians has progressed sufficiently far – not only in one country but in all the leading countries of the world – that competition between the proletarians of these countries ceases and at least the decisive forces of production are concentrated in the hands of the workers. (Marx and Engels 1973:323–4)

This striking passage contains three of the fundamental themes that Trotsky would later develop in *Results and Prospects*: (1) the uninterrupted development of the revolution in a semi-feudal country, leading to the conquest of power by the working class; (2) the need for the proletarian forces in power to take anti-capitalist and socialist measures; (3) the necessarily international character of the revolutionary process and of the new socialist society, without classes or private property.

The idea of a socialist revolution in the backward periphery of capitalism – although not the term 'permanent revolution' – is also present in Marx's late writings on Russia: the letter to Vera Zasulich (1881) and, together with Engels, the preface to the 1882 Russian edition of the *Communist Manifesto*: 'If the Russian revolution sounds the signal of a proletarian revolution in the West so that each complements the other, the prevailing form of communal ownership of land in Russia may form the starting point for a communist course of development' (Marx and Engels 1953:217).

With the exception of Trotsky, these ideas seem to have been lost to Russian Marxism in the years between the end of the nineteenth century and 1917. If we leave aside the semi-Marxists in the populist camp, such as Nicolaion, or the 'legal Marxists' such as Piotr Struve, there remain four clearly delimited positions inside Russian social democracy:

1. The Menshevik view, which considered the future Russian revolution as bourgeois by its nature and that its driving force would be an alliance of the proletariat with the liberal bourgeoisie. Plekhanov and his friends believed that Russia was a backward, 'Asiatic' and barbarous country requiring a long stage of industrialism and 'Europeanisation' before the proletariat could aspire to power. Only after Russia has developed its productive forces, and passed into the historical stage of advanced capitalism and parliamentary democracy, would the requisite material and political conditions be available for a socialist transformation.

2. The Bolshevik conception also recognised the inevitably bourgeois–democratic character of the revolution, but it excluded the bourgeoisie from the revolutionary bloc. According to Lenin, only the proletariat and the peasantry were authentically revolutionary forces, bound to establish through their alliance a

common democratic revolutionary dictatorship. Of course, as we know, Lenin radically changed his approach after the *April Theses* of 1917.

3. Parvus and Rosa Luxemburg, while acknowledging the bourgeois character of the revolution in the last instance, insisted on the hegemonic revolutionary role of the proletariat supported by the peasantry. The destruction of Tsarist absolutism could not be achieved short of the establishment of a workers' power led by social democracy. However, such a proletarian government could not yet transcend in its programmatic aims the fixed limits of bourgeois democracy.

4. Finally, Trotsky's concept of permanent revolution, which envisaged not only the hegemonic role of the proletariat and the necessity of its seizure of power, but also the possibility of a 'growing over' of the democratic into the socialist revolution.

Curiously enough, Trotsky does not mention, in *Results and Prospects*, any of the above-mentioned pieces by Marx and Engels. He probably ignored the *Address* of March 1850: the re-edition of 1885 in Zurich, in German, was not well known in Russia. His immediate source for the term 'permanent revolution' in 1905 seems to have been an article by Franz Mehring (1905) on the events in Russia, 'Die Revolution in Permanenz', published in the *Neue Zeit*, the theoretical organ of German Social Democracy. Mehring's article was immediately translated in 1905 in Trotsky's paper *Nachalo* in Petrograd, and in the same issue there appeared also the first article in which Lev Davidovitch used the term 'permanent revolution': 'Between the immediate goal and the final goal there should be a permanent revolutionary chain.' However, a close reading of Mehring's piece shows that the German Marxist used the words, but was not really a partisan of permanent revolution in the same sense as Trotsky in 1905–06. The vital kernel of the theory, its concept of the uninterrupted going-over of the democratic towards the socialist revolution, was denied by Mehring. This was well understood by Martov, the great Menshevik leader, who, in a work written many years later, recalled Trotsky's piece as a disturbing 'deviation from the theoretical foundations of the programme of Russian Social Democracy'. He clearly distinguished between Mehring's article, which he considered acceptable, and Trotsky's essay, which he repudiated as 'utopian', since it transcended 'the historical task which flows from the existent level of productive forces' (Martov 1926:164–5).

The ideas suggested in various of Trotsky's articles in 1905 – particularly in his preface for the Russian translation of Marx's writings on the Paris Commune – were then developed, in a more systematic and coherent way, in *Results and Prospects* (1962). However, this bold piece of writing remained for a long time a forgotten book. It seems that Lenin did not read it – at least not before 1917 – and its influence over contemporary Russian Marxism was desultory at best. Like all forerunners, Trotsky was in advance of his time, and his ideas were too novel and heterodox to be accepted, or even studied, by his party comrades.

DIALECTICS AND REVOLUTION

How was it possible for Trotsky to cut the Gordian knot of Second International Marxism – the economistic definition of the nature of a future revolution by 'the level of productive forces' – and to grasp the revolutionary possibilities that lay beyond the dogmatic construction of a bourgeois democratic Russian revolution which was the unquestioned problematic of *all* other Marxist propositions?

There seems to exist an intimate link between the dialectical method and revolutionary theory: not by chance, the high period of revolutionary thinking in the twentieth century, the years 1905–25, are also those of some of the most interesting attempts to use Hegelo-Marxist dialectics as an instrument of knowledge and action. Let me try to illustrate the connexion between dialectics and revolution in Trotsky's early work.

A careful study of the roots of Trotsky's political boldness, and of the whole theory of permanent revolution, reveals that his views were informed by a specific understanding of Marxism, an interpretation of the dialectical materialist method distinct from the dominant orthodoxy of the Second International and of Russian Marxism. The young Trotsky did not read Hegel, but his understanding of Marxist theory owes much to his first readings in historical materialism, namely the works of Antonio Labriola. In his autobiography he recalled the 'delight' with which he first devoured Labriola's essays during his imprisonment in Odessa in 1893. His initiation into dialectics thus took place through an encounter with perhaps the least orthodox of the major figures of the Second International. Formed in the Hegelian school, Labriola fought relentlessly against the neo-positivist and vulgar-materialist trends that proliferated in Italian Marxism, for example Turati. He was one of the first to reject the economistic interpretations of Marxism by attempting to restore the dialectical concepts of *totality* and *historical process*. Labriola defended historical materialism as a self-sufficient and independent theoretical system, irreducible to other currents; he also rejected scholastic dogmatism and the cult of the textbook, insisting on the need for a *critical* development of Marxism (Labriola 1970:115, 243).

Trotsky's starting-point, therefore, was this critical, dialectical and anti-dogmatical understanding that Labriola had inspired. 'Marxism', he wrote in 1906, 'is above all a method of analysis – not analysis of texts, but analysis of social relations' (Trotsky 1962:196). Let us focus on five of the most important and distinctive features of the methodology that underlies Trotsky's theory of permanent revolution, in distinction from the other Russian Marxists, from Plekhanov to Lenin and from the Mencheviks to the Bolsheviks (before 1917).

1. From the vantage point of the dialectical comprehension of the unity of the opposites, Trotsky criticised the Bolsheviks' rigid division between the socialist power of the proletariat and the 'democratic dictatorship of workers and peasants', as a 'logical, purely formal operation'. This abstract logic is even more sharply attacked in his polemic against Plekhanov, whose whole reasoning can be reduced to an 'empty syllogism': our revolution is bourgeois, therefore we should support the Cadets, the constitutionalist bourgeois party. Moreover, in an astonishing passage from a critique against the Menchevik Tcherevanin, he explicitly condemned the *analytical* – i.e. abstract–formal, pre-dialectical – character of Menshevik politics: 'Tcherevanin constructs his tactics as Spinoza did his ethics, that is to say, geometrically' (Trotsky 1971:289, 306–12). Of course, Trotsky was not a philosopher and almost never wrote specifically philosophical texts, but this makes his clear-sighted grasp of the methodological dimension of his controversy with stagist conceptions all the more remarkable.

2. In *History and Class Consciousness* (1923), Lukács insisted that the dialectical category of totality was the essence of Marx's method, indeed the very principle of revolution within the domain of knowledge (Lukács 1971:ch.1). Trotsky's theory, written 20 years earlier, is an exceptionally significant illustration of this Lukácsian thesis. Indeed, one of the essential sources of the superiority of Trotsky's revolutionary thought is the fact that he adopted *the viewpoint of totality*, perceiving capitalism and the class struggle

as a world process. In the preface to a Russian edition (1905) of Lassalle's articles about the revolution of 1848, he argues:

Binding all countries together with its mode of production and its commerce, capitalism has converted the whole world into a single economic and political organism... This immediately gives the events now unfolding an international character, and opens up a wide horizon. The political emancipation of Russia led by the working class...will make it the initiator of the liquidation of world capitalism, for which history has created the objective condition. (Trotsky 1962:240)

Only by posing the problem in these terms – at the level of 'maturity' of the capitalist system in its *totality* – was it possible to transcend the traditional perspective of the Russian Marxists, who defined the socialist–revolutionary 'unripeness' of Russia exclusively in terms of a *national* economic determinism.

3. Trotsky explicitly rejected the undialectical economism – the tendency to reduce, in a non-mediated and one-sided way, all social, political and ideological contradictions to the economic infrastructure – which was one of the hallmarks of Plekhanov's vulgar materialist interpretation of Marxism. Indeed, Trotsky's break with economism was one of the decisive steps towards the theory of permanent revolution. A key paragraph in *Results and Prospects* defined with precision the political stakes implied in this rupture: 'To imagine that the dictatorship of the proletariat is in some way automatically dependent on the technical development and resources of a country is a prejudice of "economic" materialism simplified to absurdity. This point of view has nothing in common with Marxism' (Trotsky 1962:195).

4. Trotsky's method refused the undialectical conception of history as a pre-determined evolution, typical of Menshevik arguments. He had a rich and dialectical understanding of historical development as a contradictory process, where at every moment alternatives are posed. The task of Marxism, he wrote, was precisely to 'discover the "possibilities" of the developing revolution' (Trotsky 1962:168). In *Results and Prospects*, as well as in later essays – for instance, his polemic against the Mensheviks, *The Proletariat and the Russian Revolution* (1971 [1906], ch. 24) – he analyses the process of permanent revolution towards socialist transformation through the dialectical concept of *objective possibility*, whose outcome depended on innumerable subjective factors as well as unforeseeable events – and not as an inevitable necessity whose

triumph (or defeat) was already assured. It was this recognition of the open character of social historicity that gave revolutionary praxis its decisive place in the architecture of Trotsky's theoretical–political ideas from 1905 on.

5. While the Populists insisted on the peculiarities of Russia and the Mensheviks believed that their country would necessarily follow the 'general laws' of capitalist development, Trotsky was able to achieve a dialectical synthesis between the universal and the particular, the specificity of the Russian social formation and the world capitalist process. In a remarkable passage from the *History of the Russian Revolution* (1930) he explicitly formulated the viewpoint that was already implicit in his 1906 essays:

> In the essence of the matter the Slavophile conception, with all its reactionary fantasticness, and also Narodnikism, with all its democratic illusions, were by no means mere speculations, but rested upon indubitable and moreover deep peculiarities of Russia's development, understood one-sidedly however and incorrectly evaluated. In its struggle with Narodnikism, Russian Marxism, demonstrating the identity of the laws of development for all countries, not infrequently fell into a dogmatic mechanisation discovering a tendency to pour out the baby with the bath. (Trotsky 1965:vol.I, 427)

Trotsky's historical perspective was, therefore, a dialectical *Aufhebung*, able to simultaneously negate/preserve/transcend the contradiction between the Populists and the Russian Marxists.

It was the combination of all these methodological innovations that made *Results and Prospects* so unique in the landscape of Russian Marxism before 1917; dialectics was at the heart of the theory of permanent revolution. As Isaac Deutscher wrote in his biography, if one reads again this pamphlet from 1906, 'one cannot but be impressed by the sweep and boldness of this vision. He reconnoitred the future as one who surveys from a towering mountain top a new and immense horizon and points to vast, uncharted landmarks in the distance' (Deutscher 1954:161).

THE ROAD TO 1917

A similar link between dialectics and revolutionary politics can be found in Lenin's evolution. Vladimir Illich remained faithful to the orthodox views of Russian Marxism till 1914, when the beginning of the war led him to discover dialectics: the study of

Hegelian logic was the instrument by means of which he cleared the theoretical road leading to the Finland Station in Petrograd, where he first announced 'All power to the soviets!'. In March–April 1917, liberated from the obstacle represented by pre-dialectical Marxism, Lenin could, under the pressure of events, rid himself in good time of its political corollary: the abstract and rigid principle according to which 'The Russian revolution could only be bourgeois, since Russia was not economically ripe for a socialist revolution.' Once he crossed the Rubicon, he applied himself to studying the problem from a practical, concrete, and realistic angle and came to conclusions very similar to those announced by Trotsky in 1906: what are the measures, constituting in fact the transition towards socialism, that could be made acceptable to the majority of the people, that is, the masses of workers and peasants? This is the road which led to the October Revolution...

REFERENCES

Deutscher, I. (1954) *The Prophet Armed* (London: Oxford University Press).

Labriola, A. (1970 [1897]) *La concepcion materialista de la historia* (La Habana: Instituto del Libro).

Lukács, G. (1971 [1923]) *History and Class Consciousness* (London: Merlin).

Martov (1926) *Geschichte der Russischen Sozialdemokratie* (Berlin).

Marx, K. and Engels, F. (1973 [1850]) *The Revolutions of 1848* (London: Penguin).

—— —— (1953 [1882]) *The Russian Menace to Europe*, edited by P. W. Blackstock and B. F. Hoselit, (London: Allen & Unwin).

Mehring, F. (1905) 'Die Revolution in Permanenz', *Die Neue Zeit*, 24/1 (1905–06).

Trotsky, L. D. (1971 [1906]) *1905* (London: Penguin).

—— (1962 [1906]) *Permanent Revolution* and *Results and Prospects* (London: New Park).

—— (1965 [1930]) *History of the Russian Revolution* (London: Pluto Press).

4

Trotsky, 1905, and the Anticipation of the Concept of Decline

Hillel Ticktin

In this chapter I argue that the theory most commonly associated with Trotsky, that of permanent revolution, has an implicit theory of capitalist decline,[1] as it was later developed. Trotsky never tried later to develop such a theory. He preferred to argue in terms of both the long wave of capitalist development and of a disintegrating or terminal capitalism, but there is little difference. His overall political economy of such a capitalism is nuanced and complex. I have discussed aspects of his political economy elsewhere, but here in honour of the hundredth anniversary of 1905 and the birth of the theory of permanent revolution I am confining myself to that period, with the odd comparison with his later years (see Ticktin 1995, where I go through different aspects of Trotsky's theory of capitalism).

1905 was a crucial year in socialist history in that the working-class movement developed two crucial aspects in its armoury: soviets, which were new, and the general strike, which was not. Since that time both political forms have been extensively used and theorised. It is curious that such basic weapons in working-class struggle either appeared first or were taken furthest in one of the least developed countries in Europe. In the opening chapters of Trotsky's work, *1905*

---

1. It should be noted that the concept of decline is not a simple empirical argument but one that takes the view that capitalism itself goes through stages and that the last stage is one of decline. It is a period of decline of the law of value, as the basic law of capitalism, i.e. a period when it is increasingly malfunctioning, and replaced by other substitutes. Imperialism and war function in this way and are a direct result of that decline. Looking deeper, it is a period in which mediations in the poles of the contradiction become increasingly difficult, leading to the use of non-value forms. None of this precludes capitalism growing, expanding or at times raising the standard of living of the population. However, there is an increasing gap between what is materially possible and what is actually produced and an increasing tendency to prolonged crisis, which may or may not be terminal (see Ticktin 1994).

(1972),[2] Trotsky develops his theory of the nature of Russian political economy, tracing its origins and its denouement in what came later to be called the epoch of capitalist decline. He does not, however, use the word decline, speaking rather of the pusillanimity of the capitalist class.

Later in the 1930s he is more explicit: 'Just as the operation of the laws of physiology yields different results in a growing organism from those in a dying one, so the economic laws of Marxist economy assert themselves differently in a developing and a disintegrating capitalism' (Trotsky 1963:29).

Trotsky is justly famous for his analysis of capitalism (see Ticktin 1995) which is partly encapsulated in his theory of permanent revolution. That, in turn, can be described as a theory of a capitalism in decline, and it is discussed below. The cycle of birth, growth, maturity, decline and death is a dialectical concept. At this point, we can define dialectics, with Trotsky, as the logic of motion or as developmental logic. What is motion? It is not simply the mechanical movement of a circular body in space but the evolution of entities over time and space.[3] Trotsky stresses this point and in so doing he is drawing out Marx's view, in his afterword to the second German edition of *Capital*, that dialectics concerns the coming into being, maturing and dying of entities. In other words, everything is born, matures, declines and dies. The implication of the sentence in the quote above is that capitalism in its decline has its own special laws, additional to the fundamental laws of capitalism. Trotsky insists that 'The law of the transition of quantity into quality is (very likely) *the fundamental law of dialectics*' (Trotsky 1986:87). On the next page he says that this 'gives us the general formula of all evolutionary processes' (Trotsky 1986:88). He argues that 'the conversion of an abstract possibility into a concrete necessity' is an important law of dialectics. For this to happen there has to be 'the strengthening

2. This book, as Trotsky makes clear (1972: p. x), was a reconstruction of his German edition of 1908–09, written in 1922. It includes chapters of his book *Our Revolution*, written in 1907, which in turn included work originally written in 1906, which is extant in his untranslated *Collected Works*. *Results and Prospects*, which is the usual work to which reference is made, was an added chapter of *Our Revolution*. Anyone looking at *1905* and *Results and Prospects* will note that the first three chapters are similar, but have been amplified in *1905*.

3. Dialectics is constructed on the transition of quantity into quality and the reverse. 'Dialectics is the logic of Darwinism,...the logic of Marxism, the logic of philosophical materialism' (Trotsky, 1986:87).

of some factors and the weakening of others' (Trotsky 1986:90). He was speaking of feudalism but the reference to the overthrow of the bourgeoisie is clear.

Trotsky is arguing, in the above quote, the importance of the concept of transition and the move to transition, with what amounts to an accompanying decline. Although he wrote these notes in the 1930s, they are consonant with his early philosophy and viewpoint and look more like reflections drawn from his earlier experience.

THE HISTORY

Hilferding's book *Das Finanz Kapital* appeared in 1910 but Hilferding did not develop a theory of decline, though he argued that finance capital is the highest stage of capitalism.[4] In his last paragraph he goes further and says that 'It [finance capital] is the climax of the dictatorship of the magnates of capital' (1985:370). Lenin's (1935b) theory of imperialism as the phase of capitalist decline only appeared six years later, in 1916. Trotsky, on the other hand, is already quite clear that capitalism has entered a new period, that of finance capital, when writing in the period 1906–09.[5] He and Parvus put forward a concept of Permanent Revolution which precisely argues that the bourgeoisie cannot fulfil its own tasks because, in effect, the decline of capitalism has made it too dangerous for it to do so, but they do not use the word decline. They argued that as a result, it falls to the working class to undertake those responsibilities. Marx had argued that the revolution became permanent only when the working class had taken power. Trotsky is arguing that the intervening phase when the bourgeoisie and/or the petty-bourgeoisie impose bourgeois democracy, removing all feudal remnants and absolutist heritage, can no longer establish itself. He developed this case in the period January to October 1905 (Trotsky 1972:vi) and was proved correct

4. 'As capital itself at the highest stage of its development becomes finance capital so the magnate of capital, the finance capitalist, increasingly con-centrates his control over the whole national capital by means of his domination of bank capital' (Hilferding 1985:225).
5. 'The new Russia acquired its absolutely specific character because it received its capitalist baptism in the latter half of the nineteenth century from European capital which by then had reached its most concentrated and abstract form, that of finance capital' (Trotsky 1972:50). Trotsky repeated his thesis on the nature of Russia several times and the three chapters involved are an elaboration of what he wrote earlier in *Results and Prospects*. It is also in the partly untranslated Russian material in the *Collected Works*.

when the Tsar granted a limited parliament, the Duma, suppressed the general strike of November–December and then withdrew most of the political concessions he had granted. The bourgeoisie were opposed to the second general strike and did little to mitigate the massive repression that followed.

This was a remarkable political evolution. The Mensheviks drew the opposite conclusion from the failure of 1905. For them, the bourgeoisie had to be on board for the revolution against autocracy to succeed. In other words, they considered the working class too weak to undertake its tasks of overthrowing the capitalist system and hence it was necessary to proceed through a capitalist stage first before undertaking a socialist revolution. If one looked at the working-class movement in the limited perspective of Russia and 1905, this seemed a necessary conclusion. It was only by putting the Russian Empire in the context of world capitalism that one could make another inference. Strangely, since they were Marxists, they did not do so. Even more strangely, for Marxists, they appeared to have no concept of the dialectics of capitalist growth, i.e. that it should go through embryonic, mature and declining phases.[6] In other words, they had no concept of decline and hence, turning the argument around, only if they had had a conception of decline could they have taken a different viewpoint.

Trotsky had stood between the Mensheviks and the Bolsheviks after 1904 and it was precisely for that reason that he was acceptable to both as the de facto leader of the Petrograd Soviet (Deutscher 1954:130–1). He was critical of Lenin for his authoritarian stance on the nature of the party, as he argued in his work *Our Political Tasks* in 1904. The Mensheviks had taken a more optimistic view of the working-class and socialist revolution until the events of 1903 (Deutscher 1954), and Trotsky went along with that, although he grew more critical of their organisational stance as well as of their gradual conversion to the support of liberals. Trotsky, therefore, stood in a very different theoretical position from either of the two factions, one which proved to be correct in 1917 and which Lenin then adopted.

In reality the nature of the Russian Revolution, as it unfolded, could give rise to three possible interpretations. One was the increasingly

6. Marx himself integrated these concepts into his method, as he himself says in the Afterword to *Capital*, where he indicates approval of a summary of his dialectical method by a Russian reviewer of *Capital*.

pessimistic Menshevik conclusion that the autocracy could only be overthrown with the help of the bourgeoisie. That was almost certainly based on their interpretation of the relative strengths of the working class and sections of the ruling class and was reinforced by the defeat of the 1905 revolution.

The second was that of Trotsky, who had observed the realities of the struggle during 1905, when the working class established itself as a self-conscious independent decision-making entity, leading the struggle. He concluded that any struggle to overthrow the autocracy would necessarily take the same form and that therefore the working class would be compelled to take that struggle to its necessary socialist conclusion.

The third was that of Lenin, who formulated the goal as the dictatorship of the working class and peasantry, arguing that there would be a bourgeois democratic phase before moving to the dictatorship of the proletariat. So far did Lenin argue this case that he even said that in 1905 the aim of the proletariat was to achieve a republic, a bourgeois republic, in which the proletarian party should take part in government (Lenin 1931:18–20). He was defying the general socialist ban on taking part in bourgeois governments by theorising that such a bourgeois government would be a revolutionary bourgeois government. This would have put him to the right of the Mensheviks and not just of Trotsky, if it were not for his insistence on and even glorification of armed struggle at the time (Lenin 1931).

It should be noted that the real difference with the Mensheviks was the less active role they attributed to the working class at the time of the overthrow of the autocracy. Both Lenin and Trotsky saw the working class as the mainstay of the revolution, but Lenin felt that it could not succeed without the support of the broad mass of the non-proletarian population, including the revolutionary section of the bourgeoisie, and hence the proletariat would subordinate its class interest until it was ready to take power in its own name.

Menshevik theory was clearly in transition and hence composed of different conflicting strands. Lenin's view was internally conflicted in that he was arguing two points. The first was that the proletariat had to engage in armed struggle, win over the army and then take power but hand it over to a Constituent Assembly as part of a bourgeois republic, because the proletariat needed allies. The second strand was that the proletariat and its parties would remain independently organised and responsible only to themselves at a time when their success in the revolution made them the most powerful parties in the country.

It is clear today that capitalism would not be able to function under those conditions. It is hard to imagine Lenin as an early market-socialist theorist, but one cannot avoid such an implication. Trotsky's view was similar to that of Lenin up to the point where a successful revolution takes place. He takes Lenin to his logical conclusion. If the bourgeoisie itself will not be the leading party in the revolution and it is replaced by the proletariat, why does the proletariat have to abstain from pursuing its own goals? If Lenin had held his later view of the decline of capitalism he ought logically to have come to Trotsky's conclusion that there could not be such a thing as revolutionary bourgeois democracy, a term he was wont to employ at this time.

There have been various theories as to why Lenin changed his programmatic viewpoint in April 1917, and fought his own party until they accepted his new strategy. Michael Löwy (1976:5–15) sees the change as being precipitated by Lenin's study of Hegel. Others have simply assumed that Lenin was a pragmatic politician and took the opportunity. Lenin was certainly the most down-to-earth revolutionary socialist politician of his time, but he was no opportunist. However, the very possibility of taking power, without the concessions he had earlier predicated, which he clearly saw, indicated that his viewpoint was outdated. Nonetheless, he needed a mental framework which allowed him to see that possibility itself. Löwy may well be right, but the whole concept of a declining capitalism on which he laid such stress in his work on imperialism, and which was inherent in his analysis of the First World War, made his earlier viewpoint of a bourgeois democratic phase dubious. In other words, a capitalism which could only survive through its brutal invasion of the Third World in order to extort tribute and which then fought a world war to re-divide the spoils had lost its earlier democratic ethos.

In contrast to Lenin, Trotsky is arguing precisely that the bourgeoisie wants and needs democracy for capitalism to operate efficiently, but fearing that capitalism itself could be overthrown it is forced to compromise and hence it does not get much of what it wants. To make it clearer, Lenin is arguing that 'the bourgeoisie will inevitably change...to the side of counter-revolution when its narrow selfish interests are satisfied' (Lenin 1935a:95, author's translation).

Neither Lenin nor the Mensheviks had a theory of the nature of the Russian autocracy. Lenin (1958:48) had criticised the Narodniki and written on the nature of Russian agriculture, but he had not tried to explain the nature and evolution of Russian history. Trotsky at the age of 26–7 had already formulated an overall political economy for the Russian Empire, which explained its dynamic (Trotsky 1972:3–10). He argued that it was not feudal but semi-Asiatic. This much he derived from Plekhanov. What was crucial was the extraction of the surplus product and its distribution. He saw Russia's defence of its borders as playing the same role as irrigation in the Asiatic mode of production. The surplus product went into the military to maintain the Russian state, besieged as it was on all sides. As a result, the peasants were reduced to a new serfdom, with a close resemblance to slavery. This in turn resulted in a low level of productivity and so a relatively small surplus product, which in turn meant that taxation was high and the state disproportionately large and bureaucratic in order to maintain the stability of the system. Unlike in the Asiatic mode of production there were landlords but they were part of the state bureaucracy. By 1905 the peasants were no longer enserfed, but their economic position was often worse than before their emancipation in 1861.

This was neither feudalism nor capitalism. It was clear that the autocracy had no place in its social structure for the rising capitalist class and the accompanying 'middle class' of professionals and others. Likewise, the autocratic social structure had no future in a capitalist society. Logically, the two sides stood opposed. Indeed, the students were overwhelmingly critical of the Tsarist autocracy. The fact that the bourgeoisie supported the October 1905 strike showed where they stood. And yet they did not carry through their demands for the full removal of the old state and its replacement by a bourgeois democratic structure, which could have provided the necessary environment for the full development of capital. Trotsky argued that they were afraid to go further because they knew that they would be replaced by the working class, once the Tsarist bureaucratic police state was removed.

Engels had remarked earlier that the bourgeoisie had lost its stomach for governing, when he was talking of German unification and noting that it was the Junkers who carried out that task. Trotsky was essentially building on this Marx–Engels conception of the bourgeois loss of courage and leadership. 'By 1848 the bourgeoisie was unable to play a similar role. It did not want to, and could not, assume a revolutionary liquidation of the social order which barred the way to its own dominance' (Trotsky 1972:52). Western Europe, including Germany, had had a long evolution of the market in which a bourgeoisie had developed, while sometimes enveloped in feudal remnants. Landlords were part of the market, even while maintaining semi-feudal aristocratic forms, so it was not surprising that the Junkers could carry through the unification of Germany. That was not the case in Russia, where the extraction of the surplus product remained bound to the old forms of the semi-Asiatic mode of production of the village commune, ties to the land and the brutal assertion of bureaucratic and landlord authority.

This meant that the rising capitalist class would have had to assert itself in revolutionary not evolutionary form in order to establish its own dominion, even though there was a world capitalist market. While it had been prepared to do so in France in earlier times, it could not do so in the Russia of the twentieth century. As noted above, it was afraid to act in case it would destroy the very bulwark which prevented its left taking power, but it also had another reason and that presaged the events of the late 1920s.

Finance capital had come to dominate modern capitalism and that meant that foreign investment in Russia played a critical role in the emerging industrial economy.

The new Russia acquired its absolutely specific character because it received its capitalist baptism in the latter half of the nineteenth century from European capital which by then had reached its most concentrated and abstract form, that of finance capital. (Trotsky 1972:50)

The short-termist nature of finance capital is its hallmark. Hilferding theorised it as abstract capital, which therefore had no place, industry or worker to which it was tied, unlike industrial capital. Its only aim was to make money out of money. This meant that it was not interested in the development of Russia, only that it made the maximum return on its investments. Logically, as today in post-Soviet Russia, it sought out extractive industry, whose output was largely exported. Nonetheless, it also financed railway and industrial expansion and as Trotsky put it: 'The European entrepreneurs took direct possession of the most important branches of Russian industry. Europe's finance capital, by assimilating the lion's share of the Russian state budget, returned in part to Russian territory in the form of industrial capital' (1972:16). However, the interests of this section of capital were much more in terms of stability and the strong state rather than the overthrow of the Tsarist system. Indigenous industrial capital was therefore too weak to assert itself. It constituted a relatively weak force within the state capitalist enterprises and the operations of foreign finance capital.

In principle Trotsky was arguing that capital wanted to remove absolutism but would be pusillanimous at best in removing the autocracy. He was essentially making the same case as modern economists, the neo-conservatives and the rest, that the development of capitalism requires the extension of civil rights to the whole population, and he makes the case explicitly (Trotsky 1925:71–9), citing case after case in which sectors of Russian capital explicitly, in prosaic language, as he says, make their case for democracy. Why then did he argue that they would not go the whole way? In 1905, once the Tsar had granted a parliamentary system and civil rights, the bourgeoisie was satisfied. Trotsky, at the time, argued that the Tsarist concessions were a sham and they had to push for immediate concessions such as an amnesty and release for political prisoners, removal of the old Tsarist ministers, the standing down of the army, in short an immediate shift in power. The promised new constitution was little more than a sham. So indeed it proved to be as the regime had prepared both a massacre and a pogrom, which was wisely avoided by the Petrograd Soviet (Deutscher 1954:128–34).

There were essentially two issues. The first was that the autocracy did not want to concede anything if it could help it and if it could undo any concessions it would do so, once it felt sufficiently strong. The bourgeoisie was not, however, prepared to fight to the bitter end for its own demands. One had, therefore, to conclude that they were prepared to accept a malfunctioning and limited market. This was not the bourgeoisie of the French Revolution but a bourgeoisie afraid of its successor.

The second issue concerned the demand for workers' rights, which were in themselves not socialist, and which the bourgeoisie of the West had implemented or conceded decades or centuries previously.

One aspect of bourgeois democracy is that labour power should be free. In Russia, however, personal rights were limited and one of the most obvious limitations, as in Stalinist Russia, was the internal passport, which was a major grievance. Censorship was another example of civil rights and the printers acted to remove it in 1905. Mass education was an elementary demand which was essential to raise the level of productivity. The demand for the eight-hour day, which a century later is still not fully implemented in many countries, clearly went further. How much further is shown by the absurd discussion in the British press in May 2005 in which it largely supported the British rejection of a maximum 48-hour week imposed by the European Union. The point, however, is that all these demands are not in themselves socialist, but the Russian bourgeoisie refused to support them when the Petrograd Soviet called the second general strike in November 1905.

One can, however, make the case that these demands are inherently favourable to workers and hence workers' issues. The problem with such an argument is that a mature capitalism with a confident bourgeoisie at its head would have no problem implementing them, and more, in its own interest. In principle capital needs conditions for abstract labour, which requires a fully flexible, fluid and well-trained labour force, and without those conditions it can only be crippled. It became clear that capital in Russia had accepted its limited role and hence could not perform its own tasks.

Trotsky does not use the actual phrase 'decline of capitalism' but that is the only conclusion that one can draw. He does, however, have all the ingredients of the conception of decline, which he later uses, as in the following quote in 1935:

History places this task squarely before us. If the proletariat is, for one reason or another, incapable of routing the bourgeoisie and of seizing power, if it is, for example, paralysed by its own parties and trade unions, the continued decay of economy and civilization will follow, calamities will pile up, despair and prostration will engulf the masses, and capitalism – decrepit, decayed, rotting – will strangle the people with increasing strength, and will thrust them into the abyss of a new war. (Trotsky 1935)

Following Trotsky's analysis, one can see why soviets and the general strike showed themselves in all their glory in the Russia of 1905. Capitalism, in its decline, had come to incorporate trade unions as tolerated non-political entities, but in Russia trade unions could not easily function as non-political entities within an autocratic police state and consequently were not tolerated, except for those few which were economistic. Migratory illiterate labour, living under appalling conditions, had little use for trade-unionist bargaining when they needed more radical solutions. Militant workers' committees at the point of work were an obvious development, not least because they immediately posed the question of power at the workplace. As long as they had the support of their constituents there was no point in arresting them. In themselves, they did not pose the question of socialism. For that there had to be direction, coming from the Marxist leaders. In the last 15 years (up to 2005), we have seen many examples of de facto soviets being set up but leading nowhere. After a time they become demoralised as they go nowhere and then they are suppressed. That did not happen in the Russia of 1905. The process snowballed in the towns and the countryside and built up through two general strikes to the point where ultimately the Bolsheviks ended up fighting the Tsarist army in Moscow.

This cannot be explained as a purely spontaneous series of actions. The first general strike, with the Petrograd Soviet at its head and Trotsky its de facto leader, made a series of demands, but the leaders called off the strike, after ten days, when the Tsar made his concessions. It was consciously and coherently led. There were, of course, a number of parties involved, not just one, but that does not alter the point. This was as far as the bourgeoisie would go. It did not want to overthrow the system.

The second general strike, now based on the working class and the support of the socialist parties, was again very consciously led. It might be argued that a fully developed, prepared and conscious underground socialist party could have succeeded where the Petrograd Soviet and the Marxists failed. As there was no such party, the argument could be regarded as speculative if it were not for the fact that just such a party succeeded twelve years later. In the upshot, the Tsarist system went for wholesale repression on an extreme scale and it took until 1912 before the left began to recover. We can ask whether the second strike was not a mistake and it is obvious that the outcome could lead to such a conclusion.[7] Yet, every revolutionary movement has to learn its lessons and every leadership has to be tested in battle. It might have been wiser to have called off the strike earlier, when it was clear that it could not succeed, but it would be hard to avoid the conclusion that it was right that it was called in the first place.

One of the features of finance capital to which Hilferding pointed was the fact that it can act as the organisational centre of capital. In its decline, capital has developed a highly conscious nucleus which can plan its defence, which in turn requires an equally conscious trained socialist nucleus.

7. Trotsky had no illusions about the results; when speaking of the 1905 revolution, he said: 'Yet at the same time there can be no doubt that no revolution in the past has absorbed such a mass of popular energy while yielding such minimal positive results as the Russian revolution has done up to the present' (Trotsky 1972:55). Later in the same book he quotes Marx to the effect that at a decisive moment in a revolution it is necessary to stake everything, whatever the chances of the struggle (Trotsky 1972:266).

CONCLUSION

Soviets or workers' committees are not enough to ensure that a general strike succeeds in overthrowing the system. Spontaneity cannot succeed against a trained, determined and highly conscious opponent. Nor is a general strike in itself sufficient to change a regime. We have to understand 1905 as the revolution which led to the evolution of the theory of permanent revolution, the need for the formation of a theoretically armed and militant working-class party, an understanding of the limited importance of soviets and a rather better appreciation of the role of the general strike.

In theoretical terms, the use of the concept of decline radically alters the perspective of the thinker. For Trotsky the bourgeoisie was getting weaker and the proletariat stronger both objectively because the categories of capital were themselves changing towards socialisation and because subjectively the bourgeoisie had lost its earlier self-confidence in opposition to the working class. Clearly, if capitalism had a long and relatively stable future then any shift to socialism would either be doomed or take a long time. Lenin had shifted to this view by the time he wrote *Imperialism, the Highest Stage of Capitalism* in 1916 and it does not seem surprising that by 1917 he would abandon the very cautious position he had held earlier. In a sense, Trotsky's understanding was a remarkable anticipation of the whole epoch in which we now exist in that he saw that the end of capitalism was a process, not a simple climax as Hilferding seems to see it – a process of decline initiated with the shift to finance capital and reflecting the weakness of the bourgeoisie. The concept of permanent revolution itself is a statement that only the working class as the universal class can change society and society is ripe for overthrow, but until it is overthrown the world is doomed to endure one struggle after another, one repression after another, until the final victory.

REFERENCES

Deutscher, I. (1954) *The Prophet Armed* (New York: Oxford University Press).
Hilferding, R. (1985 [1910]) *Finance Capital* (London: Routledge and Kegan Paul).
Lenin, V. I. (1935a [1905]) *Two Tactics of Social Democracy in the Democratic Revolution*, Polnoye Sobraniye, *Sochinenie*, viii, 3rd edn. (Moscow: Partizdat).

—— (1935b [1916]) *Imperialism, the Highest stage of Capitalism*, Polnoye Sobraniye, *Sochinenie*, xix (Moscow: Partizdat).

—— (1931 [1905]) *The Revolution of 1905, The Revolutionary Democratic Dictatorship of the Proletariat and Peasantry*, Vperyod, 14 (12 April 1905) (Little Lenin Library).

—— (1958 [1899]) *Razvitie Kapitalizma v Rossii* (Development of Capitalism in Russia), Pol'noe Sobranie, *Sochinenie*, iii, 3rd edn. (Moscow: Partizdat).

Löwy, M. (1976) 'From Hegel to the Finland Station', *Critique*, 6.

Ticktin, H. (1994) 'The Nature of an Epoch of Declining Capitalism', *Critique*, 26:69–93.

—— (1995) 'Trotsky's Political Economy of Capitalism', in H. Ticktin and M. Cox (eds), *Trotsky's Ideas* (London: Porcupine Press).

Trotsky, L. (1925 [1906]) *Our Revolution: Capital in Opposition, Sochinenie*, ii (Moscow).

—— (1935) *Once Again, Whither France?* part I, March 28, available at <http://www.marxists.org/archive/trotsky/works/1936/witherfrance/>.

—— (1963 [1939]) 'Presenting Karl Marx', in *Leon Trotsky presents the Living Thoughts of Karl Marx* (Fawcett).

—— (1972 [1922]) *1905* (London: Allen Lane/The Penguin Press).

—— (1986 [1933–35]) *Notebooks 1933–1935*, edited by Phil Pomper (New York: Columbia University Press).

5

Results and Prospects:
Trotsky and his Critics[1]

Paul Blackledge

Despite being widely referred to by his interlocutors, it is a peculiarity of Trotsky's theory of uneven and combined development that it has received little by way of systematic consideration in the century since its first formulation in 1906. The initial lack of impact of Trotsky's thesis can largely be explained by the combined consequences of censorship alongside an unfortunately timed publication. The selection of Trotsky's writings, *Our Revolution*, which included *Results and Prospects*, was quickly seized by the Tsarist police, and those few copies which escaped detection found their target audience dispersed across Europe and America in the wake of the post-revolutionary reaction. Trotsky's misfortune was further compounded by the fact that the book was in the main a collection of previously published pieces, which meant that Russian socialists tended not to go out of their way to find a copy. Consequently, few of Trotsky's contemporaries actually read his argument before the October Revolution. This is almost certainly true of Lenin, whose critical comments on Trotsky's theory before 1917 seem to have been made against quotations taken from works of others (Deutscher 1954:162; Carr 1950:71).

If Trotsky was hard done by in this respect before the revolution, it was as nothing compared to the virulence of the attacks made upon him generally, and his strategy of permanent revolution[2] specifically, as part of Stalin's struggle for power from the mid-1920s onwards. It was not until the rebirth of an anti-Stalinist Marxism after 1956 that Trotsky's contribution to historical materialism began to be taken seriously, and even this impetus has not proved to be enough to salvage his reputation within the academy. If Jon Elster is

1. Thanks to Bill Dunn and Kristyn Gorton for their comments on this chapter in draft.
2. Permanent revolution is perhaps best understood, as Ernest Mandel has suggested, as the strategic counterpart to Trotsky's theory of combined and uneven development (Mandel 1979:84).

unrepresentative in so far as he actually engages with the theory of uneven and combined development, his argument that this theory was 'rather vapid' and did 'not make any positive contribution' is typical of academic assessments of Trotsky's Marxism (Elster 1986:55). Elsewhere I have argued that Trotsky did make a powerful contribution to historical materialism, which acted as a theoretical corollary to his political break with Second International fatalism without succumbing to political voluntarism (Blackledge 2005, cf. 2006a, 2006b). In this chapter, I argue that those of Trotsky's interlocutors who have taken his ideas seriously have concluded, either implicitly or explicitly, that his characterisation of Stalinism contradicts his model of uneven and combined development, such that one or other of these must be jettisoned if his contribution to Marxism is not to fall into incoherence. Concretely, the medium- to long-term survival of the Soviet Union as, in Trotsky's analysis, a 'degenerate workers' state', was incompatible with the theory of uneven and combined development, so long as the Soviet state remained isolated from successful *socialist* revolutions in the West.

DEBATING TROTSKY'S MARXISM

If the events of 1956 opened up a space within which Trotsky's ideas began, in narrow circles, to attain a fair hearing, amongst the first to reassess the concepts of uneven and combined development was George Novack. Novack argued, in an essay first published in 1957, that uneven and combined development was a universally valid model 'rooted in features common to all processes of growth in nature as well as society' (Novack 1980:85). Thus, whereas Trotsky developed the theory of uneven and combined development to explain the concrete mechanisms at play in Russia and internationally at the beginning of the twentieth century, and from which, in the context of a failed revolution, he derived the strategy of permanent revolution, Novack naturalised the concept of uneven and combined development and deployed it as a theoretical prop for a fatalistic model of revolutionary change. Specifically, he argued that Trotsky's theory could explain both the degeneration of Soviet communism after the revolution and the underlying causes of 'the process of de-Stalinisation' (Novack 1980:112). Novack argued that Stalinism combined 'socialist...economic foundations' alongside 'a political superstructure showing the most malignant traits of the class dictatorships of the past' (1980:101). However despotic its nature,

Novak expected this peculiar structure to reform itself in the direction of 'socialist democracy' in response to the 'extension of the revolution to Eastern Europe and Asia after the Second World War, the expansion of Soviet industry, and the rise in numbers and cultural level of the Soviet workers' (1980:111). While history falsified this prediction, Novack's deployment of the concept of uneven and combined development also appears to evacuate the content of Trotsky's Marxism. For whereas Trotsky was adamant that socialism was on the agenda in Russia in 1917 only because the proletariat would be in the forefront of the revolution (Trotsky 1973:307–11; Knei-Paz 1978:47–57), the social transformations in Eastern Europe and China after the Second World War, which Novack described as socialist, involved at best only a minor role for the proletariat. Moreover, on the basis of the theory of uneven and combined development, Trotsky had imagined the survival of the Soviet Union for years, not decades, before international revolutions saved it, and certainly not against an onslaught from the Wehrmacht. Thus, in 1928, he approvingly quoted Lenin's earlier statement that 'without timely aid from the international revolution, we shall be unable to hold out' (Trotsky 1974:13). Indeed, while the events of 1917 confirmed the power of Trotsky's analysis of the Tsarist state, the continuing vitality of the Soviet Union in the 1930s, during the war and in the post-war years, seemed to falsify its basic predictions. This was one of the key criticisms of Trotsky's Marxism made by Nicolas Krasso in a famous exchange with Novack's collaborator Ernest Mandel in the late 1960s.

In an article first published in *New Left Review* in 1967, Krasso argued that *Results and Prospects* was 'undoubtedly a brilliant prefiguration of the main characteristics of the October Revolution of 1917' (Krasso 1971a:15). However, while Trotsky had accurately predicted the class dynamic of the coming revolution, Krasso commented that his discussion of the 'role of political organisation in the socialist struggle' was as inept as his discussion of the class struggle was profound (1971a:16). This weakness was no mere error that was overcome once Trotsky joined the Bolshevik Party in 1917, but rather reflected a deep-seated tendency on Trotsky's part towards 'sociologism'; a concept which Krasso explained by reference to that of economism (1971a:22). Whereas economistic Marxism tended to reduce politics to an epiphenomenon of the economy, sociologistic Marxism reduced politics to class structure: 'Here it is not the economy, but social classes, which are extracted from the complex historical totality and hypostatised in an idealist fashion as the demiurges of a given political situation' (1971a:22). This weakness in Trotsky's Marxism was not overcome in 1917, but rather remained as a consistent feature of his thought up until his murder in 1940. Moreover, or so Krasso maintained, this flaw in Trotsky's method resulted in a general lacuna in his political perspectives: he consistently 'underestimated...the autonomous power of political institutions' (1971a:29). Indeed, Krasso explained both Trotsky's defeat at the hands of Stalin after Lenin's death, and his misunderstanding of the prospects for revolution in the West after 1917, in relation to this basic failing.

With reference to the conflict between Stalin and Trotsky, Krasso claimed that the dialectical unity of hope and realism that was a characteristic of Lenin's thought was split asunder within the Communist Party after his death. On the one hand, the realistic Stalin dismissed the perspectives for world revolution to concentrate on socialist construction in Russia, while, on the other hand, the naively optimistic Trotsky dismissed the hopes of socialist construction at home without the success of revolutions abroad. The relative power of Stalin's position in this debate was proved not only by his success in constructing socialism in the Soviet Union, but also by the failure of Trotsky's predictions for a Western revolution. In fact, Krasso claimed that by contrast with Stalin's realistic appraisal of the prospects for world revolution, there was no 'substance in Trotsky's thesis that socialism in one country was doomed to annihilation' (1971a:34). Finally, Trotsky's attempt to form the Fourth International in the late 1930s was 'destined to failure' as he understood Lenin's conception of socialist organisation only in 'caricature'. Therefore, while he 'brilliantly' analysed the class dynamic of the October Revolution in his *History of the Russian Revolution*, his lack of an adequate model of the autonomy of politics precluded him from making a sufficiently scientific analysis of the requirements of Western revolutionary organisations. Consequently, despite the 'prescience' of his analysis of German fascism, in light of his general inability to comprehend the specifics of national politics in the West his conceptualisation of political leadership was too voluntaristic to offer a viable alternative to Stalin's Comintern.

Krasso's article sparked a debate on the nature of Trotsky's Marxism in the pages of *New Left Review*. In his first contribution to this debate, Mandel argued, quite reasonably, that Krasso's praise of Trotsky's analysis of German fascism sat uneasily with his overarching dismissal of Trotsky's conceptualisation of the national specificities of politics. 'How could Trotsky succeed' in correctly analysing German politics in the period between 1929 and 1933, he asked, 'without a minute examination and understanding not only of social classes and groupings but also of parties?' (Mandel 1971a:49–50).

On the question of political organisation, Mandel suggested that the 'rational kernel' of Trotsky's rejection of Lenin's approach to this question before 1917 'was based upon' a reasonable 'distrust of Western social democratic apparatus' (Mandel 1971a:45). Moreover, Mandel pointed out that Lenin, for whom the epoch of imperialism was one of wars and revolutions, shared with Trotsky the basic assumption, as Lukács argued, that politics in the present period should start from 'the actuality of the revolution' (Lukács, quoted in Mandel 1971a:64). Developing this claim in a rejoinder to Krasso's reply to his first essay, Mandel pointed out that to reject Trotsky's assessment of the epoch implied the rejection of Lenin's account of the same (Mandel 1971b:116). Irrespective of the validity of the claim that Trotsky and Lenin were at one on this issue, Mandel's argument highlights the fact that the debate on Trotsky's conceptualisation of the nature of socialist organisation was premised on a prior analysis of the prospects for revolution in the West. Against Krasso's dismissal of this perspective, Mandel argued three points: first, that in Germany, Spain, France and Italy, amongst other countries, there had developed revolutionary or pre-revolutionary situations on several occasions between 1917 and 1945; second, that in all but the earliest of these conjunctures Stalin's Comintern acted to suppress the revolutionary energy of the workers' movements; and third, in contrast to the misrepresentation of Trotsky as an ultra-leftist, in the early 1920s he was at the forefront, with Lenin, of those within the Comintern who argued that Western capitalism had gained a breathing space after the immediate post-war upheavals (Mandel 1971a:64–7). Mandel thus pointed out that to label Stalin's perspective as pragmatic or realistic, as did Krasso, involved both caricaturing Trotsky's position and eliding Stalin's role in the failure of the Russian Revolution to spread from the early to mid 1920s. Further, Mandel insisted that Krasso obscured the mechanism upon which Stalin's successful rise to power was premised, not upon his more realistic analysis of the international conjuncture in the 1920s, but on the way his policies reflected the interests of an emerging 'special social grouping inside Soviet society: the Soviet bureaucracy' (Mandel 1971a:68).

Despite the power of this argument, a fault-line ran through Mandel's defence of Trotsky. Because Trotsky's perspectives regarding the long-term viability of socialism in Russia were, as Krasso correctly pointed out, predicated upon the success of a revolution in the West, Trotsky insisted that without one or more such revolutions the Soviet regime was bound to collapse. 'His whole discussion' of the world system, in *The Permanent Revolution*, 'assumes that the capitalist world market is the economic system rendering socialism impossible in one country' (Krasso 1971b:83). Returning to his critique of Trotsky's supposed 'sociologism' in a rejoinder to Mandel, Krasso maintained that Trotsky's underestimation of 'the autonomy of the political institution of the nation state' led to a lacuna in his Marxism regarding the continuing vitality of the Soviet regime (Krasso 1971b:88). In a second reply, Mandel argued that Trotsky did not exhibit one 'atom of the historical pessimism' attributed to him by Krasso, and that there is 'no foundation' within *The Permanent Revolution* 'of any conception of "inevitable collapse" of the Soviet Union' (Mandel 1971b:110).

Unfortunately, despite the general power of Mandel's critique of Krasso, this argument is somewhat disingenuous; for by narrowing his discussion of Trotsky's analysis of the prospects for the Soviet system to comments made in *The Permanent Revolution*, Mandel elided a flaw in Trotsky's analysis that Krasso had justifiably highlighted. The continued existence of the Soviet Union as some form of workers' state appeared to negate Trotsky's claim that socialism in one country was an impossible dream. This was the thrust of Monty Johnstone's contribution to this debate: 'A serious examination of what Trotsky actually said about building socialism in Russia reveals a fundamental and unresolved contradiction in his position.' Johnstone went on to suggest that Trotsky, from the perspective of the theory of uneven and combined development, was unable to account for the vitality of the Soviet state from the 1920s to the 1960s (Johnstone 1971:129–30). From a diametrically opposed position, Duncan Hallas similarly pointed out that in the late 1930s Trotsky predicted that the bureaucracy was 'becoming ever more the organ of the world bourgeoisie in the workers' state' and, either it 'will overthrow the new forms of property and plunge the country back to capitalism; or the working class will crush the bureaucracy and open the way to socialism'. 'Each day added to its domination helps to rot the foundations of the socialist elements of economy and increases the chances for capitalist restoration' (Hallas 1971:8). Commenting on these arguments, Hallas suggested that Trotsky's characterisation of the Soviet regime as both exceptional and unstable had become indefensible in the wake of, first, its victory over the Wehrmacht, and, second, its imperial expansion, including the reproduction of its social structure, across Eastern Europe after 1945.

Trotsky's *analysis* of the class struggle in the USSR after 1927 has clearly been shown to be erroneous. The point is important. No 'orthodox' Trotskyist tendency today in fact defends Trotsky's *analysis* – they substitute a label for the analysis. And this label covers a confused and shifting content. (Hallas 1971:8)

Mandel's reply to Krasso failed, therefore, to recognise that the resilience of the Soviet regime for half a century after the 1930s, and against incredible external pressures, posed testing problems for Trotsky's analysis of Stalinism. Further, Mandel's denial of Trotsky's 'pessimism' vis-à-vis the long-term future of the Soviet Union in the absence of European socialist revolutions does not bear scrutiny. As Michael Burawoy has suggested, a model of the Soviet regime's terminal degeneration, in the context of failed revolutions elsewhere in Europe, was anticipated in *Results and Prospects* (Burawoy 1989:785). More generally, Burawoy has argued that the strength of Trotsky's analysis of the pre-revolutionary Russia is evidenced in the power of the novel predictions that his analysis suggested. In a comparison of Trotsky's analysis of the Russian Revolution with that offered by Theda Skocpol, Burawoy argues that whereas Skocpol maintained an explicit attachment to induction, Trotsky's deductive approach foreshadowed the theory of research programmes as developed by Imre Lakatos. In addition, while Trotsky sometimes 'sunk below' his method and Skocpol often rose above the limitations of hers, 'Trotsky still makes the greater scientific advance, underscoring the superiority of research programs over induction' (Burawoy 1989:763).

Lakatos argued that any 'research programme' could be differentiated between its 'hard core' and its 'protective belt'. Hypotheses contained within the protective belt could be falsified without necessarily undermining the hard core; however, if hard core hypotheses were falsified then the research programme as a whole would be falsified. Thus, Lakatos differentiated his version of falsification theory from a version that he believed was sometimes present in Popper's work, which he called 'dogmatic falsification' (Lakatos 1970:95). For where, in dogmatic falsification, the falsification of any hypothesis could lead to the rejection of the general scientific framework from which it originated, in his sophisticated falsificationist model, a research programme could survive the falsification of many of the hypotheses that it generated. Lakatos argued that 'the main difference from Popper's original version is, I think, that in my conception criticism does not – and must not – kill as fast as Popper imagined' (1970:179). Lakatos argued that a scientific theory should contain both a positive and a negative heuristic. The positive heuristic would be that element of the theory which suggested further areas for research. The negative heuristic, meanwhile, was that element of the research programme that could not be challenged. A strong scientific research programme would, Lakatos argued, generate a positive heuristic through which novel facts would be predicted (1970:155).

Whereas Stinchcombe argued that Trotsky had followed the inductive method in the formulation of his theory of uneven and combined development (Stinchcombe 1978:53), Burawoy suggests that Trotsky elaborated this theory as an implicit response to the generation of anomalies within the Marxist research programme. Against Second International orthodoxy, socialist revolutions seemed to be on the agenda in relatively backward sectors of the world system, and Trotsky's method aimed at both accounting for this anomaly and underpinning a realistic strategic orientation for the Russian socialist movement. According to Burawoy, Trotsky takes Marxism's hard core to include the statement, made in Marx's famous 1859 preface to *The Contribution to the Critique of Political Economy*, that revolutions occur in epochs when the further development of the forces of production come into conflict with the existing relations of production, and that no social order perishes before it has fostered all the development of the forces of production of which it is capable. For Burawoy, Trotsky's analysis of the prospects for the Russian Revolution 'aimed to protect the hard core of Marxism from refutation by the failure of revolution in the most advanced capitalist countries' (Burawoy 1989:781). The power of Trotsky's analysis of world history, when compared to Skocpol's, lay in the way that whereas she 'freezes history, for Trotsky: "History does not repeat itself. However much one may compare the Russian Revolution with the Great [French] Revolution, the former cannot be transformed into the latter. The 19th century has not passed in vain"' (Burawoy 1989:782; cf. Trotsky 1969:52). Hence, in contrast to Skocpol's static comparisons of the French, Russian and Chinese revolutions, Trotsky was aware of the degree of change, alongside continuity, between the contexts within which the first of these two great social upheavals were played out. Accordingly, whereas the theory of uneven development explained the temporal, but not social, variation in world history, the theory of combined development explained both temporal and social historical divergences.

Nevertheless, Burawoy argues that of the two novel predictions made by Trotsky in *Results and Prospects*, only one was realised. For whereas Russia's industrial proletariat did lead the revolution in 1917, and while the bourgeois revolution did therefore spill over into a proletarian revolution placing a mass revolutionary workers' party, the Bolsheviks, in power, Trotsky's hoped for Western revolution failed to materialise. Accordingly, if Trotsky 'is successful in anticipating the Russian Revolution, he is wide of the mark in his anticipation of revolution in Western Europe' (Burawoy 1989:788).

Paralleling Novack's similar claims, and explicitly following Deutscher, Burawoy extends this argument to suggest that once the Russian Revolution was isolated, 'the permanent revolution' was forced 'inwards, where it took the form of Stalin's revolution from above' (1989:785). Burawoy thus praises the power of Trotsky's theory of uneven and combined development, and its parallel strategy of permanent revolution – even going so far as to recruit Stalin as a closet Trotskyist. However, Burawoy combines this praise for one element of Trotsky's theory with a dismissal of another: Trotsky's perspectives for the West in the inter-war years were, he argues, mistaken. Indeed, he uses the same example as did Krasso: Trotsky understood, as did no one else, the 'true significance' of the events in Germany in the years running up to 1933, but his 'faith that the German working class would rise up against Hitler' was misplaced (Burawoy 1989:789).

Burawoy's critique of Trotsky's European perspectives is open to the charge made by Mandel against Krasso: that his approach was fatalistic and therefore implicitly apologetic of the role of the Stalinist parties in consistently undermining European revolutionary movements from the early-mid 1920s onwards. In contrast to this approach, the great lesson that Trotsky learnt in 1917 was of the importance of political leadership within the class struggle (Geras 1986:162). This is the thrust of his discussion of the crucial role played by Lenin in 1917. He argued that without the political reorientation led by Lenin, the Bolsheviks would not have seized the revolutionary opportunity in October; and, as the alternative to their rule was a military coup, fascism would have had a Russian precursor (Trotsky 1977:343, 1947:205). Similarly, he argued that the crucial role of political leadership had been negatively evidenced through the loss of a number of revolutionary opportunities in the 1920s and 1930s as a result of the Comintern's increasingly 'counter-revolutionary role' after 1923 (Trotsky 1990:25).

The irony of Burawoy's defence of Trotsky's theory of uneven and combined development is therefore that, whereas he praises Trotsky's break with the fatalistic Marxism of the Second International, his discussion of Western Europe's missing revolutions, like Krasso's before him, betrays an implicit retreat back towards just the form of mechanical fatalism from which Trotsky had broken between 1906 and 1917. While Mandel and Novack shared neither Krasso's nor Burawoy's dismissal of both the revolutionary events of the 1920s in Western Europe, and the conservative role played by the Comintern therein, their own discussions of Trotsky's Marxism are no less problematic. In the case of Novack, this weakness takes the form of fatalistic hopes for the regeneration of Soviet Communism after 1953, whereas Mandel's defence of Trotsky's characterisation of Stalinism in a context explicitly precluded by Trotsky tends to preserve the form of Trotsky's mature thought at the expense of its content. Consequently, whereas the theory of uneven and combined development was premised upon the insight that capitalism tended to unify the global labour process (Harman 1983:67–8, 75), a dogmatic attachment to Trotsky's characterisation of Stalinism opens the door to the theory of socialism in one country, and therefore involves a tacit rejection of this assumption. Similarly, in contrast to Trotsky's commitment to the idea of socialism as the self-emancipation of the working class, Mandel's defence of Trotsky's classification of the Soviet Union leads him to describe Maoist China, and other similar states, as examples of the dictatorship of the proletariat, despite the fact that the proletariat played little or no active role in the social transformations through which these states were formed (Mandel 1995:102; cf. Löwy 1981:213ff). Therefore, both analytically and politically, Trotsky's model of Stalinism tends to negate the power of his theory of uneven and combined development.

CONCLUSION

The related weaknesses of all of these criticisms appear to confirm Hallas's opinion that Trotskyism found itself at an impasse after the war. Russia's victory over Germany negated the content of Trotsky's characterisation of the Soviet regime as a degenerate workers' state, whilst, simultaneously, the resilience of the Soviet state seemed to negate the implications of the theory of uneven and combined development: that socialism in one country is impossible. Interestingly, one prominent intellectual who took the falsification of Trotsky's predictions seriously was Alasdair MacIntyre, who explicitly linked his break with Marxism to this fact (MacIntyre 1985:262). Nevertheless, as MacIntyre had previously suggested, there did exist a way out of this conundrum. The problem with Trotsky's key predictions after 1906 lay not in a failure of the Western working class to act as prescribed in the 1920s, but rather in a failure of the Soviet state, in the 1940s and beyond, to react to severe external pressure as Trotsky had expected (MacIntyre 1971). The power of the theory of uneven and combined development, suitably deepened with Trotsky's post-1917 embrace of Bolshevism, was demonstrated in the period after 1917, when revolutions occurred not only in Russia but also across Europe; and the fact that most of these revolutionary movements were defeated confirms only the importance of revolutionary leadership in such situations. Conversely, the weakness of Trotsky's analysis of Stalinism was confirmed by the successes of the Soviet Union between 1941 and 1948. Chris Arthur engaged with this problem from a different angle when, in his contribution to the debate occasioned by Krasso's essay, he argued that Trotsky's claim that the coming Russian Revolution would be political rather than social in nature skirted over the fact that a socialist revolution in Stalinist Russia would be forced to confront the social basis of the Soviet bureaucracy (Arthur 1971:154–5). Unfortunately, Arthur rejected the logic of his own argument, that Trotsky's characterisation of the Soviet state was of little help to our understanding of the course of its development after his death.

Paralleling Burawoy's discussion of Trotsky's Lakatosian problem shift in 1906, Alex Callinicos argues that Tony Cliff made a similar contribution to Marxism in 1948, when, building on Trotsky's theory of uneven and combined development, he rejected Trotsky's characterisation of the Soviet Union as a degenerated workers' state (Callinicos 1989:79ff). Cliff argued that Stalin's forced industrialisation programme marked not the deepening inwards of the permanent revolution, but rather the counter-revolutionary negation of that project. While this process confirmed Trotsky's pessimistic prognosis of the perspectives for the Soviet regime, given the failure of supporting revolutions abroad, it did so at the expense of his model of Stalinism (Cliff 2003:1). By contrast with Trotsky, Cliff characterised the Soviet state that emerged from Stalin's counter-revolution as a form of 'bureaucratic state capitalism'. According to Callinicos, this theory not only provided a more powerful model of the Soviet system, it also entailed the novel prediction of the post-war boom. Moreover, one of the effects of this boom was to mediate against the emergence of revolutionary workers' movements in the West in the two decades after the war. Therefore, just as Trotsky's method allowed him to predict novel facts by breaking with the degeneration of Marxism, so too did Cliff by breaking with the degeneration of Trotskyism. By disassociating Trotsky's powerful analysis of uneven and combined development from his weak characterisation of Stalinism, Cliff reconfirmed the power of Trotsky's key contribution to historical materialism.

REFERENCES

Arthur, C. (1971) 'The Coming Soviet Revolution', in N. Krasso (ed.) *Trotsky: The Great Debate Renewed* (St Louis: New Critics Press).

Blackledge, P. (2005) 'Leon Trotsky's Contribution to the Marxist Theory of History', *Studies in East European Thought*, 57.

—— (2006a) *Reflections on the Marxist Theory of History* (Manchester: Manchester University Press).

—— (2006b) 'Karl Kautsky and Marxist Historiography', *Science and Society*, 2006.

Burawoy, M. (1989) 'Two Methods in Social Science: Skocpol versus Trotsky', *Theory and Society*, 18.

Callinicos, A. (1989) *Trotskyism* (Buckingham: Open University Press).

Carr, E. H. (1950) *The Bolshevik Revolution*, i (London: Penguin).

Cliff, T. (2003 [1948]) 'The Nature of Stalinist Russia' in T. Cliff, *Marxist Theory after Trotsky* (London: Bookmarks).

Deutscher, I. (1954) *Trotsky: The Prophet Armed* (London: Oxford University Press).

Elster, J. (1986) 'The Theory of Combined and Uneven Development: A Critique', in J. Roemer (ed.) *Analytical Marxism* (Cambridge: Cambridge University Press).

Geras, N. (1986) *Literature of Revolution* (London: Verso).

Hallas, D. (1971) 'Introduction', in D. Hallas et al. *The Fourth International, Stalinism and the Origins of the International Socialists* (London: Pluto Press).

Harman, C. (1983) 'Philosophy and Revolution', *International Socialism*, 21.

Johnstone, M. (1971) 'Trotsky and the Debate on Socialism in One Country', in N. Krasso (ed.) *Trotsky: The Great Debate Renewed* (St Louis: New Critics Press; first published in *New Left Review*, 50 (1968)).

Knei-Paz, B. (1978) *The Social and Political Thought of Leon Trotsky* (Oxford: Oxford University Press).

Krasso, N. (1971a) 'Trotsky's Marxism', in N. Krasso (ed.) *Trotsky: The Great Debate Renewed* (St Louis: New Critics Press; first published in *New Left Review*, 44 (1967)).

—— (1971b) 'Reply to Ernest Mandel', in N. Krasso (ed.) *Trotsky: The Great Debate Renewed* (St Louis: New Critics Press; first published in *New Left Review*, 48 (1968)).

Lakatos, I. (1970) 'Falsification and the Methodology of Scientific Research Programmes', in I. Lakatos and A. Musgrave (eds) *Criticism and the Growth of Knowledge* (Cambridge: Cambridge University Press).

Löwy, M. (1981) *The Politics of Combined and Uneven Development* (London: Verso).

MacIntyre, A. (1971) 'Trotsky in Exile', in A. MacIntyre, *Against the Self-Images of the Age* (London: Duckworth).

—— (1985) *After Virtue* (London: Duckworth).

Mandel, E. (1971a [1968]) 'Trotsky's Marxism: An Anti-Critique', in N. Krasso (ed.) *Trotsky: The Great Debate Renewed* (St Louis: New Critics Press).

—— (1971b [1969]) 'Trotsky's Marxism: A Rejoinder', in N. Krasso (ed.) *Trotsky: The Great Debate Renewed* (St Louis: New Critics Press).

—— (1979) *Revolutionary Marxism Today* (London: Verso).

—— (1995) *Trotsky as Alternative* (London: Verso).

Novack, G. (1980) 'Uneven and Combined Development in World History', in *Understanding History: Marxist Essays* (New York: Pathfinder).

Stinchcombe, A. (1978) *Theoretical Methods in Social History* (New York: Academic Press).

Trotsky, L. (1947 [1940]) *Stalin* (London: Hollis & Carter).

—— (1969 [1906]) 'Results and Prospects', in L. Trotsky, *The Permanent Revolution* and *Results and Prospects* (New York: Pathfinder).

—— (1973 [1907]) *1905* (London: Penguin).

—— (1974 [1928]) *The Third International After Lenin* (London: New Park).

—— (1977 [1931–3]) *The History of the Russian Revolution* (London: Pluto Press).

—— (1990 [1939]) 'Again and Once More Again on the Nature of the USSR', in L. Trotsky, *In Defence of Marxism* (New York: Pathfinder).

6

The Baggage of Exodus

Daniel Bensaïd

Certain 'Trotskyist' theses, such as the theory of permanent revolution, first appeared at the beginning of the twentieth century in relation to the Russian Revolution of 1905. However, the term 'Trotskyism' only appeared, as a banal term of bureaucratic jargon, in 1923–24. After the victorious civil war, and still more in 1924 after the failure of the German October and Lenin's death, the leaders of Soviet Russia and the Communist International were in an unforeseen situation of relative international stabilisation and the lasting isolation of the Soviet Union. It was no longer the social base which supported the state superstructure, but the will of the superstructure which sought to engage the base.

After his first stroke in March 1923, Lenin urged Trotsky to begin fighting Stalin on the questions of the foreign trade monopoly, nationalities and especially the internal party regime. In a letter to the Central Committee in October 1923, Trotsky (1975a) denounced the bureaucratisation of state institutions. In December of the same year, he assembled these criticisms into a series of articles calling for a *New Course*. This provoked the fight against 'Trotskyism' and its demands: the re-establishment of internal party democracy and the adoption of an economic plan to control the uneven and centrifugal effects of the New Economic Policy. In December 1924, in *Pravda*, Stalin (1976) personally characterised Trotskyism as 'a variety of Menshevism' and as 'permanent despair'. He opposed to this the daring construction of 'socialism in one country', rather than waiting to be rescued by an extension of the revolution elsewhere that might never actually happen.

After the massive recruitment of the 'Lenin levy' in 1924, the few thousand veterans of October no longer weighed very heavily in the party's membership relative to the hundreds of thousands of newcomers, amongst whom were many last-minute careerists. In a country lacking democratic traditions, and following the slaughter of the Great War, the hardships of the civil war left a people accustomed to extreme forms of social and physical violence. The upheavals of war and civil war led to a 'great leap backwards' and a reversion to an archaic level of development compared to that reached before 1914. Of the 4 million inhabitants of Petrograd in 1917, there remained no more than about 1.7 million in 1929. More than 380,000 workers left production and only 80,000 remained at work. The workers' citadel, the Putilov works, lost four-fifths of its employees, while more than 30 million peasants experienced food shortage and famine. The devastated cities lived on the back of authoritarian campaigns of requisition. The historian Moshe Lewin (1975) argues that in truth the state was formed on the basis of regressive social development.

Privilege thrives on scarcity: therein lie the fundamental roots of bureaucratisation. In a journal dictated in 1923 to his secretaries, Lenin, already sick, deemed that 'the apparatus we call ours is, in fact, still quite alien to us; it is a bourgeois and tsarists hotchpotch' (1922). That year, the prices of manufactures had practically tripled compared to pre-1914 levels, whereas farm prices had increased by less than 50 per cent. This disproportion explains the imbalance between city and countryside, and the refusal of the peasants to deliver their harvests at imposed low prices while there was nothing to buy.

The Bolshevik leaders had always conceived the revolution in Russia as the first step towards a European revolution or, at least, as a prelude to German revolution. The question put in 1923 was therefore: how to hold on until a possible resumption of the revolutionary movement in Europe? In 1917, all the Russian parties admitted that the country was not ripe for socialism. However, the 'democrat' Miliukov himself estimated that it was no more ready for democracy. He saw no alternative between the military dictatorship of Kornilov and that of the soviets. This meant a pitiless fight between revolution and counter-revolution.

From before Lenin's death, responses diverged. The strategy of 'construction of socialism in one country', defended by Stalin and his allies, subordinated the chances of world revolution to the interests of the Soviet bureaucracy; that of 'the permanent revolution', developed by Trotsky and the Left Opposition, subordinated the future of the Russian Revolution to the extension of the world revolution. These strategies implied divergent answers in relation to the principal international events: Anglo-Russian relations in 1926, the second Chinese revolution of 1927, the rise of Nazism in Germany, and later the radically contrary attitudes towards the Spanish civil war, the German–Soviet pact of 1939 and preparations for war.

The two strategies were equally opposed on the Soviet Union's policies at home. Trotsky and the Left Opposition proposed after 1924 a 'new course' aimed at reviving Soviet democracy and the role of the party. They put forward policies of planning and industrialisation aimed at reducing the tensions between agriculture and industry. However, they came to oppose Stalin's brutal about-turn of 1928 from Bukharin's 'socialism at a snail's pace' to forced collectivisation and the accelerated industrialisation of the first Five-Year Plan, which denuded the countryside and led to the great famine of 1932 in the Ukraine.

Faced with such clear alternatives, some historians have wondered about Trotsky's relative passivity immediately after Lenin's death, his reluctance to start a ruthless fight against Stalin, his agreeing to sweep Lenin's testament under the carpet. Self-interest provides plausible, and logical, explanations. He was, in the mid-1920s, perfectly conscious of the brittleness of a revolution whose working-class and urban base was thin, and of the need to work with a backward peasantry which constituted the overwhelming majority of the population. Given such an unstable equilibrium, favourable to authoritarian Bonapartist solutions, he refused to be pushed by the army (where his popularity remained high) and by the officer caste, because a military *coup d'état* would only have accelerated the process of bureaucratisation.

However, the political struggle had in fact been joined from 1923. By 1926, a united opposition was established which saw itself as a tendency that respected the legal authority of the party; their perspective was one of redirecting and reforming the regime. In May 1927, after the defeat of the second Chinese revolution, they called for a militant mass mobilisation. In October of the same year, on the tenth birthday of the revolution, Zinoviev and Trotsky were excluded from the party. The latter was exiled to Alma Ata, while more than 1,500 oppositionists were deported. The purges began.

In 1929, faced with a catastrophic economic situation, Stalin turned against the right of the party. He seemed, by instituting the first Five-Year Plan, to be adopting certain suggestions of the opposition. This turn precipitated a split among the opposition. Some of its most prestigious leaders saw in this 'revolution from above' a swing to the left. Capitulations and defections followed one after another. For Trotsky, those reconciled with the Thermidorean regime were from now on 'lost souls': planning without the restoration of socialist democracy would only further reinforce the power of the bureaucracy. Thus began a long exodus, forced to the margins of the mass movement.

These tragic inter-war struggles shaped the original defining characteristics of Trotskyism. Its essence can be summarised in four points.

1. THE OPPOSITION OF THE THEORY OF PERMANENT REVOLUTION TO THAT OF 'SOCIALISM IN ONE COUNTRY'

The elements of this strategy had emerged from the earlier Russian revolution of 1905. They were elaborated during the 1920s and found their full expression in Trotsky's theses on the second Chinese revolution of 1927:

> With regard to countries with a belated bourgeois development, especially the colonial and semi-colonial countries, the theory of the permanent revolution signifies that the complete and genuine solution of their tasks of achieving democracy and national emancipation is conceivable only through the dictatorship of the proletariat as the leader of the subjugated nation, above all of its peasant masses.... The conquest of power by the proletariat does not complete the revolution, but only opens it. Socialist construction is conceivable only on the foundation of the class struggle, on a national and international scale.... The completion of the socialist revolution within national limits is unthinkable. One of the basic reasons for the crisis in bourgeois society is the fact that the productive forces created by it can no longer be reconciled with the framework of the national state. From this follow...imperialist wars.... Different countries will go through this process at different tempos. Backward countries may, under certain conditions, arrive at the dictatorship of the proletariat sooner than advanced countries, but they will come later than the latter to socialism. (Trotsky 1962: 152–5)

In his introduction to the 1930 German edition of his texts on *Permanent Revolution*, Trotsky denounces the Stalinist amalgam of 'messianic nationalism...supplemented by bureaucratically abstract internationalism' (Trotsky 1962:25). He maintains that the socialist revolution remains, even after the seizure of power, 'a continual internal struggle' through which society 'continues to change its complexion', and within which inevitable shocks arise from 'the various groupings within this society in transformation'. This theory is imbued with a nonlinear and non-mechanical conception of history, where the law of 'combined and uneven development' determines only a range of possibilities whose outcome is not determined in advance. 'Marxism', writes Trotsky, 'takes its point of departure from world economy, not as a sum of national parts but as a mighty and independent reality which has been created by the international division of labour and the world market, and which in our epoch imperiously dominates the national markets' (1962:22)

2. ON TRANSITIONAL DEMANDS, THE UNITED FRONT AND THE FIGHT AGAINST FASCISM

The questions put in the light of the Russian Revolution were: how to mobilise the greatest possible numbers; how to raise the level of consciousness through action; and how to create the most effective alliance of forces for the inescapable confrontation with the ruling classes. This is what the Bolsheviks had known how to do in 1917 around the vital questions of bread, peace, land. It was a question of moving beyond abstract discussion of the intrinsic virtue of the claims, whether reformist by nature (because compatible with the established order) or revolutionary by nature (because incompatible with this order). The appropriateness of the demands depended on their mobilising value in connection with a concrete situation, and on their educational value for those who entered into struggle. The concept of 'transitional demands' overcame sterile antinomies between a reformist gradualism, which believed in changing society without revolutionising it, and a fetishism of the 'glorious day', which reduced revolution to its climactic moment, to the detriment of the patient work of organisation and education.

This debate is directly related to the one at the centre of strategic discussions on the programme of the Fifth and the Sixth Congresses of the Communist International. Reporting on the question in 1925, Bukharin reaffirmed the validity of 'the tactics of the offensive' of the beginning of the 1920s. On the other hand, at the Fifth Congress, the German representative Thalheimer supported the idea of the united front and transitional demands. He argued in particular:

One only has to look at the history of the Second International and its disintegration to recognise that it is precisely the separation between day-to-day questions and broad objectives which constituted the starting point of its descent into opportunism [...] The specific difference between us and the reformist socialists lies not in the fact that we want to eliminate from our programme demands for reform, by whatever name we give them, in order to distance ourselves from them. Rather, it consists in the fact that we locate these transitional demands in the closest relationship to our principles and our aims.

The question was again on the agenda of the Sixth Congress of 1928, under profoundly different conditions. Exiled in Turkey since 1929, Trotsky benefited from his enforced retreat to assess more deeply the previous ten years of revolutionary experiences. This reflection provided the material for the texts on *The Third International after Lenin* (1996). In his critique of the programme of the CI, published in Constantinople in 1929, Trotsky condemned the abandonment of the slogan of the Socialist United States of Europe. He rejected any confusion between his theory of permanent revolution and Bukharin's theory of the permanent offensive. He again characterised fascism as a 'state of civil war' carried out by capitalism against the proletariat.

Immediately after the Congress, through an about turn which ran in parallel with the policy of liquidation of the kulaks and forced collectivisation in the Soviet Union, the CI adopted an orientation of 'class against class'. This made social democracy the principal enemy and produced a fatal division in the German labour movement faced with the rise of Nazism. In a booklet entitled *The Third Period of Error of the Communist International*, Trotsky denounced this disastrous course not as a relapse into revolutionary enthusiasm, explicable as youthful leftism, but as a senile and bureaucratic leftism subordinated to the interests of the Kremlin and the zig-zags of its diplomacy. In his *History of the Russian Revolution*, he insisted on the serious study of indices of mass radicalisation (the evolution of trade-union power, electoral results, the strike rate) instead of abstractedly proclaiming the constant possibility of revolutionary action:

the activity of the masses can take very different forms according to conditions. At certain times, the masses can be completely absorbed by economic struggles and express very little interest in political questions. Alternatively, after having undergone several important reverses on the economic front, they can abruptly shift attention onto the political field.

His *Writings on Germany* day-by-day advance proposals for united action to overcome the resistible rise of Nazism. They provide a brilliant example of concrete political thought adjusted to the changes in the economic situation. They were thunderbolts hurled at German Communist Party 'orthodoxy', which was wedded to the stupid prophecy according to which 'after Hitler, comes the turn of Thälmann [then Secretary-General of the German CP]'.

In 1938, the founding Programme of the Fourth International (or Transitional Programme) summarised the lessons of these experiences:

It is necessary to help the masses in the process of the daily struggle to find the bridge between present demands and the socialist program of the revolution. This bridge should include a system of transitional demands, stemming from today's conditions and from today's consciousness of wide layers of the working class and unalterably leading to one final conclusion, the conquest of power by the proletariat... The Fourth International does not discard the program of the old 'minimal' demands to the degree to which these have preserved at least part of their vital forcefulness. Indefatigably, it defends the democratic right and social conquests of the workers. But it carries on this day-to-day work within the...revolutionary perspective. (1973a:75–6)

The programme included demands for sliding scales of wages and hours, for workers' control of production (a school for the planned economy) and financial transparency, for 'the expropriation of certain groups of capitalists', for the nationalisation of credit. It attached particular importance to democratic and national claims in the colonial and semi-colonial countries. This programme did not constitute a ready-made model of society; rather it developed a way of understanding action in which the emancipation of the workers remained the task of workers themselves.

3. THE FIGHT AGAINST STALINISM AND THE BUREAUCRACY

At the beginning of the 1920s, certain Soviet economists saw the world capitalist economy plunging into endless stagnation. Trotsky was one of the first to analyse its relative revival. In this context, he came to think of the Soviet economy not as a socialist economy, but as an 'economy in transition' in a country subjected to constant military threats and forced to devote a disproportionate share of its meagre resources to defence. It was thus not a question of building an ideal society in one country, but of gaining time, while awaiting the ebb and flow of the world revolution on whose final authority the future of the Russian revolution depended. The Russian revolution would remain constrained by the world market, and by competition with countries with more developed technology and higher labour productivity, for as long as it remained unsupported by the revolutionary movement of more developed countries.

Within the framework of these contradictions, Trotsky was one of the first to perceive the danger of the bureaucracy as a new social force enjoying social privileges related to its monopoly of political power. If, at the time of the civil war and war communism, he had been in favour of authoritarian methods, as testified by his worst book, *Terrorism and Communism* (1975b), since 1923 he had started to analyse bureaucratisation as a social phenomenon, even if in his eyes the 'new middle-class' of the kulaks and Nepmen still remained the principal danger. This decisive question of the periodisation of the bureaucratic counter-revolution continued to confront the Russian and international revolutionary movements. It was a question of knowing if the 'Soviet Thermidor' was already achieved or yet to come.

The bureaucratic counter-revolution was not a single event, symmetrical to that of October, but a drawn-out, cumulative process of different levels and stages. From October 1917 to the Stalinist Gulag there is no simple continuity but different levels of repression by, and weight of, the bureaucracy. At the same time as forced collectivisation, a crucial reform of the detention system came into effect in June 1929, generalising work camps for all condemned prisoners with more than three-year sentences. Confronted by the great famines of 1932–33 and the importance of internal migrations, a decision of December 1932 introduced internal passports. The law of 1 December 1934 introduced procedures that provided the legal instruments of the great terror. Then began the genuinely terrorist cycle marked by the great purges of 1936–38. More than half the delegates to the congress of 1934 were eliminated; more than 30,000 cadres from an army of 178,000 were killed. In parallel, the bureaucratic state apparatus exploded: according to the statistics of Moshe Lewin, the numbers of administrative staff went from 1,450,000 in 1928 to 7,500,000 in 1939, while the number of white collar workers leaped from 4 million to nearly 14 million. The state apparatus devoured the party, which thought it had the power to control it.

Under the bureaucratic knout, the country thus witnessed an upheaval without equivalent in the world. Between 1926 and 1939, the cities grew by 30 million inhabitants, and their paid labour force went from 10 to 22 million. It resulted in a massive ruralisation of the cities and the despotic imposition of a new work discipline. This transformation by forced march was accompanied by the exaltation of nationalism and a massive rise in careerism. In this great social and geographical whirl, as Moshe Lewin comments ironically, society was in a certain sense 'classless', because all classes were formless, in perpetual fusion.

Despite the differences in their outlooks, authors as different as Trotsky and Hannah Arendt agree that the first Five-Year Plan and the great purges of the 1930s were the qualititative turning-point after which it became possible to speak about bureaucratic counter-revolution (for Trotsky) or totalitarianism (for Arendt). Trotsky's contribution was to provide the elements of a materialist understanding of the bureaucratic counter-revolution, where social and historical conditions took precedence over palace intrigues or the psychology of the actors. He does not reduce colossal events involving multitudes to the whims of a 'history from above', made by supreme guides or great helmsmen. His contribution therefore does not end the debate, and definitely does not solve the historical problems which continued to divide his 'orthodox' and 'heterodox' heirs.

He particularly sought to locate the stages of the process by which the bureaucracy became autonomous and power became concentrated in the hands of one individual. The extent of crystallisation of privileges, the relationship between classes, Party and State, and the bureaucratic orientation of international politics represent various indicators which he combined to try to determine these stages. The most telling element of this reactionary break, however, was not sociological, but political: it lay in the bankruptcy of the Communist International in relation to the rise and victory of Nazism in Germany. In 1937, when the Moscow trials and the great terror were in full swing, Trotsky corrected his vision: 'I once defined Stalinism as bureaucratic centrism...[T]his definition...is obviously obsolete today. The interests of the bonapartist bureaucracy can no longer be reconciled with centrist hesitation and vacillation...the counter-revolutionary character of Stalinism on the international arena [is definitively established]' (1973b:311). From this followed the need to give up the position of realignment and reform of the USSR: 'the central task from now on becomes that of overthrowing the thermidorian bureaucracy itself'. This revolution qualifies as political insofar as it is supposed to be based on existing social rights (state property and planning). In his essay on Trotsky, Ernest Mandel uses the paradoxical formula for Stalinism of 'political counter-revolution in the revolution'. Such ambiguous formulae led to an insistence on characterising the state as a bureaucratically degenerated workers' state, thus attributing to it a social content that gave rise to many ambiguities.

The programme of the political revolution still included a series of democratic claims already advanced in 1927 in the Platform of the Joint Opposition: '(1) Strike at the root every inclinaton to lengthen the eight-hour day...(2) ...the raising of wages at least to correspond to the achieved increase in the productivity of labour...(5) A systematic improvement in housing conditions...' (1927). This platform categorically condemned the practice of removing elected trade-union representatives under the pretext of internal party dissent. It advocated full independence for factory committees and local committees with respect to the state administration. On the other hand, it did not call into question 'the position as a single party occupied by the Communist Party of Soviet Union'. It was satisfied to announce that this situation, 'absolutely essential to the revolution', generated a series of 'particular dangers'. The *Transitional Programme* (1973a) of 1938 marks a fundamental change on this point. There, political pluralism, the independence of the trade unions from the Party and the state and democratic freedoms become questions of principle, insofar as they express the heterogeneity of the proletariat and the conflicts of interests likely within it that are likely to persist well beyond the conquest of power. In *The Revolution Betrayed*, Trotsky had shown the theoretical bases of this principled pluralism. Classes are not homogeneous as if 'the consciousness of a class strictly corresponds to its place in society'. They are

torn by inner antagonisms, and arrive at the solution of common problems no otherwise than through an inner struggle of tendencies, groups and parties. It is possible, with certain qualifications to concede that 'a party is part of a class'. But since a class has many 'parts'...the same class may create several parties. (1967:267)

Thus the proletariat of the Soviet society 'is at least incomparably more heterogeneous and complicated than the proletariat of capitalist countries, and consequently can furnish adequate nourishing soil for several parties' (1967:268). Trotsky concluded from this that the democratisation of the soviets was from now on 'inconceivable without the right to the multi-party system'.

4. THE QUESTION OF THE PARTY AND THE INTERNATIONAL

This is the fourth great question constitutive of original 'Trotskyism'. It is the organisational corollary of the theory of the permanent revolution, and of understanding the revolution as an international process. Trotsky's last fight for a new International, which he regarded as the most important of his life, was against the nationalist evolution of the Soviet regime and its foreseeable consequence: the liquidation of the Communist International itself, made official in 1943.

REFERENCES

Lenin, V.I. (1922) 'The question of nationalities and "autonomisation"', available at <http://www.marxists.org/archive/lenin/works/1922/dec/testament/autonomy.htm>.

Lewin, M. (1975) *Le dernier combat de Lénine* (Paris: Minuit).

Stalin, J. (1976 [1924]) *Problems of Leninism* (Peking: Foreign Languages Press).

Trotsky, L. D. (1927) *Platform of the Joint Opposition*, available at <http://www.marxists.org/archive/trotsky/works/1927/opposition/ch02.htm>.

—— (1962 [1930/1906]) *The Permanent Revolution* and *Results and Prospects* (London: New Park).

—— (1967 [1936]) *The Revolution Betrayed: What is the Soviet Union and Where is it Going?* (London: New Park).

—— (1973a [1938]) *The Transitional Program for Socialist Revolution* (New York: Pathfinder).

—— (1973b [1931–39]) *The Spanish Revolution* (New York: Pathfinder).

—— (1975a [1923–25]) *The Challenge of the Left Opposition* (New York: Pathfinder).

—— (1975b [1920]) *Terrorism and Communism: a Reply to Karl Kautsky* (London: New Park).

—— (1996 [1929]) *The Third International After Lenin* (New York: Pathfinder).

7

Beyond Trotsky: Extending Combined and Uneven Development[1]

Colin Barker

Neil Davidson's first chapter in this volume offers an interpretation of the two concepts 'uneven development' and 'combined development'. In what follows, I suggest a case not so much opposed to Neil's as moving in further directions.

As Davidson points out, the logic of the twin concepts, 'uneven development' and 'combined development', has hardly been explored in the literature. Yet the ideas embodied in them offer us an extraordinarily rich and fruitful set of tools with which to crack a few theoretical nuts.

Here, I argue for an extension of the idea of 'combined and uneven development' to a different area of problems from that indicated in Neil's chapter, and indeed in Trotsky's writings. 'Combined development' is the more problematic term, though I suggest that my second, extended sense is *implicit* in Trotsky's thinking.

THE CLASSICAL (RESTRICTED) VIEW

Davidson and others have shown the continuing relevance of 'uneven and combined development', as applied by Trotsky and others to questions of national capitalist development and the

1. I offered a version of the argument in this chapter at the conference on 'Towards a Cosmopolitan Marxism' hosted by Historical Materialism/ Socialist Register, London, 4–6 November 2005. My thanks to those who participated in the discussion. I have accumulated many debts to people who have corresponded with me. Thanks are due – for references, hints, questions, ideas and more besides – to Sam Ashman, Paul Blackledge, Adrian Budd, Gareth Dale, Neil Davidson, John Game, Derek Howl, Annie Nehmad, Justin Rosenberg, Heike Schaumberg, Mandy Turner and Andrew Wright. Appropriately to the subject matter, I have ruthlessly borrowed and assimilated from them all, producing a combination for which none but myself can be held in any way responsible. I would welcome comments and criticism: c.barker@mmu.ac.uk.

prospects, in some backward countries, for permanent revolution. In this perspective, the term 'combined development' is *restricted* in its application within national frontiers, referring in essence to the potentially explosive political consequences of a *combination* of 'archaic' and 'modern' elements within a single country.

Trotsky's originality consisted in part in his emphasis on capitalism as a world system:

Marxism takes its starting point from world economy, not as a sum of national parts but as a mighty and independent reality which has been created by the international division of labour and the world market and which in our epoch imperiously dominates the national markets. The productive forces of capitalist society have long ago outgrown the national boundaries. (Trotsky 1962:22)

Trotsky's insistence on locating the question of capitalist development in world economy sets his work apart from and in advance of work by other Russian Marxists, notably Lenin, who had focussed his efforts to discredit the Russian populists of his day by stressing *domestic* changes alone (Blackledge 2005). The brutal fact of uneven world development exerts pressure – 'the whip of external necessity' – on backward countries, compelling them to attempt to 'catch up' with their threatening rivals. Overcoming backwardness is difficult, but not impossible in all cases. It is possible for those ruling backward countries to borrow and assimilate selected elements of advanced technique, organisation, ideas, etc., without needing to go through the trouble of inventing them all over again. They are thus able to 'skip over stages', *combining* in a single national system these imported elements of advanced culture along with older, inherited social forms.

Trotsky had in mind, of course, Tsarist Absolutism, which developed an advanced machine-based industry, with the aid of foreign capital, while at the same time maintaining its old structures of repressive politics. That combination had a revolutionary political consequence, for the authoritarian politics of Tsarism had now to deal with a suddenly expanded modern working class. In the later 1920s, Trotsky extended the argument for 'permanent revolution' to China, in the light of the Third International's disastrous policies there (Trotsky 1957). Thereafter, organised Trotskyism's practical defeats as a political current (Callinicos 1990) meant that, for a long period, few people even *heard about* Trotsky's ideas, while even fewer met them in anything but pejorative terms. As a *strategy* guiding revolutionary movements in the decades since Trotsky's murder, 'permanent revolution' has been notably absent, even if we can still attribute the *causation* of those revolutions to the same 'uneven and combined development' to which Trotsky pointed (Cliff 2003).

While 'uneven and combined development' took flight as an idea linked to an argument for *proletarian revolution* in a relatively backward country, the concept is not relevant to those conditions alone. Davidson himself has brilliantly deployed it in accounting for the paradoxes of seventeenth- and eighteenth-century Scotland, whose location within a European-wide historical context helps make sense of its peculiar 'bourgeois revolution' and its precocious capitalist development (Davidson 2000, 2003). *Similar* patterns of theorisation would illuminate many other cases: for example, the French Revolution of 1789, the 1848 revolutions, the Tsarist emancipation of the serfs in 1861, the unifications of Germany and Italy, and the Meiji Restoration in Japan. In every case, the 'whip of external necessity' compelled ruling classes to attempt to adopt and assimilate elements of technique, organisation and ideas from their more advanced rivals; and the contradictions of the 'combinations' thus effected were real causal elements in the crises that ensued. In the post-war period, likewise, one could hardly begin to analyse the conditions giving birth to the anti-colonial revolutions, or indeed the revolutionary movements that destroyed Stalinism in Eastern Europe, without reference to just the matters to which Trotsky drew attention.

As Davidson emphasises, the conceptual order in Trotsky is clear: uneven development in world economy generates the conditions for combined development within various nations. Combined development, in that sense, grows out of and completes uneven development.

EXTENDING THE VIEW

There's a question: are we bound to this conceptual order in all cases? Might 'combined and uneven development' be applied in a broader field of inquiry, not necessarily restricted to specific national contexts, or to issues of revolutionary prospects within backward capitalist countries? Can we extend the reach of these terms beyond the matters so far addressed?

Trotsky offers a possible starting-point when he remarks that *uneven development* is 'the most general law of the historic process' (Trotsky 1965:27). That sounds like an invitation to apply *uneven development* to other modes of production than the capitalist. We might also ask, can we apply it to other phenomena within capitalism itself than national state development?

That might seem relatively uncontroversial. But what about *combined development*? Must we follow Davidson and confine its application within national frontiers, and to the linking together of 'archaic' and 'modern' in these settings? Could it conceivably *also* be a 'general law of the historic process'?

BEYOND TROTSKY?

I am indebted to Chris Harman for my initial stimulus. Almost in passing he remarked, in a 1983 article on 'Philosophy and revolution', that 'uneven development' marks the whole history of pre-capitalist societies. But capitalism's rise changes the situation: 'For now the massive growth of the forces of production in some societies enables them to undermine all the others. Uneven development becomes *combined and uneven development*.... Capitalism inexorably moves towards being a world system' (Harman 1983:67–8). A few pages later, Harman wrote:

The capitalist exploitation of labour dissolves all pre-existing social forms, transmuting them into elements of a single capitalist world. Every tangible object is continually being reduced to a simple expression of a single, unitary substance – abstract labour. Every element of unevenness is continually being combined with every other element of unevenness to provide the totality which is the world market. (1983:75)

At the time I read this, I picked up no more than a vague notion, of 'combined and uneven development' as a general feature of capitalist world economy (and not just of individual nation states). That notion underpinned some critical reflections on work by Ellen Wood that I penned in 1997 (Barker 1997). However, correspondence with Neil Davidson forced me to recognise that I was using the term differently from Trotsky, whose 'combined development' was, as Davidson insists, confined to the linking together of elements in the *interior* of nation states. I'd used it to refer to interactions *between* states – to their *exterior* relations as these made up the 'interior' of the overall, encompassing, world system. Nor, I discovered when my circle of correspondence expanded, was I alone in this usage. Finally, I came across two recent papers by Justin Rosenberg, which further blew the question wide open (Rosenberg 2005; Rosenberg forthcoming).

There's a problem with Harman's early formulation. It seems to make 'combined and uneven development' a feature only of the history of *capitalism*, when the possibility still remains that it is a 'general law of the historic process'.[2] But Harman did offer a different account of what 'combined development' could refer to: namely, the interactive relations between human productive units. In *capitalism*, these are dominated by the practices of *competition, abstract labour, the law of value*. But these social practices were not dominant in other periods of human history nor – any Marxist worth their salt will insist – will they be in the future. If we want to treat combined development as a 'general law', we must specify it with care.

This brings me to Justin Rosenberg, who begins by identifying a general intellectual problem, inherited from classical social theory. That body of theory

never formulated theoretically the multilinear and interactive dimensions of social development as an historical phenomenon... [R]emarkable as it seems in retrospect, none of the major classical social theorists systematically incorporated the fact of inter-societal co-existence and interaction into their theoretical conception of social causality – with regard either to explaining the constitution of social orders, or to theorizing the dynamic process of their ongoing historical development. (Rosenberg forthcoming)[3]

Since the 1970s, in different ways, this problem has been *noticed*, but hardly solved, both within Marxism (Barker 1978a, 1978b; Braunmühl 1978) and within 'neo-Weberianism' (Skocpol 1979; Mann 1984, 1988; Giddens 1985). The field of the international has, in Rosenberg's phrase, stayed 'analytically unpenetrated'.

Rosenberg suggests that 'uneven and combined development' offers potential solutions to the general problem, especially (but not only) within 'international relations'. He considers the different terms.

First, *uneven development* is indeed what Trotsky suggested, 'a general law of the historic process'. The whole of human history is marked by 'unevenness' in its development. Here a little differentiation is needed.

2. Chris Harman has pointed out to me that his great opus, *A People's History of the World* (Harman 1999) is no longer constrained by any such assumption.
3. Rosenberg's stricture also applies to Marx and Engels, certainly so far as theorising the international state system (Barker 1998). However, in *methodological* terms, Marx came closest to a solution to the *general* problem in at least two respects: firstly, his conception of the individual as an active 'nexus of social relations'; secondly, his conception of capitalist commodity production and circulation, dominated by the law of value.

There are two senses in which we can treat the enormous variability in human social development across the globe as 'uneven'.

In one sense, 'unevenness' exists only in the eye of the beholder, in that some development occurred 'differently' in some ecological regions without any apparent interaction with other such regions. The millennia of separation between Eurasia and the Americas offer an obvious example. America did not develop the wheel, but did develop a whole range of food and other crops unknown in Eurasia. The populations of each land mass lacked immunity to some diseases common in the other.

The other sense concerns unevenness arising in the context of actual social interactions between different communities. It is this second sense of 'uneven development' that brings us to *combined development*. Here, the fundamental observation is that what we call 'societies' do not, in the immense majority of cases, develop in isolation from each other, nor, as Rosenberg puts it, do they merely 'co-exist in some passive way'. They *actively interact* with each other. Each exists in a field of forces, such that development in any one of them is – positively or negatively – a condition for development in others. Indeed, we may say that development in one 'social entity' enters into the conditions of development of others, so that they 'inter-penetrate' each other. In *that* sense – of 'social entities' being bound together in an interacting whole – their development is '*combined*'.

There are immediate implications for their 'internal' social organisation. Rosenberg cites anthropological work suggesting that all social entities in this situation have developed internal mechanisms for handling their relations with other such entities. The generic term he suggests for this is 'diplomacy', but that must be a very provisional term. A whole battery of types of social interaction – from gift exchange to commodity exchange, from kinship and intermarriage to feuds and their management, from ritual assembly to capital investment, from diplomacy to many forms of warfare, etc., etc. – could be identified and explored. In every case, the entities engaged in these 'inter-entity' social practices will have developed informal or formal means (rules, personnel, roles, customs and manners, institutions) for handling the relevant interactions. Further, these means will make up necessary parts of their own 'constitutive structures'. Thus their 'external' ties condition their 'internal' forms of social organisation. This is not a matter, necessarily, of 'borrowing and assimilating' elements from others, but of developing – mutually, and potentially differently – social mechanisms for responding to the effects of ongoing 'external' interactions.

Theoretical effects follow: this approach throws into question simple assumptions about the 'boundaries' between social entities. 'Society', 'community', 'nation' no longer look like entities that can be explored in isolation from others around them. Rosenberg rightly points out that we can't, in such a view, consider a concept like 'society' as constituted analytically prior to its interaction with other 'societies'; rather, the 'intra-societal' and the 'inter-societal' are 'analytically coeval'.

In processual terms, we should expect to find that developments occurring in one social setting will have 'knock-on' effects that ripple outwards, gaining force or dissipating, changing in their character as they progress, and impacting more or less indirectly on remote social settings whose members played no part in the *genesis* of the relevant causal process. Rosenberg's striking conclusion is that too little attention has been paid in the human sciences as a whole to the 'inner multilinearity and interactivity' of human social processes, a suggestion with a generality far beyond 'international relations'.

The above argument clearly goes beyond Trotsky. Yet, I suggest, something like it is nonetheless *implicit* in his case. And Trotsky's very terms logically demand this kind of extension. Only from the angle of world economy, of the *combined development* of the different countries within it, do words like 'advanced' and 'archaic' have any meaning, as measures of *coercive comparison* within a larger system of competitive interactions. Nothing *intrinsic* makes a thing 'backward'. We can turn a horse-drawn gun carriage every way up, subject it to all manner of chemical and other tests, and nothing 'backward' will appear in its make-up. But set it against a motorised tank, and its backwardness soon appears. Trotsky's specific usage of 'combined development' *assumes* a wider field of combined and uneven development, in the 'extended' sense.

COMBINED AND UNEVEN DEVELOPMENT
AND MODES OF PRODUCTION

'General laws of the historic process' may – like 'production in general' or 'labour process' – be rational abstractions, but are insufficient. On that, Marx is definite and clear:

[Some] determinations belong to all epochs, others only to a few. No production will be thinkable without them; however, even though the most developed languages have laws and characteristics in common with the least developed, nevertheless, just those things which determine their development, i.e. the elements which are not general and common, must be separated out from the determinations valid for production as such, so that in their unity – which arises already from the identity of the subject, humanity, and of the object, nature – their essential difference is not forgotten. (Marx 1973a:85)

'Uneven development' and 'combined development' remain empty terms unless we specify what *scales* of development and what kinds of *entity* we are considering, what socially developed *needs* promote ongoing interactions and in what *forms* of combinatory relations (or what 'mechanisms of combination'), and what the particular *social dynamics* of that form of combined development may be. In short, if 'combined development' in general refers to the social integration of apparently discrete entities, it needs further specification through conceptual integration with a theory of *modes of production*.

That's a large question. All I can note here is that the social interdependence captured by 'combined development' has many different social faces. It is, for instance, not inherently *conflictual*. As in other aspects of the critique of political economy, we must be careful not to 'read back' (or indeed 'read forwards') features of social production within modern society into other historical and future social settings. Thus, the social arrangements which gathering and hunting bands made for the mutual exchange of their young men and women, and for mutual assistance in situations of difficulty, were *cooperative* rather than *competitive*. The laws of commodity production did not rule every form of 'exchange' in history. Different developmental dynamics governed conquest and tribute collection in ancient empires from those marking modern capitalist imperialism. In like manner, the fact that a *multiplicity* of producing units coexists cannot, in itself, generate any assumption about competition: as Weeks points out, the fact that there were *many* feudal manors does not mean they competed with each other (Weeks 1981:158).

Indeed, the general fact of 'combined development' does not necessarily generate the kinds of *systematic* 'uneven development' we find within capitalism, or indeed in other forms of class society. In its *cooperative* forms, indeed, combined development is a means of *general, mutual development*, a means of enlarging the powers of the combined individuals or groups.[4] Its tendencies may indeed be 'levelling'.

4. See, for example, Marx's discussion of the *general* effects of 'cooperation' in *Capital*, i: ch. 13.

COMBINED AND UNEVEN DEVELOPMENT, AND CAPITALISM

As Harman suggests, capitalism has unified the whole globe into a single interactive productive system, under the dominance of capital. Capitalist industry tends to create a world market. Expanding productivity creates a rapidly growing flow of commodities whose value must be urgently realised, pressing capital to seek markets beyond its national limits. In its money form, capital seeks profitable investment outlets across the globe. Its cheapened commodities 'batter down Chinese walls', undermining pre-capitalist production systems and dislocating national economies. Mutual competition between capitals within a single 'domestic' market translates into 'international' pressure on the nations and industries of the entire world.

Pre-capitalist 'uneven development' became universally 'combined development', complexly integrated by historically new mechanisms, the precise topic of Marx's *Capital*. No part of the world was now exempt from their increasingly direct influence.

If one single 'law' expresses the capitalist form of combined and uneven development in summary manner, it is 'the law of value'. That law has two main clauses: 'competition forces all producers to produce with the minimum input of concrete labour time, and forces a tendency toward a normal rate of profit in all industries' (Weeks 1981:40). Each clause, however, could only become a coercive rule of social interaction among producers once capital established its dominance over the sphere of production. For the first clause, the necessary condition is that all inputs become commodities, requiring money to obtain them, thus drawing all production into capital's circuits; for the second, the condition is capital's movement between industries, made possible by 'freeing' labour from the means of production. Both clauses of the law of value have convulsive effects on all those subject to their power, generating uneven development among them.

The 'combined' character of capitalist development consists in a form of social interchange that imposes itself on producers who are formally autonomous, yet necessarily interdependent, bound together, through the movement of their products, in competitive antagonism.

Existing levels of development of the productive forces shape the *validation* of products via socially necessary labour time, a measure given by the whole, *combined* level of societal development. Producers are *compelled* to try to catch up with the latest technique, under a definite threat of punishment for non-compliance – in the form of non-validation of their productive activity and thus economic failure. The law of value, this modern expression of combined and uneven development, is not merely a 'description of regularities' but a *prescriptive command*, more generally powerful in its real effects on behaviour than any edict or fatwa. It subordinates not only workers and employers, but the mightiest governments. Yet its forces derive, not from any powerful deliberative agency, but from the impersonal workings of the capitalist form of combined development.

One 'sub-clause' of the law of value deals with the law of the 'tendency of the rate of profit to decline, and its counteracting tendencies'. The interaction of capitals, through the circuit of production and circulation, involves unevenly advantaged capitals which differentially invest in new means of production, thus tending to cheapen commodities at the point of sale. They act this way because of competition between them, and because, in any case, technical change does not occur evenly. Those capitalists who advance their productive technique and thereby reduce the value of the relevant commodities deliver a nasty shock to those who stick with old methods of production. For now these find, when they come to market, that the general price has fallen and their output of commodities (and thus their capital) has been devalued. The antagonistic process of combined development that defines the relations between the 'enemy brothers' (Marx) who constitute the capitalist class not only assumes a starting point of unevenness but, more to the point, *generates* uneven development among them, in the shape of what Weeks terms a 'stratification of capitals' within the industry, and a redistribution of capital among participating capitalists. As Weeks comments, 'The law as such and the counteracting tendencies...come into play as a result of a dynamic process of uneven development.... the process of accumulation has within it the devaluation of existing capitals' (1981:204–5).

Here is a neat dialectic indeed, where one process, accumulation, engenders through its very logic its opposite, devaluation. In its combined capitalistic form, uneven development generates new forms out of itself.

There are other directly contradictory tendencies arising from the form of combined and uneven development we find within capitalism. Let me draw attention to just two.

First, there is the contradiction noted vividly by Trotsky, between a tendency to 'equalisation' and a counteracting tendency to 'differentiation' within the very expansiveness of capitalism:

By drawing the countries economically closer to one another and levelling out their stages of development, capitalism...operates by methods of *its own*, that is to say, by anarchistic methods which constantly undermine its own work, set one country against another, and one branch of industry against another, developing some parts of world economy, while hampering and throwing back the development of others. Only the correlation of these two fundamental tendencies – both of which arise from the nature of capitalism – explains to us the living texture of the historical process. (Trotsky 1957:19)

And, Trotsky continues, imperialism – itself, of course, the outgrowth of the workings of capitalism's inner tendencies to expansion and centralisation – 'lends vigour to *both these tendencies*'. In linking the world together it both makes its methods and forms more identical and, simultaneously,

it attains this 'goal' by such antagonistic methods, such tiger-leaps, and such raids upon backward countries and areas that the unification and levelling of world economy which it has effected, is upset by it even more violently and convulsively than in the preceding epochs. (1957:19–20, emphasis in original)

Bukharin is the author who, most sharply, records the second contradictory tendency in world economy and imperialism (Bukharin 1971, 1972). First, capital tends to spill over national borders and to 'internationalise' its circuits of production and circulation. But, second, that very tendency generates, above all in the era of imperialism, a counter-tendency to 'nationalisation' of capital and the formation of 'state capitals'. Actual historical development consists in the continual contradictory interplay of these two tendencies, and in no sense is one of them rendering the other ineffectual.

COMBINED AND UNEVEN DEVELOPMENT AND STATES

The starting point for both Trotsky's and Bukharin's account of modern capitalism is 'world economy'. This totality – a vast system of antagonistic interdependence – is bound together by capital accumulation, whose dynamics produce a continuously shifting unevenness of development as between its various national economies, states, regions and the like. The relations between producing units are governed by competition, which – most explicitly in Bukharin – takes both 'economic' and 'military' forms. These very drives are what produce the various national 'amalgams' to which Trotsky drew theoretical attention, and which reveal explosive political potentials.

These accounts rest on an unstated but necessary assumption. Adopting the angle of the world, rather than its national parts, combined and uneven development has implications for the way Marxism theorises *states*. There is an inherited problem here. We can approach it by considering a famous passage from *Capital*, iii. Marx discusses in general terms how to differentiate modes of production:

The specific economic form, in which unpaid surplus-labour is pumped out of direct producers, determines the relationship of rulers and ruled, as it grows directly out of production itself and, in turn, reacts upon it as a determining element. Upon this, however, is founded the entire formation of the economic community which grows up out of the production relations themselves, thereby simultaneously its specific political form. (Marx 1981:927)

If we ask about capitalism, what is the 'economic community' founded on the extraction of surplus value? the obvious answer is the whole *world economy*. As for its 'specific political form', we must conclude that it is the modern *system of nation states*. Yet, curiously, neither Marx nor Engels seems ever to have explored the implications of this elementary fact (Barker 1998). Both tended to write about 'the state' in the singular, and not about the relations *between* states.[5]

This gap in their theorisation has been replicated in most Marxist writings on 'the capitalist state' ever since. One could fill a small library with the plethora of articles and books which set out to explain the form of the modern state as if it existed in the singular. Many take their starting point from Marx's critiques of 'political revolution', treating the claims made by states to 'sovereignty' as rooted in the rise of a distinct 'economic sphere'. From this, some extrapolate what they see as a necessary feature of capitalism, a tendency to 'separation of economics and politics' (see, for example, Wood 1995; Barker 1997). Yet there are problems. Sovereignty consists not only in a claim to authority over a state's subjects, but also in the maintenance of 'sovereign borders' (predicated on *other* states). Further, this perspective

5. The major exception is Engels, who offers a brilliant account of the dialectic of modern industry and arms races as these shape European state competition in the later nineteenth century (Engels 1959), but does not explore the implications for the way we theorise the state form.

faces difficulties in relation to the contradictory tendency to the *fusion* of political and economic power, noted for example by Bukharin. More generally, the exercise of *force* in capitalist development should not be regarded as merely a 'founding moment' (as in Marx's account of 'primitive accumulation') but continues as an essential feature of all stages of capitalist development, summed up in Harvey's nice phrase 'accumulation by dispossession' (Harvey 2003).

All these matters make more sense if we approach them in the light of the combined and uneven development of *states* in their relations with each other, within the economic framework of a *global* economy. As with other social entities, their 'external' relations enter into their very definition. Their very interactions generate unevenness of development among them.

In this light, geopolitical competition, the predominant feature of 'international relations', is itself an inherent aspect of capitalist world society. The particular institutional shapes and powers of states give this competition a duality of forms which requires incorporation into Marxist theory. For states compete both by 'economic' and also by 'military and diplomatic' means, and these two forms of competition, moreover, both depend on each other and – in particular contexts – may also contradict one another. The pursuit of military power depends on access to the advanced technologies and thus to the development of adequate productive bases; but that very pursuit may – for it is costly – induce contradictions in that productive development, as the histories of both the United States and the former Soviet Union attest in different ways.

Modern states are 'Janus-faced', staring both downwards at their subjects and outwards at their current rivals and allies alike. In this sense, modern states mirror the political relations that Marx decoded within capitalist production relations: states like capitals stand in a hierarchical and despotic relation to those they rule, while between their many units there is 'anarchy' (Marx 1976:477). Rivalry between states is matched by their exploitative relations with their subjects. Just as a *commodity* can only be defined by its relation to other commodities, so too with a capitalist state.

Taking account of this has significant implications for Marxist politics, for long dominated by arguments about 'reform or revolution'. An essential question here was and is: can the modern state be an instrument of emancipation? From the angle of *the world*, the debate takes on new colours. Various claims and justifications for the state become bankrupt and empty. In particular, a notion – shared by thinkers from Hobbes to Hegel and from Stalin to Blair – collapses: namely, that the state can represent the 'common interest' as against the 'private interests' of civil society. Each state is only *local*, merely 'national', is *limited*. All idolatry of 'the state', whether from right or left, turns out to be worship of a merely partial, petty thing with no sustainable claims to *generality* or *universality*.

One element uniting classical social democracy and Stalinism is the claim that *state property* is the negation of private property, even its solution. From a *world* perspective, the notion appears thin and ridiculous. States and their property do not negate private property; they are merely one of its forms.

Marx's early writings undermine the pretensions of the state, by revealing its connections with private property. From the angle of the world, Marx's attitude seems correct, but only one-sidedly. Once we recognise the state's mere localism, we impart new force to Marx's insistence that the state offered no key to the solution of major social problems, and that the greatest contribution it could make to human welfare was 'suicide' (Marx 1975).

IN PLACE OF A CONCLUSION

A pedant might object that my argument has applied 'combined and uneven development' to issues far beyond anything Leon Trotsky meant by the term. Were there an afterlife, I doubt his dialectical spirit would be much troubled by most of my argument here.

Every matter raised here demands further development. There are issues, too, that the editors' strict word limits have excluded. I should have liked to say something about combined and uneven development as it applies to the *geography* of capitalism (but see, for example, Smith 1984; Harvey 1996).

The 'extended' view of combined and uneven development contains still more possibilities. The most general principle, that human development is *combined and interdependent* in its very essence, and necessarily *uneven and differentiated* in its movement, offers openings for the analysis of social phenomena still further removed from Trotsky's starting point: for example, the growth and potentials of local and global social movements, or indeed the very development of human personality. It even adds illumination to Marx's characterisation of communism, as 'an association, in which the free development of each is the condition for the free development of all' (Marx 1973b:87)

REFERENCES

Barker, C. (1978a) 'A Note on the Theory of Capitalist States', *Capital and Class*, 4:118–26.

—— (1978b) 'The State as Capital', *International Socialism*, second series, 1.

—— (1997) 'Some reflections on two books by Ellen Wood', *Historical Materialism: Research in Critical Marxist Theory*, 1 (autumn):22–65.

—— (1998) 'Industrialism, Capitalism, Value, Force and States: Some Theoretical Remarks', in *Anglo-Bulgarian Comparative History Seminar* (Wolverhampton University).

Blackledge, P. (2005) 'Leon Trotsky's contribution to the Marxist theory of history', *Studies in East European Thought*, 57:1–31.

Braunmühl, C. von. (1978) 'On the analysis of the bourgeois nation state within the world market context', in J. Holloway and S. Picciotto (eds) *State and Capital. A Marxist Debate* (London: Arnold), 160–77.

Bukharin, N. (1971 [1920]) *Economics of the Transformation Period, with Lenin's Critical Remarks* (New York: Bergman).

—— (1972 [1917]) *Imperialism and World Economy* (London: Merlin).

Callinicos, A. (1990) *Trotskyism* (Milton Keynes: Open University Press).

Cliff, T. (2003 [1963]) 'Permanent Revolution', in *Selected Writings*, iii: *Marxist Theory After Trotsky* (London: Bookmarks), 187–201.

Davidson, N. (2000) *The Origins of Scottish Nationhood* (London: Pluto Press).

—— (2003) *Discovering the Scottish Revolution* (London: Pluto Press).

Engels, F. (1959 [1877–78]) *Anti-Dühring: Herr Eugen Dühring's Revolution in Science* (Moscow: Foreign Languages Publishing House).

Giddens, A. (1985) *A Contemporary Critique of Historical Materialism*, ii: *The Nation-State and Violence* (Cambridge: Polity).

Harman, C. (1983) 'Philosophy and revolution', *International Socialism*, second series, 21:58–87.

—— (1999) *A People's History of the World* (London: Bookmarks).

Harvey, D. (1996) *Justice, Nature and the Geography of Difference* (Oxford: Blackwell).

—— (2003) *The New Imperialism* (Oxford: Oxford University Press).

Mann, M. (1984) 'Capitalism and militarism', in *War, State and Society*, edited by M. Shaw (Houndmills: Macmillan).

—— (1988) *States, War, Capitalism: Studies in Political Sociology* (Oxford: Blackwell).

Marx, K. (1973a) *Grundrisse* (Harmondsworth: Penguin).

—— (1973b [1848]) 'Manifesto of the Communist Party', in *Marx: The Revolutions of 1848*, edited by D. Fernbach (Harmondsworth: Penguin), 62–98.

—— (1975 [1844]) 'Critical Notes on the article "The King of Prussia and Social Reform". By A Prussian', in *Marx: Early Writings*, edited by L. Colletti (Harmondsworth: Penguin), 401–20.

—— (1976 [1887]) *Capital: A Critique of Political Economy*, i (Harmondsworth: Penguin).

—— (1981 [1894]) *Capital: A Critique of Political Economy*, iii (Harmondsworth: Penguin).

Rosenberg, J. (2005) 'The concept of uneven and combined development', in *International Studies Association Conference* (Hawaii).

—— (forthcoming) 'Why is there no international historical sociology?' *European Journal of International Relations*.

Skocpol, T. (1979) *States and Social Revolutions: A Comparative Analysis of France, Russia and China* (Cambridge: Cambridge University Press).

Smith, N. (1984) *Uneven Development: Nature, Capital and the Production of Space* (Oxford: Blackwell).

Trotsky, L. (1957 [1928]) 'The draft program of the Communist International – A criticism of fundamentals', in *The Third International After Lenin* (New York: Pioneer), 3–230.

—— (1962 [1930/1906]) *The Permanent Revolution* and *Results and Prospects* (London: New Park Publications).

—— (1965 [1932–3]) *A History of the Russian Revolution* (London: Gollancz).

Weeks, J. (1981) *Capital and Exploitation* (Princeton: Princeton University Press).

Wood, E. M. (1995) *Democracy Against Capitalism: Renewing Historical Materialism* (Cambridge: Cambridge University Press).

8

From World Market to World Economy

Sam Ashman

Michael Mann does more than most to adequately sum up what is commonly called 'globalisation' when he writes that northern capitalism 'unevenly but simultaneously integrates, dominates and ostracizes across the world' (2001:72). One of the strengths of Marxist political economy is its history of understanding capitalist development precisely in these terms – in terms of its combination of integration, domination and unevenness. Uneven development is not a term exclusively confined to the Marxist tradition, of course, and there is relatively little scholarship of its genealogy within this tradition (Smith 1984: pp. xi–xii). Nonetheless the Marxist tradition of understanding uneven development is both important and potentially extraordinarily fertile analytically, particularly through Trotsky's notion of uneven and combined development.

This chapter seeks to clarify the importance of this notion through looking briefly at the strengths and the limitations in Marx's conception of world market, the significance of the notion of uneven and combined development in relation to it, and why we need to move from *world market* to *world economy*, a category which seeks to integrate states and imperialism into an understanding of accumulation and competition. It concludes by suggesting some ways this analysis is useful in relation to debates about globalisation (greater economic integration) today.

MARX AND THE WORLD MARKET

How is an emphasis on uneven development to be squared with Marx's views about capital's powerful expansionary dynamic, particularly as famously expressed in the *Communist Manifesto*?

Constant revolutionizing of production, uninterrupted disturbance of all social conditions, everlasting uncertainty and agitation distinguish the bourgeois epoch from all earlier ones... The need of a constantly expanding market for its products chases the bourgeoisie over the whole surface of the globe. It must nestle everywhere, settle everywhere, establish connections everywhere. The bourgeoisie has through its exploitation of the world market given a cosmopolitan character to production and consumption in every country. (Marx and Engels 1996:8–9)

This view of Marx and Engels as the original 'hyper-globalisers' is taken to extreme and fanciful lengths by Meghnad Desai, who argues that, 'If it came to a choice between whether the market or the state should rule the economy, modern libertarians would be as shocked as modern socialists...to find Marx on the side of the market' (2002:3).

The world market clearly has a huge presence in Marx's analysis of capitalism. The globe is presented as the ultimate horizon of capital as exploitation and competition drive capital beyond geographical boundaries. Capital exhibits such a powerful impulse to grow that 'everything becomes saleable and purchasable': nothing is immune, not even the 'bones of the saints' can withstand the process (1976:229). This inherent expansionary dynamic is summed up simply by Marx when he writes, 'The tendency to create the world market is directly given in the concept of capital itself' (1973:408).

This is particularly so in the era of 'machinofacture' (or industrialisation) when the production of relative as opposed to absolute surplus value dominates. Trade is transformed into a servant of industrial production, 'for which the constant expansion of the market is a condition of existence' (Marx 1981:454). An increasing mass of production swamps the existing market and works to widen the market so as to absorb production, thus breaking through its barriers. What limits this production is not trade, but the scale of capital functioning and the productivity of labour. Alienation is also raised to the level of the world market as:

Their own exchange and their own production confront individuals as an *objective* relation which is *independent* of them. In the case of the *world market*, the *connection of the individual* with all, but at the same time also the *independence of this connection from the individual*, have developed to such a high level that the formation of the world market already at the same time contains the conditions for going beyond it. (Marx 1973:161)

But whilst the world market may well be contained within the concept of capital, as Marx suggests, questions remain about precisely what *sort* of world market it is and what is the role of the national and of states within it? Marx's analysis, in *Capital* in particular, may be the 'indispensable basis' on which to develop less abstract analysis, but it remains nonetheless at a high level of abstraction (Fine and Harris 1979:vii; Callinicos 2001). The state is present – without doubt – as when Marx (1976:580) suggests that the international division of labour is 'one suited to the requirements of the main industrial countries'. But Marx's goal is the delineation of the abstract tendencies and laws of motion of the capitalist mode of production (Callinicos 2001). Crucially, Marx abstracts capitalist economic reproduction from social reproduction in general; from particular periods of capitalist development; and from the existence of nation states (Fine and Harris 1979). He writes:

> In order to examine the object of our investigation in its integrity, free from all disturbing subsidiary circumstances, we must treat the whole world of trade as one nation, and assume that capitalist production is established everywhere and has taken possession of every branch of industry. (1976:727)

Marx suggests at one point that the industrial capitalist 'must compare his own cost prices not only with domestic market prices, but with those of the whole world' (1981:455).

Surely the phenomenon of uneven development suggests a considerably more complex picture than certainly this single quotation from Marx implies? Not all areas of the world are penetrated by capitalist relations of production to the same extent, and not all areas penetrated by capitalist relations of production operate with the same level of productivity. Local conditions mediate the impact of capitalism's 'laws of development'. Or, put another way, heterogeneous conditions of production serve only to reproduce heterogeneity (Bettelheim 1972).

But there is far more entailed in Marx's analysis of the world market than we have so far suggested. Whilst Marx does not explicitly theorise uneven development, the analysis he develops, particularly in *Capital*, is underpinned by a whole series of assumptions about uneven development at the economic level, particularly once competition (or many capitals) is introduced. Capitals (plural) are inherently uneven given they operate in different sectors, with varying degrees of technological development and levels of productivity. Moreover, they are organised in different forms, with different degrees of mobility, and all these factors change, at varying rates. But competition also ties capitals together, as it connects them within a framework in which the behaviour of each is governed by the coercive comparison with the others and technological innovation in any one centre can threaten production in another. Weeks therefore argues that,

far from establishing a harmonious equilibrium, capitalist competition disrupts, eliminates the weak, challenges the strong, to force upon industry a new standard of efficiency and cost. The movement of capital to equalise profits across industries is the process of generating uneven development: equilibrium in exchange (a single price in a market) hides the generation of uneven development in production. (1997:105)

This analysis suggests a heterogeneity of units, but also of their interaction – interaction which is conditioned by their combination and mutual awareness, or by what might be called their *combined and uneven development*. Competition, both in terms of battles for markets between different firms in the same industry and in the sense of the ebb and flow of capital from less profitable to more profitable sectors, leads to the formation, according to Marx, of a general rate of profit. Competition is in this sense a force for equalisation. Technological change, however, compelled by competition, disrupts this equalisation, producing new unevenness. A process of equalisation and differentiation results as each capital, by raising the productivity of labour in its own unit of production, aims to realise an extra profit.

But this process of equalisation and differentiation does not simply imply constant flux. Some stay ahead in the race. Those units of capital with access to advanced research and development are in a better position to win surplus profits. They are in a better position to establish a virtuous circle, in that surplus profit enables further research and development and further research and development enables further surplus profits. Those sections of capital without access to research and development are therefore hindered in ability to innovate and to get above average profit and this further hinders research and development. The result is a process of differentiation, not of equalisation. These processes can also to be connected to the development of patent laws and intellectual property rights, and the utilisation of the power of the state. Tony Smith therefore argues that, 'The drive to appropriate surplus profits through technological innovation – an inherent feature of capitalist property relations – thus tends to systematically reproduce and exacerbate tremendous economic disparities in the world market over time' (Smith 2004:233).

Smith also rightly suggests that Marx's theory of technological change remains superior to Schumpeterian perspectives that seek to explain economic development in evolutionary terms because of the way Marx understands the subsumption of technological change under the valorisation imperative and the connection between technological change and the relation between capital and wage labour. Technological change can only be understood in the context of specific social relations. And so even in this brief and limited discussion we can see that Marx provides critical analytical tools for understanding how accumulation or the law of value generates uneven development and not the simplistic levelling of economic life. How does Trotsky develop this?

UNEVEN AND COMBINED DEVELOPMENT

The further elaboration of the concept of world market into that of world economy is closely associated with the first explicit formulation of uneven and combined development by Trotsky. How to relate national social formations and the interconnections of the world market is the question addressed by Trotsky and other successors of Marx. Indeed it is arguably the very process of uneven and combined development which produces 'a *consciousness* of backwardness' and which explains why the idea of uneven development was common in Russia as it experienced 'late' capitalist development (Knei-Paz 1977:73). Vorontsov, for example, wrote in 1882:

The historical peculiarity of our large-scale industry consists in the circumstance that it must grow up when the other countries have already achieved high levels of development. It entails a two-fold result: firstly, our industry can utilize all the forms which have been created in the West, and, therefore can develop very rapidly, without passing at a snail's pace through all the successive stages; secondly, it must compete with the more experienced, highly industrialized countries, and the competition with such rivals can choke the weak sparks of our scarcely awakening capitalism. (Cited in Walicki 1989:115–16)

Lenin, in debate with Populists like Vorontsov, similarly recognised that capitalism was not following a linear pattern of development and uneven development would later form an important dimension of his pamphlet on imperialism. Parvus too wrote a series of articles in 1904 to which Trotsky was indebted (Deutscher 1987). And a few years later, Hilferding would analyse institutional unevenness in the provision of finance, recognising that capitalism in different countries had become interdependent. Rather than developing from handicrafts, industry could now be imported in its most advanced form and so exert 'its revolutionary effects far more strongly and in a much shorter time' (1981:322–3).

Trotsky (1977) most clearly expresses and synthesises such insights when accounting for the 'peculiarities of Russia's development'.

A backward country assimilates the material and intellectual conquests of the advanced countries... repetition of the forms of development by different nations is ruled out. Although compelled to follow after the advanced countries, a backward country does not take things in the same order. The privilege of historic backwardness – and such a privilege exists – permits, or rather compels, the adoption of whatever is ready in advance of any specified date, skipping a whole series of intermediate stages... The development of historically backward nations leads necessarily to a peculiar combination of different stages of the historic process. Their development as a whole acquires a planless, complex, combined character. (Trotsky 1977:26–7)

And so, as Trotsky continues, it is possible for 'savages' to go from bows and arrows to rifles in one move or for Germany and the United States to catch up and overtake Britain, and, concomitantly, for the British coal industry to suffer as a consequence of having 'played too long the role of capitalist pathfinder' (1977:27). Yet Trotsky immediately introduces qualifications which complicate this process and mean that it is not simply an analysis of skipping stages as part of an overall dynamic of moving forwards. On the contrary, Peter I imported Western military and industrial techniques and loans and in so doing strengthened serfdom and Tsarism.

The possibility of skipping over intermediate steps is of course by no means absolute. Its degree is determined in the long run by the economic and cultural capacities of the country. The backward nation, moreover, not infrequently debases the achievements borrowed from the outside in the process of adapting them to its own more primitive culture. In this the very process of assimilation acquires a self-contradictory character... The laws of history have nothing in common with a pedantic schematism. Unevenness, the most general law of the historic process, reveals itself most sharply and complexly in the destiny of the backward countries. Under the whip of external necessity their backward culture is compelled to make leaps. From the universal law of unevenness thus derives another law which, for the lack of a better name, we may call the law of combined development – by which we mean the drawing together of the different stages of the journey, a combining of separate steps, an amalgam of archaic with more contemporary forms. (1977:27)

The amalgam of the archaic and the contemporary does not necessarily produce a forward impetus. It may instead serve to cement the reactionary. The conditions of the backward country itself are critical.

This analysis has enormous implications. It affects whether we conceive capitalist development in linear terms and it affects how we conceive the role of the state in this. It further recognises the connections between states, capital (particularly finance) and uneven development. But there are also ambiguities and limitations as well as possibilities in Trotsky's account.

Knei-Paz (1977:72–3) suggests that the process of uneven and combined development seems to refer primarily to the processes which take place *within* a national formation (see also Davidson, this volume) as the advanced and the backward struggle for domination.[1] This, however, seems an unduly narrow conception of uneven and combined development. We would suggest a broader conception, with the 'combinedness' created by the world economy that links together national (or regional) formations. Indeed, that different stages can be combined within a country is only rendered possible by the broader conception of uneven and combined development (see Barker, this volume). The geographical expansion of capitalism according to a single logic of accumulation produces social and political differentiation. An emerging capitalist core becomes part of a causal mechanism. The totality, the international, interacts with the parts, the national, in complex ways which render unilinear models of development redundant (Rosenberg 1996). There are no linear scales for social development, but there are only structural imperatives.

Trotsky explicitly criticises Marx in this respect:

'The industrially more developed country shows the less developed only the image of its own future.' This statement of Marx, which takes its departure methodologically not from world economy as a whole but from the single capitalist country as a type, has become less applicable in proportion as capitalist evolution has embraced all countries regardless of their previous fate and industrial level. England in her day revealed the future of France,

1. These terms are used comparatively, not pejoratively.

considerably less of Germany, but not in the least of Russia and not of India. (Trotsky 1977:1219)

So, methodologically, does Trotsky insist we put the world economy first as our starting point, instead of the nation? Trotsky's analysis is ambiguous in this respect. At times he clearly suggests that world economy dominates the parts (Trotsky 1962:22). But at other times he contradicts this, suggesting we see national formations and world economy as interwoven. He writes at one point that *'national peculiarity is nothing else but the most general product of the unevenness of historical development, its summary result'* (1962:24, emphasis in the original).

Trotsky's analysis, we would suggest, when taken as whole, is that the national and the international are coeval – or of the same epoch. Nations are to be seen as critical constituents, evolving and differentiated parts of a broader totality. 'The national peculiarities represent an original combination of the basic features of the world process [but] the economic peculiarities of different countries are in no way of a subordinate character' (Trotsky 1962:23–4). The relation between whole and parts is not one of domination (world economy over states) but of determination in a specific sense – that the world economy (the whole) sets limits to what can be done at the national (part) level. National states are not pre-formed essences which then interact nor are they unimportant or inconsequential in relation to the global. Is class formation global or national? The answer must be both.

There are further variables which Trotsky introduces to his understanding of world economy. Already we have world economy, states and also finance. He further considers a worldwide division of labour propelled by the dynamic development of the forces of production and the tendency of capitalist development 'toward a colossal growth of world ties' as expressed through trade and capital export (1962:28). Credit and finance in general play critical roles for developing countries (1962:29). He presents a vision of the combination of mutual interdependence between nations but also of the uneven development of nations and of culture. A further variable 'is the productivity of labour, which in turn depends upon the relative weight of the industries in the general economy of the country' (1977:31), though Trotsky is ambiguous about whether he is discussing technological productivity or the form of social relations.

So we see that a number of variables interact: world economy, a hierarchy of nations, the productivity of labour, the international division of labour, the state, finance. We cannot develop the analysis further, however, without introducing the role of states and imperialism in both the creation and structuring of world economy. More specifically we are speaking of a hierarchy of states (what Trotsky refers to as an imperialist chain). Not all capitals, and not all capitalist states, have the same power to structure the world market in their favour. Trotsky, in a passage worth citing at length, clearly points to how this is a contradictory nature of capitalist development in terms of its simultaneous tendencies to equalisation and differentiation:

Capitalism gains mastery only gradually over its inherited unevenness, breaking and altering it, employing therein its own means and methods. In contrast to the economic systems which preceded it, capitalism inherently and constantly aims at economic expansion, at the penetration of new territories, the surmounting of economic differences, the conversion of self-sufficient provincial and national economies into a system of financial interrelationships. Thereby it brings about their *rapprochement* and equalizes the economic and cultural levels of the most progressive and the most backward countries... By drawing the countries economically closer to one another and levelling out their stages of development, capitalism, however, operates by methods *of its own*, that is to say, by anarchistic methods which constantly undermine its own work, set one country against another, and one branch of industry against another, developing some parts of world economy, while hampering and throwing back the development of others. Only the correlation of these two fundamental tendencies – both of which arise from the nature of capitalism – explains to us the living texture of the historical process. (1957:19–20)

Moreover, as he continues, imperialism grows out of these twin tendencies to expansion and to centralisation and reinforces them. It links together units (be they national, subnational or continental) into a single entity, but does so by such antagonistic methods as to undermine this unification and levelling. As such, there are limits to capital's 'universalizing pretensions' (Kaiwar 2004:235). Its development is contradictory – 'creating, overcoming, and recreating obstacles to itself, thus leaving in its wake not only a highly uneven, and polarised, world geography but also highly localised social formations which appear to share very little in common with each other' (2004:236).

Mandel's interpretation of uneven development hangs on the role of imperialism as simultaneously uniting and differentiating, creating a world economy of interdependent parts but not a single world society or 'homogenous capitalist milieu' (Mandel 1970:22). This is precisely what is disputed in contemporary literature on globalisation, including Marxist literature (see for example Sklair 2001). As Sutcliffe has commented, 'the hard-core version of globalization' argues that 'the world is not only an economic unity but also a social unity with a unified global class structure' (2002:54).

However, there are limitations in Trotsky's analysis. We have already considered whether uneven and combined development should be seen in narrow or broad terms. There are further grey areas. Firstly, uneven development implies difference, it implies hierarchy, but it also implies a totality: uneven development within something – the world market or world economy – a single articulated unity or order that generates systematic inequalities between its parts. What are the mechanisms which generate this unevenness? Trotsky does not explore the latter beyond introducing the variables we describe above. We need to complement Trotsky with an understanding of Marx's analysis of accumulation in the manner suggested briefly above if we are to understand specifically capitalist combined and uneven development.

Secondly, and connected, Rosenberg (forthcoming) raises the question of its status as a law. Trotsky at one point refers to the unevenness as 'the most general law of the historic process' (1977:5). Mandel (1970) has also referred to 'the laws of uneven development'. Knei-Paz (1978) suggests that 'law' here should be understood not as causal determination but as descriptive generalisation. As Rosenberg notes, 'laws of history' are regarded with suspicion within the social sciences (forthcoming:7). Interpreting uneven and combined development as a descriptive generalisation is, therefore, a way to assert that there has never been a single path of development but a multiplicity of forms of society. This latter point is surely correct, but, as Rosenberg rightly concludes, it is also too limited. If uneven and combined development is rooted in an analysis of 'laws' of accumulation – in all their complexity and contradictoriness, their development through the interplay of tendencies and counter-tendencies, their openness and contingency – then this suggests more than a mere sociological generalisation. It suggests generative mechanisms which systematically, not contingently, generate and reproduce uneven development.

Thirdly, Trotsky's analysis is ambiguous about what precise view of world economy emerges. Does it commit him to a version of what would become world systems or dependency theory? Again, we need a more thorough understanding of accumulation to develop a response to these questions. Finally, Trotsky's analysis leaves the origins of nations assumed and unexplored, though this is not so in later Marxist debates about the state and capital. As a result of these weaknesses uneven and combined development is potentially fertile but it needs to be filled out.

WORLD ECONOMY – GLOBAL AND NATIONAL

We see above the difficulty in separating uneven development at the economic level (accumulation) with uneven development politically (states and imperialism). Imperialism is not a term used by Marx – though in places he comes close (see Harrison 2005). It is also the subject of considerable dispute concerning both how to understand the term and whether or not it is still of relevance given the emergence in the post-war era of a much greater degree of internationalisation of productive capital and, under US hegemony, a much greater emphasis on cooperation between the advanced capitalist states of the West than on rivalry. We suggest, notwithstanding these changes and other weaknesses, that Lenin (1982) and Bukharin (1987) provide a number of insights of lasting relevance that we need to add to Trotsky's account of uneven and combined development.

The first generation of theorists of imperialism located the roots of the phenomenon in a number of new features arising out of capitalism's developmental tendencies. Lenin's definition of imperialism as the monopoly stage of capitalism was remarkably short (Fine 2004). It was based on: the concentration of production into monopolies; the merging of banking and industrial capital; the export of capital becoming more important than the export of commodities; the formation of international capitalist combines; the territorial division of the whole world. Imperialism is the process through which large nationally based monopolies compete on a world stage and enlist states in their support. Rivalries between national monopolies become rivalries between states, producing expansion and war. Lenin and Bukharin 'tie capitalism as a social system to the rise of national rivalries on a global scale' (Harrison 2005:83). This analysis thus points to the process of the economic growth and expansion of capital and to the mechanisms through which capital expands on a world scale, mechanisms which include violence, war, conflict and dispossession.

Bukharin (1987) saw national economies as units in a world economy defined as '*a system of production relations and, correspondingly, of exchange relations on a world scale*' (1987:26, emphasis in the original). It is a 'special medium' in which nations 'live and grow' (1987:17). Anarchy prevails, given the unregulated nature of production, but the result is the 'intertwining of "national capitals"' and 'the "internationalisation" of capital' (1987:41). Moreover, this developing world economy is not composed of only one tendency but of two contradictory ones.

Firstly, there is the internationalisation of economic life and the integration of capital, the breaking down of barriers, the extension of the sphere and the interconnection of commodity production rooted in the transition to capitalist industrialisation, the production of relative surplus value, and a range of technological developments which follow – electricity, water power, water turbines, steam turbines, motors, transport. Secondly, there is the simultaneous nationalisation of economic life; the erection of barriers against the competitive expansion of other capitals; and the formation of state capitalism or state capitalist trusts. Both tendencies are a consequence of the drive to accumulate competitively. Competition between capitals is thus mediated by a system of states and geopolitical competition between states takes place within the context of economic and social uneven and combined development. One critical outcome of this analysis is that world economy is not a 'smooth space' as Hardt and Negri argue (2000:327). 'The process of the internationalisation of economic life is by no means identical with the process of the internationalisation of capital interests' (Bukharin 1987:61). This point is critical. The development of the world market or the internationalisation of economic life (and competition on a rising scale) increases tension and vulnerability, forcing reliance on states for protection and advancement.

This expresses in different form what Marx and Trotsky also point to, in different ways, that the nature of the world market is politically structured by states in the context of both exploitation and competition. As capital develops in scale and scope, the era of world economy is one of rivalries and clashes. These underpinned the great power rivalry that produced the wars of 1914–18 and 1939–45.

There are weaknesses in the analysis. Bukharin in particular exaggerates the extent to which differences are levelled out; both Lenin and Bukharin suggest that competition no longer takes place at a national level; both stress too much the extent to which national states and capitals fuse; and both endorse an unequivocally instrumentalist view of the state. Moreover, and critically, capitalism has changed in many significant ways since the beginning of the twentieth century.

Yet there are lasting insights we should not discard too hastily. Firstly, the internationalisation of world economy shapes national paths of development, which simultaneously shape the direction of world economy. This world economy is not a smooth space because of the constant tensions which competition between capitals gives rise to. Secondly, the growing interpenetration of state and capital, the fusion of economics and politics, whilst at times exaggerated and conceived simplistically in Lenin and Bukharin, is nonetheless a critical feature of the development of capitalism, particularly in the post-war period. Thirdly, the historical process out of which a capitalist world economy emerges is one which involves war, conflict and violence.

Harrison suggests that

Lenin establishes a global image: a critique of capitalism as an international system which produces a radical disjuncture between capital's 'Lockean heartlands' ...and the spaces outside these relatively small parts of the world which, nevertheless, also constitute the very being of capitalism. (Harrison 2005:84–5)

In this light he suggests that the early theorists of imperialism remain relevant in that they 'define two key disjunctures' in the foundation of global capitalism:

1. The radically unequal constitution of a system of nation-states as a result of the historic processes of the emergence of capitalism and imperial projects in various parts of the world. This has produced a modern system of formal sovereign equality underpinned by a political economy which remains (albeit dynamically and in complex ways) clustered around certain capitalist cores.

2. The violent deconstruction and reconstruction of societies (more or less purposefully) as capital expands, deepens, or changes throughout global space. This has produced modern liberal bourgeois discourses of modernity, stability and rational instrumentalism which ideologise processes of violence, imposition, and dispossession. (Harrison 2005:87)

World economy needs to be understood as based on capitalist relations of production; created through the historical process whereby capitalist relations of production are created in one corner of the globe and spread in complex, uneven and combined ways, particularly once the transition to capitalist industrialisation has taken place – the formation of world economy is thus critically in the era of the production of relative surplus value (machinofacture) and imperialism. The exploitation of wage labour in capital's 'heartlands' and the violent integration of large areas of the world initially dominated by non-capitalist relations are therefore *connected* developments (Davis 2001).

But to what extent is it possible to talk of a genuinely unified world economy given the uneven spread of capitalist relations from the areas of its origins in north-west Europe and the survival of large areas of 'peasant' production or of production which is undertaken in non-capitalist (if not pre-capitalist) relations? This is an extraordinarily complex question but nevertheless it is one our analysis raises. It is tempting to respond by saying the answer is 'yes' and 'no': 'no' in the sense that the very uneven development of capitalism produces complex amalgams of old and new and because it also, in the course of its development, acts to reinforce elements of the old; 'yes' in that the coexistence of non-capitalist forms and of complex amalgams does not mean that capitalism is not a global mode of production. The complexity of these forms and how they arise cannot be grasped in isolation (see Bernstein 2000). The significance of Trotsky's contribution lies precisely in its insistence that we analyse the complexity of the whole in its 'living texture'. What is capitalism after all? A pure and very abstract concept of a mode of production at a lower level of abstraction is a much more messy reality which can only emerge and develop historically. But despite the complexity of forms which arise over the course of the uneven development of capitalism, capitalism is nonetheless an integrated, but differentiated, world economy. It is clumpy and territorialised, but dynamically so and in complex ways, clustered around certain capitalist cores and states. It is a combined and uneven social entity – to which we should add, one that generates movement of resistance and opposition.

CONCLUSIONS

This chapter has sought to clarify the following. Firstly, the importance of Marx's conception of world market, and how Marx roots his understanding of the world market in his analysis of the tendencies of accumulation, but also the limitations in this understanding.

Secondly, the importance of the notion of the combined and uneven development of capitalism as developed by Trotsky. This introduces the complexity of different economic, social and cultural structures which are brought into contact with each other through the world economy, but how, simultaneously, world economy does not create homogenisation, but complex and varying amalgams between old and new. This perspective locates the state more centrally in relation to development. Thirdly, in the light of this is stressed the importance of moving from a conception of world *market* to world *economy*, a category which combines states and imperialism more thoroughly into an understanding of competition and accumulation. This category, by integrating states within it, necessarily operates at a lower level of abstraction than that of a world market arising out of the unmediated workings of capital or the law of value. Moreover, underpinning this notion of world economy is that of its combined and uneven character which arises out of the accumulation process itself. Of course many questions remain about the relationship between the state and capital and the relationship between economic competition between capitals and the separate but connected process of geopolitical rivalry between states (Harvey 2003) but even this limited discussion opens up a rich perspective through which to view the world.

Finally, it is worth spelling out a few implications of this analysis, particularly with current debates about globalisation and the nature of growing economic integration in mind. Firstly, globalisation is clearly not new to anyone concerned with the uneven and combined development of capitalism. As Bromley (1999) has suggested, globalisation and modernity are broadly coterminous, globalisation and neoliberalism are not. Secondly, globalisation or economic integration is not a process which produces homogenisation or the levelling of the globe. Accumulation systematically, not contingently, produces uneven development. Thirdly, the process of the globalisation of capitalist relations of production is uneven, forced and at times violent. Imperialism is, in Bromley's phrase, a 'major vector of globalisation, bringing the world market and the states system to vast reaches of the non-European world' (1999:288). And fourthly, it is not a process which results in the declining power of the nation state. The global and the national are not in conflict; the nation state is both a product and an agent of globalisation. Both are aspects of the social forms through which the worldwide expansion of capitalism has been constructed and reproduced.

REFERENCES

Bernstein, H. (2000) '"The Peasantry" in Global Capitalism: Who, Where and Why?' in L. Panitch and C. Leys (eds) *Socialist Register 2001: Working Classes, Global Realities* (London: Merlin).

Bettelheim, C. (1972) 'Appendix I: Theoretical Comments by Charles Bettelheim', in A. Emmanuel, *Unequal Exchange: A Study in the Imperialism of Trade*, translated by B. Pearce (London: NLB).

Bromley, S. (1999) 'Marxism and Globalisation', in A. Gamble, D. Marsh and T. Tant (eds) *Marxism and Social Science* (London: Macmillan).

Bukharin, N. I. (1987 [1917]) *Imperialism and World Economy* (London: Merlin).

Callinicos, A. (2001) 'Periodizing Capitalism and Analysing Imperialism: Classical Marxism and Capitalist Evolution', in R. Albritton, M. Itoh, R. Westra and A. Zuege (eds) *Phases of Capitalist Development* (Basingstoke: Palgrave).

Davis, M. (2001) *Late Victorian Holocausts: El Nino Famines and the Making of the Third World* (London and New York: Verso).

Desai, M. (2002) *Marx's Revenge: The Resurgence of Capitalism and the Death of Statist Socialism* (London and New York: Verso).

Deutscher, I. (1987 [1954]) *The Prophet Armed: Trotsky 1879–1921* (Oxford: Oxford University Press).

Fine, B. (2004) 'Examining the Ideas of Globalisation and Development Critically: What Role for Political Economy?' *New Political Economy*, 9/2: 213–31.

—— and Harris, L. (1979) *Rereading Capital* (London: Macmillan).

Hardt, M. and A. Negri (2000) *Empire* (Cambridge, Mass.: Harvard University Press).

Harrison, G. (2005) 'Imperialism', in G. Blakeley and V. Bryson (eds) *Marx and Other Four-Letter Words* (London and Ann Arbor, Mich.: Pluto Press).

Harvey, D. (2003) *The New Imperialism* (Oxford: Oxford University Press).

Hilferding, R. (1981 [1910]) *Finance Capital: A Study of the Latest Phase of Capitalist Development*, edited and introduced by T. Bottomore, translated by M. Watnick and S. Gordon (London: Routledge & Kegan Paul).

Kaiwar, V. (2004) 'Towards Orientalism and Nativism: The Impasse of Subaltern Studies', *Historical Materialism*, 12/2:189–247.

Knei-Paz, B. (1977) 'Trotsky, Marxism and the Revolution of Backwardness', in S. Avineri (ed.) *Varieties of Marxism* (The Hague: Martinus Nijhoff).

—— (1978) *The Social and Political Thought of Leon Trotsky* (Oxford: Clarendon Press).

Lenin, V. I. (1982 [1917]) *Imperialism: The Highest Stage of Capitalism* (Moscow: Progress).

Mann, M. (2001) 'Globalization and September 11', *New Left Review*, 2/12: 51–72.

Mandel, E. (1970) 'The Laws of Uneven Development', *New Left Review*, 1/59:19–38.

Marx, K. (1973 [1953]) *Grundrisse: Foundations of the Critique of Political Economy (Rough Draft)* translated and foreword by M. Nicolaus (London: Penguin/NLR).

—— (1976 [1867]) *Capital: A Critique of Political Economy*, i, introduction by E. Mandel, translated by B. Fowkes (London: Penguin/NLR).

—— (1981 [1894]) *Capital: A Critique of Political Economy*, iii, introduction by E. Mandel, translated by D. Fernbach (London: Penguin/NLR).

—— and F. Engels (1996 [1847]) *The Communist Manifesto* (London: Phoenix).

Rosenberg, J. (1996) 'Isaac Deutscher and the Lost History of International Relations', *New Left Review*, 1/215:3–15.

—— (forthcoming) 'Why is There No International Historical Sociology?' *European Journal of International Relations*.

Sklair, L. (2001) *The Transnational Capitalist Class* (Oxford: Blackwell).

Smith, N. (1984) *Uneven Development: Nature, Capital and the Production of Space* (Oxford: Blackwell).

Smith, T. (2004) 'Technology and History in Capitalism: Marxian and Neo-Schumpeterian Perspectives', in R. Bellofiore and N. Taylor (eds) *The Constitution of Capital: Essays on Volume I of Marx's Capital* (Basingstoke: Palgrave).

Sutcliffe, B. (2002) 'How Many Capitalisms? Historical Materialism in the Debates about Imperialism and Globalization', in M. Rupert and H. Smith (eds) *Historical Materialism and Globalization* (London and New York: Routledge).

Trotsky, L. (1957) 'The Draft Programme of the Communist International: A Criticism of Fundamentals', in *The Third International After Lenin* (New York: Pioneer).

—— (1962 [1930/1906]) *The Permanent Revolution* and *Results and Prospects*, translated by J. G Wright and B. Pearce (London: New Park Publications).

—— (1977 [1932–33]) *The History of the Russian Revolution*, translated by M. Eastman (London: Pluto Press).

Walicki, A. (1989 [1969]) *The Controversy Over Capitalism: Studies in the Social Philosophy of the Russian Populists* (Notre Dame, Ind.: University of Notre Dame Press).

Weeks, J. (1997) 'The Law of Value and the Analysis of Underdevelopment', *Historical Materialism*, 1/1:1–112.

9

Trotsky, Social Science and Irish Revolution

Michael Hanagan

Leon Trotsky's *Results and Prospects* (R&P) is his broadest and most comprehensive depiction of Russian historical development. Although he did not use the term until the 1930s, R&P contained his first detailed statement and most concrete illustrations of the 'laws of uneven and combined development' (LUCD). Focussing exclusively on R&P, this chapter (1) briefly reviews the developmental theories of Marx and Engels; (2) shows how Trotsky developed a theory of the Russian case to modify Marx and Engels' theory of stages; and (3) locates Trotsky's approach within the context of modern social science approaches to social change. (4) It further applies the LUCD to the Irish revolution of 1916–23 to provide an illustration of their use in contemporary social analysis.

MARX AND ENGELS ON STAGES OF CAPITALIST DEVELOPMENT

From the late 1840s to the early 1870s Karl Marx and Friedrich Engels argued that development occurred in a series of well-defined stages, identical in each state. In the preface to *Capital*, Marx discerned 'tendencies working with iron necessities towards inevitable results. The country that is more developed industrially only shows, to the less developed, the image of its own future' (Marx 1967:8–9).

To explain the growth of capitalism Marx and Engels sometimes emphasised the role of international trade and at other times the importance of capitalist reorganisation of industry. In any case, as the economic power of capitalists grew, capitalists fought to expand the markets for their products and to create a wage labour force. Over the course of centuries capitalists sought to restrict or abolish serfdom, the guild system, aristocratic legal privileges, and royal monopolies. They fought for the creation of a bourgeois state with some form of representative government, open to bourgeois manipulation and free from the control of religious bureaucracy.

The *Communist Manifesto* of 1847 established the idea of a bourgeois revolution as a central concept in Marxist theory. In early modern Europe, according to Marx and Engels, revolutions had involved cross-class alliances in which capitalists participated to attain their own ends. As bourgeois economic power grew, its role within revolutionary coalitions increased. The German Reformation, the English Civil War and the French Revolution were all seen as parts of a unified and continuous revolutionary process, each revolution bringing more benefits to capitalists than the last and each bringing capitalists closer to their goals of free markets, free labour and non-arbitrary limited government. For Marx and Engels, the French Revolution was and always remained the fullest example of a bourgeois *political* revolution. The bourgeois, according to Marx and Engels, were hardly champions of democracy but, as in France, elements of the bourgeois might support universal suffrage in order to rally the people against aristocracy and absolute monarchy. In 1847, Marx and Engels classified England and France as bourgeois nations liable to socialist proletarian-led revolution while for other major European states bourgeois revolution remained on the agenda.

While the emphasis on stages clearly predominated in Marx and Engels' thinking, it was never the only element; there were less-developed channels that offered alternative perspectives on capitalist development. Even in the *Communist Manifesto* Marx and Engels had suggested that stages could be shortened and trimmed in Germany. In his later years Marx famously began to consider whether Russia might skip the capitalist stage altogether. In the process of studying Russia Marx elaborated a different, more comparative, approach to analysing capitalist development. In a letter written in 1877 but not published until 1886, Marx rejected efforts 'to metamorphose my historical sketch of the genesis of capitalism in western Europe into a historico-philosophical theory of general development, imposed by fate on all peoples, whatever the historical circumstances in which they are placed'. Instead Marx argued for a comparative approach:

By studying each of these evolutions of its own, and then comparing them, one will easily discover the key to the phenomena, but it will never be arrived at by employing the all purpose formula of a general historico-philosophical theory whose supreme virtue consists in being supra-historical. (Marx 2001:71–2)

In such a view, the specific trajectory of Western capitalism offered less an 'iron' law of development than a useful model for identifying similarities and differences with developments outside Western Europe.

LUCD IN RUSSIA

Trotsky's LUCD shared much in common with the comparative approach to social development advocated by Marx in 1877. While the Russian revolutionary accepted the Marxist theory of transition from feudalism to capitalism as an adequate description of trends in Western Europe, he modified it in fundamental ways with respect to Russia. Trotsky agreed with Marx and Engels that cities, guilds, autonomous religious institutions, a powerful independent landlord class and representative estates had been prerequisites for the path of Western European development. Lacking these prerequisites, Trotsky argued that Russia was forced to develop a new path when thrown into contact with the capitalist state system.

The law of uneven development (LUD) rests on the proposition that backward states, those lacking the requisite conditions to follow the European path, must innovate to survive. Very early on, from at least the mid fifteenth century, a Russian state came into contact with the Western state system. Already, however, the problems confronting Russia's rulers were radically different from those confronting Western Europeans. For centuries, Russia had been under pressure from the Mongols and Tatar khanates as well as from Sweden, the Polish–Lithuanian kingdom and the Austrian Empire. Economically the Russian Empire had been moulded by pressure from Western European financiers and demands for cheap Eastern European grain. The Russian state retained its sovereignty by straining all its resources under autocratic direction to become a military power. Nearer to the West, the Polish kingdom had collapsed under Western pressure. But the Russian Empire, argued Trotsky, survived by a process of *state militarisation*, making extraordinary demands on society, forcing levies from urban bourgeois, aristocracy and peasantry, exactions that produced a gigantic Russian state and a weakened bourgeoisie.

The same powerful despotic Russian state that dominated the military machine also promoted an accelerated industrialisation using the latest Western technologies. Trotsky described Russia's extraordinary industrial expansion as a *privilege of backwardness*, by which he meant that backward states can draw on the example of the advanced states and adopt the latest methods, be they technologies or social institutions. Russian metallurgy did not follow stages of development. It did not first imitate English practices in the first Industrial Revolution and employ wrought-iron making with its artisanal labour force before switching over to steelmaking with its mass proletariat. Instead, Russian metallurgy largely skipped the metalworking technologies of the first Industrial Revolution to adopt the technologies of the second Industrial Revolution.

This skipping of technological stages had important political consequences, Trotsky argued. Drawing on the example of the French Revolution, Marx and Engels had believed that the bourgeois could only win the support of the popular classes by granting democratic concessions and some measure of social protection to the urban masses and peasantry in return for their political support. Politically, the bourgeoisie merely demanded some form of consultative political assembly to check arbitrary state power. But in 1793–94 a section of the French middle classes, the Jacobins, offered cheap bread and manhood suffrage to secure the allegiance of the Parisian sans-culottes, a cross-class social formation of masters and skilled workers.

The Tsarist state's appropriation of advanced technologies and the development of a new labour force made a repetition of the French democratic coalition unlikely in Russia. Drawing on the lessons of Russia in 1905, Trotsky doubted that any section of the Russian bourgeoisie would adopt the pro-democratic strategies of the militant French revolutionary bourgeois because, in Russia, state-supported industrialisation created a proletariat based on large factories concentrated in great cities. Dealing with a militant socialist-inclined Russian labour force would be infinitely more difficult for bourgeois elites than manipulating French sans-culottes. A large working class located in the political capital would, Trotsky believed, inevitably demand social reforms during the course of the struggle. Demands for an eight-hour day, which had emerged during the revolution of 1905, would enrage the middle classes and throw them to the side of reaction. Here Trotsky annunciated a *dynamic of revolutionary coalitions*; workers might be induced to participate in revolutionary coalitions led by the bourgeoisie but the bourgeoisie could not be induced to participate in coalitions led by workers.

Trotsky emphasised that the Russian Empire lacked the requisite conditions to follow the Western path but that prolonged contact with the West pointed Russia in a different direction. The LUCD explain why Russia followed a different path and suggest the general direction of deviations from the Western path. A concatenation of state militarisation, the privileges of backwardness and the dynamic of revolutionary coalitions help us understand the particular path that Russia did follow.

LAWS AND MECHANISMS

Although R&P concentrated on the Russian case, Trotsky cast his theory very generally. Our argument is that the expansion and development of Trotsky's LUCD should follow his practice in R&P. It should comparatively examine starting points and transnational influences on developmental patterns. Explaining divergent patterns requires elaborating concrete explanations – some derived from Trotsky but others drawn from different sources and others invented on an ad hoc basis. Such an approach has roots in modern scientific and social scientific approaches (Stinchcombe 1978:31–3).

With the philosopher of science Mario Bunge, let us define laws as 'recurrent patterns within a defined system' (Bunge 2004). Following R&P, the social system within which the LUCD apply is that of an early modern Europe in the transition from feudalism to capitalism, an advanced Western Europe thrown into contact with backward countries.

Trotsky's law of uneven development (LUD) asserts that backward nations lacking specific developmental prerequisites will follow different paths from those of Western and Central Europe. The task of Russian Marxists was not to impose a dogmatic theory of stages but 'to discover the "possibilities" of the developing revolution by means of an analysis of its internal mechanism' (Trotsky 1965:168). LUD generates questions based on *different starting points*. How did the lack of cities and an urban mercantile class, or the lack of artisans and a guild tradition, or the control of state administration by bureaucrats rather than landlords shape economic development and class relations in an evolving backward state?

Complementing the LUD, Trotsky's law of combined development (LCD) asserts the inadequacy of the state as a site for studying the development of backward states. LCD maintains that interactions can occur between backward and advanced countries within capitalist state systems that will alter the developmental path of backward countries. It generates questions about the role of *transnational processes* in development. Typical questions include: how did the cross-border transmission of technologies, the spread of socialist parties, or the influence of international financial institutions affect the course of development in backward countries? Within their specified domain, the variation suggested by the LUCD should be empirically identifiable.

If the LUCD identify patterned variations in capitalist development, they acquire intellectual strength and credibility when joined with causal mechanisms that explain these patterns. In some ways the most interesting aspects of the LUCD are the causal mechanisms generated to explain the larger patterns uncovered. Causal mechanisms are 'a delimited class of events that alter relations among specified sets of elements in identical or closely similar ways in a variety of situations' (McAdam et al. 2001:24). Examples of causal mechanism were identified in the preceding section: *state militarisation*, the *privileges of backwardness* and the *dynamics of revolutionary coalitions*. More will be offered as we proceed. The operations of mechanisms are subject to empirical investigation.

Bunge adds that the relation of mechanisms to laws is many to one because many mechanisms may contribute to patterned behaviour. As we have seen, Russia follows the LUCD by deviating from the Western paths along lines determined by state militarisation, the privileges of backwardness and the dynamic of revolutionary coalitions. A different mix of causal mechanisms may come into play in explaining another state's path. Causal mechanisms that figure in one case may not figure in another. 'State militarisation' might be used to explain developments in China or the Ottoman Empire but not Saint-Domingue or Ireland. The more frequently a causal mechanism is used to explain different patterns identified by the LUCD the more general it may be said to be.

While Trotsky's LUCD are based on specifically Marxist assumptions, they raise some issues relevant to any developmental theory. Recently issues of uneven development have acquired new interest among institutionalist sociologists. Scholars such as Peter A. Hall and David Soskice argue that a nation's institutions are 'created by actions, statutory or otherwise, that establish formal institutions and their operating procedures' and that 'repeated historical experience builds up a set of common expectations that allows the actors to coordinate effectively with each other' (Hall and Soskice 2001:12–13). Their work suggests that differences established at early stages of capitalist development persist even in quite advanced capitalist countries. Trotsky's writings suggest the value of extending these comparisons more widely and pursuing them in greater depth.

IRELAND

The application of the LUCD to Irish revolution is challenging because Ireland and Russia differed in so many respects. In the years between 1916 and 1923, Russia witnessed a socialist revolution, Ireland, a colonial revolution. Although certainly a backward country in tight interaction with a more advanced country, Ireland was backward in very different ways than Russia. While the bare framework of the Irish state survived it had been subordinated to a mighty empire: Russia was a mighty empire. Except in Ulster where participation in the revolution was least, Ireland was not an advanced industrial economy. And in striking contrast with Russia, the Irish labour movement did not play a significant role in the revolutionary struggle.

Like the Russian Revolution of 1917–21, the Irish Revolution of 1916–23 did not proceed in neat stage-by-stage fashion. Russian revolution ended in 1921 with a socialist regime in power in a Russia devastated by civil war. Ireland too emerged from revolution with a shattered economy (although not nearly as weakened as Russia). Irish revolution ended in 1923 with a conservative nationalist regime in power in a state that had suffered partition and the loss of its only industrialised region as well as humiliating restrictions on its sovereignty and continued domination by English capital.

Despite Ireland's weakly developed capitalist class, its large rural population, the power of religious institutions, and internal dissensions, the new Irish state yielded a viable democracy that survived the inter-war period when democracy collapsed in all the agrarian states that emerged from the Versailles Conference. And in spite of revolution and democratisation the Irish state remains one of the most conservative democracies in Europe. How to explain this mix of social backwardness and political advance?

THE IRISH CONTEXT

A look at Ireland in the nineteenth and early twentieth century reveals many examples of the workings of the LUCD, but space requirements limit our discussion to providing the context for the events of 1916–23. Key points are: (1) the character of the Irish colonial state, (2) the growth of public politics in the colonial Irish state, and (3) the accelerated growth of an Irish diaspora, particularly in the United States.

Where the Tsarist state possessed a great deal of autonomy from Russian society, the Irish colonial state per se lacked both autonomy and integrity. It was a divided structure with important portions subject to local control, while other portions were subject to centralised control from a London-appointed Lord Lieutenant in Dublin. Unlike Russia, the Irish landed aristocracy had early carved out an independent political space in local government.

England's struggle with the French Revolution and its brutal repression of the Irish rebellion of 1798, a rebellion profoundly influenced by American and French examples, had led British leaders to partially merge Ireland into a United Kingdom. In 1800 Ireland exchanged its parliament in Dublin for parliamentary participation in London.

The inclusion of an Irish deputation in Parliament provided opportunities for alliances with English reformers, but the mobilisation of the countryside by Daniel O'Connell was equally important to the emergence of Irish democracy. From the 1820s to the early 1840s Daniel O'Connell mobilised masses of Irish proletarians, not only helping invent the modern social movement but reshaping the relationship between Irish politics and society. Faced with O'Connell-led movements, traditional Irish landlords proved unable to control their tenantry. The tenantry's struggles against tithes, for the disestablishment of the Church of Ireland, and for Catholic emancipation, when supported by the Catholic Church and reinforced by urban middle-class nationalists, were powerful enough to shake landlord control and restructure Irish politics. This restructuring has been formulated in mechanism form by Charles Tilly, who labels it 'the insulation of categorical inequalities from public politics' (Tilly 1995). Tilly's formula gets at the key O'Connell achievement: after Catholic emancipation in 1829, though Irish wealth remained concentrated among aristocratic large landowners, Irish electoral politics was no longer an automatic reflection of largeholder power. Catholic church spokesmen, nationalists and eventually land reformers were all able to establish a place for themselves within the electoral field. The independent political space in local politics, created by the aristocracy, was partly captured by O'Connell and in the last quarter of the nineteenth century was occupied by Charles Stewart Parnell and Michael Davitt and the Irish Land League. Throughout the whole period, Irish voters also benefited from suffrage expansions won by English political struggles.

The outbreak of famine temporarily ended the era of mass politics, but disaster ultimately brought new political opportunities. In Ireland seventeenth- and eighteenth-century civil wars had helped create a proletarianised agricultural workforce in much of Ireland. The economy that emerged in the first decades of the nineteenth century witnessed the growth of an export-oriented agricultural economy side by side with a subsistence economy increasingly based on the potato. Unlike in Russia in the 1840s and 1850s distressed Irish agriculturalists were free to leave and the onset of potato blight and the failure of British policy in 1846–51 produced a great diaspora of proletarian labour, particularly to the United States. The presence of large numbers of disaffected Irish–American proletarians concentrated in US cities, who often supplied the leadership of urban political machines, exerted considerable influence on Irish politics in the pre-revolutionary and revolutionary periods.

IRISH REVOLUTION: 1916–23

Our illustration of the law of combined and uneven development in a very different setting than Russia, that of revolutionary Ireland between 1916 and 1923, makes three points: (1) it shows the peculiar character of the Irish state and how its reaction to revolution influenced the nationalist struggle; (2) it underlines the importance of transnational social movements in the emergence of an independent Ireland; and (3) it examines why the Irish labour movement abstained from the nationalist struggle and how this shaped an Ireland both democratic and conservative.

First, the distinctive characteristics of the Irish state, a state sustained by imperialism but transformed by popular struggles, led to an unusual form of disintegration during the revolution, one with consequences for Irish democracy. Stage theories that treat states as sturdy containers miss insights available to theorists of uneven development who see them as fluid bodies traversed by currents and counter-currents. In Russia the Tsarist state dissolved under the force of defeat in war and agrarian unrest while a Bolshevik-led soviet challenged its claims to rule. In Ireland, under the pressure of war and revolution, the state itself divided in two, a mechanism that we will label *state bifurcation*. Ireland's pre-existing democratic state institutions, with their rootedness in the locality, turned towards the revolution and supported the struggle against colonial-controlled institutions. The 1920 municipal elections brought nationalists sympathetic to Sinn Fein to power in eleven out of twelve cities and most municipalities. Later, republicans triumphed in elections for county and district councils and for poor law guardians. Local government securely in the hands of revolutionaries led to strange anomalies. County councils levied taxes for the British government to fight the revolution, but money returned in grants to councils went to Dail Eireann, the revolutionary alternative government. The strong republican sentiment in most of the country inclined many judges and juries to leniency when dealing with republicans (Hart 1998:79).

While democratised traditional institutions conciliated revolutionary forces, the centrally controlled police force, the Royal Irish Constabulary (RIC), was the cutting edge of repression. Unsurprisingly then, much revolutionary violence targeted the RIC. Despite the bitterness of civil war, existing democratic institutions not only continued to function but played a key role in linking the revolutionaries to pre-existing political actors. The end of British control meant the extension of the established national political order to areas of government formerly dictated by British governors.

The second point concerns the transnational forces behind Irish revolution. Stage theorists treat development as the unfolding of internal processes within a national framework. In the case of Irish revolution an exclusive focus on internal processes seriously distorts our understanding of events; students of uneven and combined development are better placed to see the full story.

Putting aside the inevitable interaction between metropole and colony, intrinsic to any anti-colonial struggle, the outcome of Irish revolution was vitally shaped by intercontinental solidarity, particularly the aid of Irish America. In the United States, Irish migrants had established a militant anti-British political identity that had little parallel elsewhere. Many Gaelic-speaking Catholic, rural migrants from the Famine only learned in Boston or Philadelphia that they were Irish; meanwhile many existing Irish Protestant migrants distanced themselves from these desperately poor migrants by labelling themselves Scots–Irish. Among the Catholic Irish as among other US ethnic groups, American experience promoted ethnic identity; among the Catholic Irish, ethnic identity was associated with hostility to England and was intensified by a general antagonism to England among the US population. This process of *ethnic labelling* to accommodate social and cultural distinctions stemmed more from conditions in the United States than from those in Ireland but it had serious transnational consequences.

Irish America was important because of the strategic importance of the United States for Britain. By 1904–05 British military planners, apprehensive of a growing German fleet, dismissed war with the United States as an eventuality to be avoided at all cost. The First World War led British political leaders to desperately seek US intervention. Between April 1916 and April 1917, as they worked to get the United States into the First World War, leading British politicians realised the need for moderation in responding to Irish rebellion. Lloyd George, then minister of munitions, noted: 'The Irish American vote will go over to the German side. The Americans will break our blockade and force an ignominious peace on us, unless something is done even provisionally to satisfy America' (Ward 1969:113). Between 1917 and 1921 English politicians sought to deepen US involvement in the war and to preserve an alliance in the immediate post-war years.

Strong political pressure from the United States, itself determined by mass mobilisation of Irish Americans, weighed heavily on British calculations. One of the leading Irish–American organisations formed to support the Irish revolution, the American Association for the Recognition of the Irish Republic, had over 700,000 members. Irish Americans lobbied Woodrow Wilson to put Irish independence on the table at the Versailles Conference. In June 1919 Joseph Tumulty, Wilson's private secretary, warned the president that: 'The Irish are united in this matter and in every large city and town are carrying out propaganda asking that Ireland be given the right of self-determination' (Tumulty 1921:403). Wilson's failure to do so swung many Irish Americans against ratification of the Versailles treaty and Irish opposition was an important factor in its defeat.

At every step Irish America influenced the course of Irish insurrection. Despite steadfast denials, the life of Eamon de Valera, a leader of the Easter Insurrection and central figure in the shaping of modern Ireland, was almost certainly saved by his American citizenship. To conciliate the United States, Britain granted early release to Easter Rising prisoners, cadres like Harry Boland, Cathal Brugha and Michael Collins, key organisers of Irish revolution.

A third and final distinctive feature of Irish revolution was the ineffectual role of labour in the national revolution.

What role labour might have played in Irish revolt demands a counterfactual hypothesis, for Irish organised labour abstained from the struggle. Despite the predominantly agricultural character of the economy, Irish labour, with old craft traditions and organised into its own independent party, was not a negligible factor in the revolutionary years. Although defeated, the 1913 Dublin lockout awakened many workers' consciousness; labour organisation developed apace following the war. Organised into its own Labour party, the labour movement represented a formidable organisation during the years of revolution. In 1921 – at the height of the Irish revolution – 300,000 workers were enrolled in the Irish Trade Union Congress – the major Irish trade union federation (Mitchell 1974:137). Irish Labour elected 14 delegates (out of 128) to the Irish parliament, the Dail Erin, in 1922 and 22 delegates in 1927.

The Irish labour movement's decision to remain aloof from a national struggle shaking the ground everywhere around it was a contingent phenomenon, partly due to a failure of leadership and tied to the absence of the two major Irish labour leaders of the twentieth century, men committed to blending nationalism with labour militancy. James Connelly had been executed for his participation in the Easter rising and James Larkin was in a US prison, convicted under the criminal syndicalism laws. The more moderate Irish leaders who controlled the movement in their absence were mainly concerned to preserve labour unity. Support for Irish nationalism would have hopelessly alienated the skilled Unionist workers who were the nucleus of the Northern Irish trade union movement. That the modern-day Irish Labour Congress is the only all-Irish institution with members in all 32 counties (the Irish Republic together with Northern Ireland) is a remarkable achievement and still a source of pride.

Yet during the revolutionary years all-Irish labour solidarity may have been attained at the price of long-term influence in Irish politics. During the revolution and civil war, Irish labour occupied itself with supporting the cause of democracy without supporting the cause of colonial revolution. The opportunity for labour to join the nationalist movement in exchange for social and political reforms never came again.

Opportunities though are not bankable. The Labour Party encountered important potential political allies among nationalists but also bitter enemies. Adopted in 1919, Labour's socialistic Democratic Programme frightened the Irish middle classes. Labour abstentionism and the resulting removal of class issues from the table facilitated the smooth transition to democracy as pre-existing democratic institutions expanded their sway in post-revolutionary Ireland. Had labour intervened directly into the struggle it might have rallied masses, supported more popular forms of protest and publicly demanded social reforms. But class struggle would also have strengthened the hand of the forces of clerical and middle-class conservatism that already occupied a prominent role in Irish politics. Irish Labour's alliance with progressive republicans and insistence on implementing elements of its Democratic Programme might well have led to the division of Irish politics along class lines and the creation of a strong alternative on the Republic's left. Defeat might well have threatened Irish democracy. Abstention meant leaving the revolution securely in the hands of the rural and urban middle classes.

Counterfactuals aside, stage theories that treat democracy as a bourgeois concession to win popular support for creation of an independent, centralised bourgeois state cannot account for the triumph of Irish democracy faced with labour's abstention from the national struggle. Nor can stage theories explain an Irish revolution both democratic and conservative. Although hardly comprehensive, *state bifurcation* and US *ethnic labelling* which link the Irish Revolution to anterior conditions, provide better elements of an explanation. Unlike stage theories with their iron laws, mechanism-based arguments have room for contingency. The failure of Irish labour, a conjunctural event rather than the outcome of a process, makes more sense in analysing a peculiar Irish path of development than as part of a stage theory.

CONCLUSION

Our survey of Trotsky's arguments in R&P and effort to employ them in a case study suggest that his approach resembles methodological approaches in current use in the social sciences. It argues that his theories are still capable of creative application. Our study encourages social analysts to follow Trotsky in looking at how historical beginnings and transnational processes shape social trajectories. To understand these patterns, mechanisms are necessary. Following Trotsky involves not only using the mechanisms that he formulated but using those of others and inventing our own. After 100 years Trotsky's work is still capable of suggesting research agendas and inspiring debates. No mean accomplishment for a centenarian!

REFERENCES

Bunge, M. (2004) 'How Does It Work? The Search for Explanatory Mechanisms', *Philosophy of the Social Sciences*, 34/2.

Hall, P. A. and Soskice, D. (eds) (2001) 'Introduction', in *Varieties of Capitalism: The Institutional Foundations of Comparative Advantage* (Oxford: Oxford University Press).

Hart, P. (1998) *The IRA and Its Enemies: Violence and Community in Cork 1916–1923* (Oxford: Clarendon Press).

Marx, K. (1967 [1867]) *Capital*, i (New York: International Publishers).

—— (2001) 'Letter to Oteschestvenniye Zapiski', in David Renton (ed.), *Marx on Globalization* (London: Lawrence & Wishart).

McAdam, D., Tarrow, S. and Tilly, C. (2001) *Dynamics of Contention* (Cambridge: Cambridge University Press).

Mitchell, A. (1974) *Labour in Irish Politics 1890–1930: The Irish Labour Movement in an Age of Revolution* (New York: Harper & Row).

Stinchcombe, A. (1978) *Theoretical Methods in Social History* (New York: Academic Press).

Tilly, C. (1995) *Popular Contention in Great Britain, 1758–1834* (Cambridge, Mass.: Harvard University Press).

Trotsky, L. (1965 [1906]) 'Results and Prospects', in *The Permanent Revolution* and *Results and Prospects* (New York: Pioneer Publishers).

Tumulty, J. (1921) *Woodrow Wilson as I Knew Him* (Garden City, N.Y.: Doubleday).

Ward, A. J. (1969) *Ireland and American Relations, 1899–1921* (London: Weidenfeld & Nicolson).

10
Uneven and Combined Development and 'Revolution of Backwardness': The Iranian Constitutional Revolution, 1906–11

Kamran Matin

Historical analogies...cannot take the place of social analysis... History does not repeat itself.

Leon Trotsky, *Results and Prospects*

The Constitutional Revolution is arguably a watershed in modern Iranian history.[1] It threw into sharp relief the developmental contradictions, tensions and challenges of the capitalist epoch which still remain at the heart of Iran's socio-political dynamism. In fact both the 1979 revolution and the reform movement of the last decade have been portrayed as attempts to complete the 'unfinished' project of the Constitutional Revolution. Yet the studies of this first democratic revolution in the Middle East, though great in number, have remained largely uncritical variations on the theme of 'bourgeois revolution' (Abrahamian 1979, 1982; Ashraf 1981; Ivanov 1978; Momeni 1978). As such, these accounts have forced the Constitutional Revolution to 'cover the buxom model of *La Révolution Française*' (Thompson 1978:78); an exercise which has led to more than just 'some splitting at the seams'. For this literature a priori imputes to the Constitutional Revolution a bourgeois (equated with capitalist) character yet simultaneously has to qualify this categorisation to the extent of problematising the initial characterisation. For neither on the bases of its causes nor of its outcomes can the Constitutional Revolution be seen as a bourgeois revolution: there was no (industrial) capitalism in Iran at the time of the revolution, while the leading agency was an alliance of traditional, non-capitalist bazaar merchants and Shia

1. I would like to thank Bill Dunn and Robbie Shilliam for their many useful comments and suggestions on an earlier version of this chapter.

119

clergy (Abrahamian 1979; Issawi 1991:604; Neshat 1981). And the subsequent political order which eventually consolidated the Pahlavi autocracy, did not remotely resemble a 'liberal democratic' state. The extant literature, therefore, tends to reduce *difference* to *anomaly*, reflected in the descriptions of 'failed' or 'incomplete' accompanying its characterisation of the Constitutional Revolution as bourgeois.

A critical reconsideration of the Constitutional Revolution is, therefore, long overdue; a task which acquires an added urgency in the light of the powerful arguments which demonstrate that the 'buxom model' itself was not quite a bourgeois revolution *in toto* after all (Comninel 1990); an important development to which the still proliferating literature on the Constitutional Revolution has remained remarkably impervious. In this chapter, drawing on Trotsky's concept of 'backwardness', central to *Results and Prospects*, I attempt to interpret the Constitutional Revolution anew. I argue that the Constitutional Revolution can be better understood as a 'revolution of backwardness' (cf. Knei-Paz 1978:113); that is to say, as the outcome of the process whereby the revolutionary moments in the developmental trajectory of a non-capitalist society, situated within, and under constant impingement of, an increasingly capitalism-dominated international space, assume a particular character underivable from the backward society's internal dynamism alone. The Constitutional Revolution can, therefore, be seen essentially as an attempt by the *non*-capitalist class of bazaar merchants and its allies at circumscribing the arbitrary power of the patrimonial state which under *geopolitical* pressure was facilitating the detrimental encroachments of foreign capital. Thus the Constitutional Revolution was not a capitalist revolution: it did not involve or entail primitive accumulation or the 'separation of the political and the economic'. But it was nevertheless generated by the impact of the geopolitically mediated capitalist relations. It is in this general abstract sense that the French and Constitutional revolutions, while defying a simple analogy, relate to capitalism and each other as specific instances of revolutions of backwardness.

THE INTERPRETATIONS OF THE CONSTITUTIONAL REVOLUTION

The extant literature on the Constitutional Revolution can be divided into two broad categories of idealist and social interpretation. The argument of the idealist approach (Kasravi 2003[1941]; Kirmani 1953; Malikzadeh 1949) is rather simple and straightforward: increasing contacts with the West 'awakened' the Iranian 'people' making them conscious of their backwardness, which was most acutely reflected in Iran's subjugation by Britain and Russia. The main cause of this condition is attributed to the backward *mentalités* of the retrograde despotism of the Qajar monarchy contrasted with the constitutionalism of the more developed countries of the West.

The idealist approach suffers from a double error: first, changes in the material condition of societies are seen as a reflection of a self-contained and autonomous process of 'progressive' changes in ideas gravitating toward 'freedom'. And second, this process towards freedom is a unilinear one. Thus revolution is reduced to merely a highly accelerated motion on a linear teleological trajectory of the growth of *mentalités nouvelles* as the basis of the economic growth. And it is this historical unilinearity which the idealist approach shares with the social interpretation.

The social interpretation is dominated by an 'orthodox' Marxist account based on an 'internalist' schema of chronological succession of the modes of production. Thus it regards the pre-revolutionary Iran as a feudalist society whose disintegration under the growing pressure of a capitalist mode of production culminated in the Constitutional Revolution; hence the latter's bourgeois character. But it then immediately proceeds to qualify it as a failed bourgeois revolution. This failure is in turn explained in terms of the socio-political immaturity of the Iranian native bourgeoisie which underlay the 'Girondist *dérapage*' of the period of the 'lesser despotism' (1908–09) and the second *majlis* (National Consultative Assembly) (1909–11). With the absence of a proletariat, the passivity of the peasant majority and an alliance of the monarchy, reactionary clergy and Tsarist Russia, tacitly supported by Britain, the native bourgeoisie retreated and the subsequent political stalemate of 1911–21 paved the way for the reincarnation of the autocracy in the Napoleonic figure of Riza Khan.

The definitional and explanatory problems of the extant accounts are ultimately rooted in their ontological and methodological 'internalism' entailed in the category of bourgeois revolution. This, in conjunction with the assumed identity of capitalist and bourgeois, of town and capitalism, produces an axiomatic concept of bourgeois revolution which, when applied to the concrete instances of revolution in non-capitalist societies, tends to analytically repel them from fitting the category of bourgeois revolution; hence the tendentious terms 'failed' or 'incomplete', which must then accompany the definition of such instances. The assumption of capitalist–bourgeois identity has been successfully challenged by the 'social property relations' approach (Brenner 1988a, 1988b, 1989; cf. Wood 1991). This is a crucial, but not sufficient, step towards removing the fetters of the concept of bourgeois revolution from the analysis of the modern social revolutions. For so long as 'sociology ...trumps geopolitics' (Teschke 2005:7), rendering international relations a contingent element to an internalist schema of social development, we cannot achieve a full understanding and adequate explanation of the revolutions of the capitalist epoch. And it is this crucial challenge that Trotsky embraces in *Results and Prospects*.

CAPITALISM AND 'REVOLUTION OF BACKWARDNESS'

It can be claimed that the summation of Trotsky's political and intellectual life is the thesis that there is no universal path of development in the capitalist epoch; that it is *through*, not despite, her peculiarities that a backward country enters the capitalist epoch. Without special features, 'the summary result of unevenness of historical development' (1969:148), 'there is no history, but only a sort of pseudo-naturalistic geometry' (1971:339). And it is the refraction of the capitalist relations through prisms of these special features that precludes historical repetition. Trotsky's concept of backwardness, therefore, captures the condition characterised by mutations in social developmental process of a polity with a lower level of social labour productivity relative to the more developed polities from which it receives constant geopolitical pressures. Thus backwardness signifies a condition of peculiar dynamism which is both constitutive of and generated by unevenness. Since unevenness and backwardness are inherently *relational* conditions, backwardness would have no pertinence to a geopolitically insulated backward society. It is precisely this relational quality which distinguishes backwardness as a unified conceptualisation of the 'internal' and 'external' in the general process of internationally mediated capitalist development that is punctuated by the revolutionary moments of 'revolutions of backwardness'.

As the product and content of unevenness, backwardness is, therefore, both the context and precondition of combined development. The relentless pressure of the more powerful capitalist societies, expressed militarily in the first instance, is the continued condition under which the backward polity strives to maintain its existence through assimilating the perceived means and sources of the power of its adversaries, turning 'the foe into a tutor' (Trotsky 1985:26). And it is this constant geopolitical exigency which peculiarly affects the development of its internal socio-political structures in such a way that it both precludes repeating the historical experience of the more advanced societies and creates new forms of revolutionary change. In short, the history of the 'revolution of backwardness' is the history of the constant impingement of the abstract universality of capitalism, in the sense of its organic tendency towards expansion, on the concrete backward non-capitalist polities.

In Trotsky's works the causality of backwardness in the process of social development, expressed through combined development, however, tends to be seen primarily in terms of 'drawing together of separate stages' and 'the solution of the problems of one class by another' (Trotsky 1985:27 and 30). These two forms are, of course, closely intertwined. The combined development means that the geopolitically compelled backward state assumes a prime role in the process of industrialisation, leading to a peculiar process of formation of classes that are characterised by an asymmetry between their social weight and their political power, particularly with respect to the proletariat. Under this condition, contextualised internationally, revolutionary potentials, ambitions and tasks of the social classes cannot be derived from their quantitative weight or an analogy with the earlier revolutions. Thus, as Trotsky concluded, it was the peculiarities of Russia's development that compelled the Russian proletariat not only to assume the tasks of the bourgeoisie in leading the democratic revolution but also immediately to move on to the socialist tasks in an uninterrupted process, the 'permanent revolution'. In this sense the permanent revolution is itself an instance of revolution of backwardness generated by uneven and combined development (cf. Löwy 1981:87). However, taking my cue from Trotsky himself I suggest that this is only one specific form of revolution of backwardness. In other words, revolution of backwardness should be seen as a concrete abstraction whose diversity of forms is ultimately rooted in the 'unevenness of the uneven development of historical development' (Trotsky 1996:34). Thus, depending on each backward country's special features *and* the broader international conjuncture, revolution of backwardness assumes different forms.

The international conjuncture and the specificities of the backward society determine the measures to which the backward state resorts in order to maintain its existence under continued geopolitical pressures. In this sense these measures are not necessarily confined to an eclectic importation of the modern end-products of the capitalist foes. Rather they are ultimately determined by a specific aspect of combined development which I call 'multiple international mediation of capital'. This notion is intended to capture the complexity of the international and geopolitical circumstances under which combined development takes place. One aspect of this condition is the fact that the militarily expressed pressure of capitalism refracts through multiple geopolitical prisms. For instance there are instances where a backward country's immediate geopolitical pressures do not arise from advanced capitalist countries but from backward, but more powerful, states which themselves have undergone, or are undergoing, combined development, e.g. Russia and the Ottoman state vis-à-vis Iran. Consequently amalgamation of the socio-political forms will assume further diversity in the weaker backward country.

Another aspect of 'multiple international mediation of capital' is that international rivalry between great powers can create a condition under which maintaining the independence of a backward state is rendered possible without its own direct intervention in the industrialisation process. For example, as I elaborate below, unlike Russia or Germany, the 'buffer state' status of Qajar Iran reduced significantly the need and capacity for a military-orientated industrialisation from above.

THE ROOTS AND CONTENT OF THE CONSTITUTIONAL REVOLUTION

So what were Iran's special features on the eve of the Constitutional Revolution? They comprise two main aspects: the comparative strength of Iran's native mercantile class and the rather unique power and autonomy of the Shia ulama.

The half-century long interregnum from the fall of the Safavids to the rise of the Qajars in the late eighteenth century was marked by instability, insecurity and political fragmentation (Humbly 1991a). This in conjunction with the prohibitive geographical and physical features of the Iranian plateau contributed to the absence of foreign capital from Iran for the greater part of the nineteenth century (Issawi 1991:590). Thus when relative security and the territorial unity of Iran were restored by the Qajar dynasty, there already existed a conducive environment for the emergence of a rather strong and entrepreneurially aggressive native mercantile class which had its origins in the thriving trade of the Safavid era.

The relative weakness of the Qajar state (Abrahamian 1974) only reinforced the power and wealth of Iran's native mercantile class under the Qajars. Moreover the practice of assignment of *tuyul* [a form of farming-out] as the main method of administration of the state revenue reinforced the fragmentation of both the state's authority and its fiscal basis.

SHIISM AND REVOLUTION

During the early stages of the formation of the Islamic community, legal, religious and political authority were fused and exercised by the person of the Prophet. The Shias believe in the extension of this singular authority to the Prophet's twelve rightful successors or *imams*. However the fact of *ghayba* (the continued occultation of the last of the twelve *imams*, Muhammad Mahdi, since AD 939) imparts on Shiism a peculiar dynamism. When the temporal power can successfully lay claim to prophetic descent, e.g. the Safavids, there emerges a form of state which can be described as 'caesaropapism' (Arjomand 1988:7), i.e. a fusion of both religious and temporal authorities. But when this is not the case, e.g. the Qajars, there emerges a 'duality' of authority which can assume two distinct forms. First, since during the period of occultation all temporal authorities for the Shias are usurpers and illegitimate, the Shia ulama may adopt quietism, and dissociation from the state. But the same fact of occultation can also become a basis for opposition and antagonism. The traditional approach towards the role of the Shia ulama in the Qajar period has been based on the second of the above possibilities (Algar 1980). But this view has been challenged by those who highlight the modality and diversity of the Shia ulama's approach toward the state at any one time (Bayat 1991).

The decades-long turmoil, civil war and lack of effective authority following the collapse of the Safavids' 'caesaropapism' strengthened the standing, prestige and authority of the Shia ulama as the people increasingly referred to them for various judicial, social and commercial matters (Algar 1991:716). This new vitality of Shiism and increasing autonomy of the ulama was further strengthened due to the fact that the ulama owned a considerable amount of *vaqf* (charitable) land which was customarily exempted from tax. This, in conjunction with the gradual institutionalisation of their originally spontaneous functions and their traditional close connection to the bazaar, reaching back to their common struggle against the encroachments of tribal nomadism and Sufism of the Safavid period, ensured an important socio-political role for the Shia ulama. The emergence of the Qajars and the re-establishment of a central authority did not reverse this trend. In fact both the Qajars' need for the legitimising blessing of the ulama due to their own lack of prophetic descent and their military defeats at the hands of the foreign powers further strengthened the social and political standing of the ulama as their fatwas (religious decrees) were repeatedly needed for the mobilisation of the people for the war efforts; wars which they could depict as a noble religious duty, a jihad (Algar 1980:82–102). All this invested the Shia ulama with a significant political power, which important sections of them used to great effect in the run up to the Constitutional Revolution and the revolution itself.

GEOPOLITICS OF THE CONSTITUTIONAL REVOLUTION

Throughout the nineteenth century Iran was the scene of battle of the 'bear and whale'; the geopolitical rivalry of Russia and Britain. Since the time of Peter the Great, Iran and the 'warm waters' of the Persian Gulf had been seen by Russia as the gates to the treasures of India. These interests had, therefore, made Iran the first line of the British defence of India against the encroaching Russia, and at one point, albeit for a short period, Napoleonic France. The ultimate outcome of the playing out of these conflictual interests was to render Iran a 'buffer state', i.e. a state militarily too weak to pose any direct danger to the interests of either great power and strong enough to maintain internal order and security; a juridical–formal independence.

Military defeats (1812 and 1826 by Russia and 1857 by Britain) led to the adoption by the Qajars of two sets of policies. The first policy, adopted in the early part of the nineteenth century, was one of rapprochement with the great European powers in order to obtain their assistance in modernising their army (Humbly 1991b:171–3). This was the content of the crown prince Abbas Mirza's (d. 1833) *nizami jadid* (new order) reforms inspired by the Ottomans' *tanzimat* reforms. The financing of these reforms necessitated improving the state revenue, badly in arrears after the territorial losses to Russia which had hitherto generated a significant part of the Qajars' tax revenue. Thus the prime minister Amir Kabir (1848–52) initiated reforms which were primarily aimed at administrative centralisation and reducing budget deficit. These included the reduction of state pensions to the courtiers and ulama. These reforms were, however, soon defeated by the opposition of various strata of the ruling classes, who had manifold bonds to the court and myriad interests in the traditional loose and patrimonial state bureaucracy. This in turn intensified the practice of sale of state offices, on the one hand, and of crown and state lands on the other. This reinforced the centrifugal tendencies which further weakened the central authority (Bakhash 1971).

The second set of policies that were adopted from the second half of the nineteenth century onwards comprised principally the granting of commercial and economic concessions to foreign capitals, primarily British. This inaugurated an era of 'concession hunting' (Keddie 1966:7). Rather than a treacherous pursuit of personal gain by the Qajar shahs, as the extant literature tends to depict, the 'concession sale' episode can be seen as primarily a response to imperatives of the geopolitical survival; faced with the impossibility of preserving their geopolitical survival militarily, having exhausted the limits of accumulation through dispossession of native mercantile class and the sale of crown and state lands and offices, the Qajar shahs deliberately attempted to associate Iran evermore closely with Britain. This was done by involving Britain directly and heavily in the Iranian economy to provide her with an incentive strong enough to protect Iran from the omnipresent Russian menace. This had also an added benefit: through the concessions, they could import Western technological and administrative achievements, hence 'turning the European threat into a source of strength' (Greaves 1991:400). This twofold process can be seen as a concrete instance of the 'multiple international mediation of capital'.

THE REFORMS AND OUTBREAK OF REVOLUTION OF BACKWARDNESS

These economic and commercial concessions had, however, many unintended adverse consequences for the Qajar state. Firstly, and most importantly, the commercial concessions to the foreign capitals had a disastrous effect on the bazaar. For even before the Qajars' enfranchisement of foreign capitals the native merchants had serious difficulty competing with Western commodities. On the other hand the increasing dispossession of the *bazaaris* by the crisis-stricken Qajar state compelled the bazaar merchants to divert their movable capital to land, which was seen as more secure and profitable (Ashraf 1970:327). This inevitably entailed a drastic deterioration in the living conditions of the urban artisans, craftsmen and petty-bourgeoisie whose livelihood was closely connected with the bazaar; hence their active participation in the constitutional movement.

Secondly, the ulama too were alarmed by the implications of the judicial and educational reforms under way. The proliferation of civil courts as a result of the measures required for the smoother function of foreign capital threatened the ulama's influence and the prestige associated with the monopoly they had hitherto held over the judicial system. Similarly education was traditionally concentrated in ulama-run *madrasas* (religious schools) which now faced competition from new schools with secular curricula.

Moreover, traditionally, an important condition under which the Shia ulama justified their tacit approval of the extant temporal power without Prophetic descent was the protection, if not the expansion, of Muslim lands and property. The Qajars were evidently unable to perform such a function. However, the ulama's opposition to the Qajars was by no means universal or consistent (Bayat 1991). Those members of the ulama who had a close association with the state and whose wealth and position were directly due to royal appointment, such as the faction led by Sheikh Fazlollah Nuri, were staunch anti-constitutionalists. Nuri articulated his opposition to constitutionalism through the notion of *mashrutey-e mashrueh* (sharia-conforming constitutionalism) (Martin 1987, 1986). His persistent opposition to the secular tone of the new constitution was in fact instrumental in the inclusion in the draft of the Supplementary Fundamental Law, passed by the first *majlis*, the controversial article which subjected all parliamentary legislations to the approval of a committee of five leading Shia ulama (Brown 1966:Appendix A).

Thirdly, the increasing contacts with Western countries and the establishment of secular schools gave rise to a small but influential stratum of the intelligentsia, whose acute 'consciousness of backwardness' (Shilliam 2005), generated by their closer exposure to Western polities and ideologies, drove them to readily attribute Iranian backwardness to the Qajars' patrimonial absolutism; hence their active role in the constitutional movement.

Finally, the dire economic situation in late-nineteenth-century Iran forced hundreds of thousands of peasants and urban poor to migrate to Russia and seek work in the oil industry and mines of Azerbaijan and Armenia, where they were exposed to the revolutionary thoughts of Russian social democracy (Adamiyat 1976:15). Elements of this 'proletariat in exile' played an important role in the Constitutional Movement (Rasulzadeh 1998).

By the early twentieth century these processes had coalesced into a revolutionary situation. The mercantile bourgeoisie and ulama had already had the successful 'dress rehearsal' of the Tobacco Boycott Movement of 1895. Moreover the international conjuncture was conducive to the democratic movements. Russia's defeat by Japan and the subsequent 1905 revolution had elevated the popular fighting spirit in Iran considerably. On the other hand the international decline of the price of silver in the late nineteenth and early twentieth century had a drastic effect on the economy of Iran, whose currency, the *qiran*, was pegged to silver while those of its main trading partners, e.g. Russia, Britain and India, were pegged to gold (Avery and Simmons 1980). This, alongside a number of consecutive bad harvests, led to a sudden rise in the price of bread and other basic items which in turn led to the widespread 'bread riots' of the early twentieth century. The government's response was a heavy-handed treatment of the bazaar merchants, whom it accused of hoarding and artificial increase of prices. This was the trigger for a popular urban movement led by the bazaar merchants, ulama and intelligentsia against the monarchy, which eventually in August 1906 forced the shah to issue a decree for the establishment of a parliament and the drafting of a constitution; Iran's combined development thus produced her first revolution of backwardness.

CONCLUSION

The foregoing analysis only highlights the most important aspects of a long and complex historical process. But the key purpose of this simplified and condensed exposition is to show that the Constitutional Revolution cannot be explained by reference to an internationally insulated conception of internal development of the Iranian polity as entailed in the concept of bourgeois revolution. For no polity develops in isolation from other polities and the broader international trends, whose geopolitical mediation has always, albeit in different ways, been instrumental in their developmental process. The revolutionary implosions generated by this condition constitute an international 'great arch' of capitalist revolution, whose components do not necessarily represent variations on the singular moment of bourgeois revolution. Rather, they should be seen as transformative moments of the modern social development that is characterised, crucially, by its *multilinearity* (Rosenberg 2006). Understanding this quality has vital importance for revolutionary praxis, particularly in terms of political programmes and the formation of alliances. The history of the Iranian left is a vivid example of the catastrophic implications of a failure in this respect. Trotsky attempted to conceptualise this quality through his theory of uneven and combined development, whose core elements are already present in *Results and Prospects*. As such, a century on, *Results and Prospects* still remains an indispensable source for a revitalised Marxist praxis.

REFERENCES

Abrahamian, E. (1974) 'Oriental Despotism: The Case of Qajars', *International Journal of Middle East Studies*, 5/1: 3–31.

—— (1979) 'The Causes of the Constitutional Revolution in Iran', *International Journal of Middle Eastern Studies*, 10/3: 381–414.

—— (1982) *Iran Between Two Revolutions* (Princeton: Princeton University Press).

Adamiyat, F. (1976) *The Idea of Social Democracy in the Iranian Constitutional Movement* (Tehran: Payam).

Algar, M. (1980) *Religion and State in Iran, 1785–1906: The Role of the Ulama in the Qajar Period* (Berkeley: University of California Press).

—— (1991) 'Religious Forces in Eighteenth- and Nineteenth Century Iran', in E. Avery, et al. (eds) *The Cambridge History of Iran*, vii: *From Nadir Shah to the Islamic Republic* (Cambridge: Cambridge University Press) 705–32.

Arjomand, S. A. (1988) 'Shiism, Authority, and Political Culture', in S. A. Arjomand (ed.) *Authority and Political Culture in Shiism* (New York: State University of New York Press) 1–22.

Ashraf, A. (1970) 'Historical Obstacles to the Development of a Bourgeoisie in Iran', in M. A. Cook (ed.) *Studies in the Economic History of the Middle East: From the Rise of Islam to the Present Day* (London: Oxford University Press) 308–32.

—— (1981) 'The Roots of Emerging Dual Class Structure in Nineteenth-Century Iran', *Iranian Studies*, 14/1–2.

Avery, P. W. and Simmons, J. B. (1980) 'Persia on a Cross of Silver, 1880–1890', in E. Kedourie and S. G. Haim (eds) *Towards a Modern Iran: Studies in Thought, Politics and Society* (London: Franc Cass) 1–37.

Bakhash, S. (1971) 'The Evolution of Qajar Bureaucracy, 1798–1879, *Middle Eastern Studies*, 7/2: 139–68.

Bayat, M. (1991) *Iran's First Revolution: Shi'ism and the Constitutional Revolution of 1905–1909* (Oxford: Oxford University Press).

Brenner, R. (1988a) 'Agrarian Class Structure and Economic Development in Pre-Industrial Europe', in T. H. Aston and C. H. E. Philpin (eds) *The Brenner Debate: Agrarian Class Structure and Economic Development in Pre-Industrial Europe* (Cambridge: Cambridge University Press) 10–63.

—— (1988b) 'The Agrarian Roots of European Capitalism', in T. H. Aston and C. H. E. Philpin (eds) *The Brenner Debate: Agrarian Class Structure and Economic Development in Pre-Industrial Europe* (Cambridge: Cambridge University Press) 213–327.

—— (1989) 'Bourgeois Revolution and Transition to Capitalism', in A. L. Beier et al. (eds) *The First Modern Society: Essays in English History in Honour of Lawrence Stone* (Cambridge: Cambridge University Press) 271–304.

Brown, E. G. (1966) *The Persian Revolution: 1905–1909* (London: Frank Cass).

Comninel, G. (1990) *Rethinking The French Revolution* (London: Verso).

Greaves, R. (1991) 'Iranian Relations with Great Britain and British India, 1789–1921', in E. Avery et al. (eds) *The Cambridge History of Iran*, vii: *From Nadir Shah to the Islamic Republic* (Cambridge: Cambridge University Press) 374–425.

Humbly, G. R. G. (1991a) 'Āghā Muhammad Khān and the Establishment of the Qājār Dynasty', in E. Avery, et al. (eds) *The Cambridge History of Iran*, vii: *From Nadir Shah to the Islamic Republic* (Cambridge: Cambridge University Press) 104–43.

—— (1991b) 'Iran During the Reigns of Fath Ali Shah and Muhammad Shah', in E. Avery, et al. (eds) *The Cambridge History of Iran*, vii: *From Nadir Shah to the Islamic Republic* (Cambridge: Cambridge University Press) 144–73.

Issawi, C. (1991) 'European Economic Penetration, 1872–1921', in E. Avery, et al. (eds) *The Cambridge History of Iran*, vii: *From Nadir Shah to the Islamic Republic* (Cambridge: Cambridge University Press) 590–608.

Ivanov, M. S. (1978) *The Iranian Constitutional Revolution* (Tehran: Shabgir).

Kasravi, A. (2003) [1941] *The History of Iranian Constitutionalism* (Tehran: Negah).

Keddie, N. (1966) *Religion and Rebellion in Iran: The Tobacco Protest of 1891–1892* (London: Cass).

Kirmani, N. (1953) *The History of the Iranian's Awakening* (Tehran: Chapkhanah-I majlis).

Knei-Paz, B. (1978) *The Social and Political Thought of Leon Trotsky* (Oxford: Clarendon Press).

Löwy, M. (1981) *The Politics of Combined and Uneven Development* (London: Verso).

Malikzadeh, M. (1949) *The History of Iranian Constitutional Revolution* (Tehran).

Martin, V. A. (1986) 'The Anti-Constitutionalist Arguments of Shaikh Fazlallah Nuri', *Middle Eastern Studies*, 22/2: 181–96.

—— (1987) 'Shaikh Fazlallah and the Iranian Revolution, 1905–1909', *Middle Eastern Studies*, 23/1: 39–53.

Momeni, B. (1978) *Iran on the Eve of the Constitutional Revolution and the Literature of the Constitutional Period* (Tehran: Diba).

Neshat, G. (1981) 'From Bazaar to Market: Foreign Trade and Economic Development in Nineteenth Century Iran', in *Iranian Studies*, 14/1–2 (Spring).

Rasulzadeh, M. A. (1998) *Reports form the Iranian Constitutional Revolution* (Tehran: Iqbal).

Rosenberg, J. (2006) 'Why is there no international historical sociology?', in *European Journal of International Relations*, 12 (forthcoming).

Shilliam, R. (2005) *Backwardness in Context: The Roots of Morgenthau's Political Realism*, unpublished Ph.D. thesis (University of Sussex).

Teschke, B. (2005) 'Bourgeois Revolution, State Formation and the Absence of the International', *Historical Materialism*, 13/2: 3–26.

Thompson, E. P. (1978) *The Poverty of Theory* (London: Merlin Press).

Trotsky, L. (1969) *The Permanent Revolution* and *Results and Prospects* (New York: Merit Publishers).

—— (1971) *1905* (London: Allen Lane).

—— (1985) *The History of the Russian Revolution* (London: Pluto Press).

—— (1996) *The Third International After Lenin* (New York: Pathfinder).

Wood, E. (1991) *The Pristine Culture of Capitalism: A Historical Essay on Old Regimes and Modern States* (London: Verso).

11

A Veteran of the Epoch of Revolution Looks Forward

Trotsky, Serge and the Soviets: In an Age of
Disintegrating Formal Democracy, Whither the Soviet?
Or, Results from the Twentieth Century and
Prospects for the Twenty-First.

Suzi Weissman

The year 1905 ushered in a century of revolutions, wars and path-breaking discoveries. A new epoch began that held out the hope that the economy and society could be organised to serve humanity and the community, and not the reverse. In Russia the first socialist revolution was attempted but failed, though it became the dress rehearsal for the successful revolution of 1917. A new democratic form of organisation emerged, workers councils (*soviets* in Russian) and with it, the hope for democratic governance from below. With the soviets, the young Russian labour movement demonstrated their creativity and capacity for self-organisation, taking even the left parties of the time by surprise, though both Lenin and Trotsky realised their revolutionary potential.[1] In the United States, 1905 marks the centenary of the Wobblies, the Industrial Workers of the World, whose imaginative and daring radical tactics changed the face of trade unionism; and this, coupled with the birth of the soviet – which was swiftly adopted by workers everywhere as an organising tool, marked the beginning of the epoch of revolution.

We don't celebrate 1905 as a year of victory, but it opened the twentieth century with the 'actuality' of revolution. There had been the Paris Commune of 1871, but that was localised in one city. The 1905 revolution took place in a truly international context of a progressive era highlighted by workers' demands for better conditions and more power in the wake of rapid industrial expansion.

1. I wish to thank Hillel Ticktin and Michel Vale for their comments on issues raised in this chapter.

SERGE AND 1905

Victor Serge wasn't in Russia for 1905 – he was a teenager beginning a life of revolutionary activity first as an anarchist, later as a Bolshevik, finally as a Left Oppositionist. Yet 1905 echoes throughout the political formation of a new generation of young militants, including Serge, who were thirsting for a society that wasn't based on exploitation and alienation, one that was capable of engendering mechanisms for popular, authentic democratic control from below.

Victor Kibalchich, later known as Victor Serge, was born in 1890 in Belgium. His parents were Russian revolutionary populists in exile for their role in the assassination of Tsar Alexander II in 1881. By the time Serge was 13, he had left home and was living on his own. He worked ten-hour days to support himself, and formed a new family with a group of very close friends that the young Kibalchich described as a 'band of brothers'. They proclaimed themselves socialists, and though their economic circumstances were difficult, they were nourished by ideas.

They joined the *Jeunes-Gardes* in Belgium. For these young militants imbibing the political culture of the period, news of the '1905 general strike, of the days of liberty' came to them from men who had escaped Russia. Serge remembers this as the first topic of a string of public discussions he initiated in his Ixelles branch of the *Jeunes-Gardes* (Serge 2002:11).

Serge was half a generation younger than Trotsky, so the cardinal experience of revolution, in which Trotsky emerged as one of the central leaders as the President of the St Petersburg Soviet, was for Serge but a formative experience at the beginning of his revolutionary career. It would be convenient to be able to say that learning of the general strike and the soviets profoundly marked Serge's ideas at the time. There is no evidence to support this. Still it was a time when socialism was being seriously discussed and, as Serge noted, 'a great age of reformism'. For the young revolutionary worker the socialism on offer was too stodgy, too stuffy. In Belgium it meant 'reformism, parliamentarism, and unrelieved Talmudism' (Serge 2002:12).

Serge and his friends fuelled their intellectual and passionate revolutionary ardour with anarchism. Serge knew many Russians, and was invigorated and inspired by their boldness and their rejection of reformist solutions. He described them:

...men and women who had been formed in ruthless battle, who had but one aim in life, who drew their breath from danger. The comfort, peace and amiability of the West seemed stale to them, and angered them all the more since they had learned to see the naked operations of a social machinery which no one thought of in these privileged lands. (Serge 2002:14)

By and large, Serge's acquaintances were anarchists and populists, and in Paris the following year Serge met with Russian SR's (Socialist Revolutionary Party) in emigration.

The exiles from the defeated first socialist revolution in Russia impressed the young Serge and his comrades in Western Europe with their daring, and likely contributed to Serge's disillusionment with the resolution-passing reformists of the day. Serge was not converted to revolutionary Bolshevism as a result, since the next chapter in his life was anarchist. We learn more about his affinity with the Bolsheviks in his *Year One of the Russian Revolution, a* history written in 1929, where he maintains retrospectively that despite the hesitation and disarray of the Bolsheviks in 1905, embroiled in internal struggles which would define the ideas of each of the tendencies, their attitude in 1905 explains their victory in 1917 (Serge 1992:40).

That attitude was one of audacity and of willingness to push for a workers' insurrection with an understanding of the requirements of leadership. As the events of 1905 accelerated, so too did the semi-legal and illegal organisations of workers. October saw the general strike and the founding of the St Petersburg Soviet (13 October) on the basis of one deputy for every 500 workers. Led by Trotsky and inspired by the Bolsheviks, the soviet tried to win the eight-hour day by strike action, but failed (Serge 1992:41).

But what of the Bolsheviks' understanding of the requirements of leadership at the time? The proletariat was numerous, powerful, politically conscious and active. The bourgeoisie in Russia was immature and incapable of completing its own tasks of development. Yet the revolutionary enthusiasm and solidarity of the workers could not make up for the Bolsheviks' weak organisation, inexperience and lack of theoretical clarity. It would take more than understanding their role to get to victory – and thus there were three revolutions in Russia instead of one. The revolution of 1905 was lost at great cost: 79,000 were arrested, 15,000 were killed, and years of repression followed (Serge 1992:42).

LESSONS AND RESULTS

The Russian Revolution of 1905 struck fear in the hearts of ruling circles all over Europe, who now had a tangible experience of revolution. The idea of revolution was no longer simply a threat – and its appearance led to an intensive reorientation of foreign policy whose aim was to buy off the discontent of their own working classes, lest they imitate the Russian workers. So the sudden revelation of Russia's weakness changed the entire European scene, and led to new alliances, new seizing of colonies, in short to the conditions which brought about the First World War.

The 1905 revolution sparked strikes and protests all over Central Europe. Finland had a general strike the same year, and German workers paid close attention to Russian events. The general strike (also known as the mass strike) of 1905 prompted Rosa Luxemburg to write one of her most significant contributions on 'The Mass Strike, The Political Party and the Trade Unions'. Luxemburg analysed the sudden appearance of the Russian strike wave which separated the wheat from the chaff: workers' political consciousness was transformed by their collective action, while the reaction of trade union and social democratic leaders exposed their bureaucratic conservatism (see Haro 2005).

The events of 1905 showed the importance of the general strike as a political weapon; this strike was not simply a general strike, but a political strike, whose demands were directed at the state itself, challenging its power and disorganising that power. The strike paralysed vital activity, the economic apparatus of the state, disrupted communications, isolated the government and rendered it powerless. It also united the mass of workers from the factories and opposed the workers' army to the state power. This created a situation of dual power; one based on the masses, whose political expression was the soviet, and the other the old power based on the army. The two can't coexist for long, as a struggle *for* the army develops between the two opposing powers, which is what happened in the successful revolution of 1917.

In addition, the 1905 revolution signalled the emergence of a new and higher form of political organisation for the working class – the soviet. The soviet is an organ of self-government of the revolutionary masses, an organ of power. Soviets were to be organised democratically, joined voluntarily, enjoying freedom of speech and representation for various political currents; they were hotbeds of revolutionary ferment. The soviet in Russia became the workers' state in embryo, functioning as an effective alternative government. Trotsky, leader of the largest soviet (the St Petersburg Soviet), recognised the importance of this new form of organisation, which he saw as 'authentic' democracy

– without chambers, without bureaucracy, with the right of recall at any time (Trotsky 1971:265–80). Soviets spread throughout Europe, and were embraced by the international working class as a tool in struggle.

Although 1905 was a defeat, much was learned from the experience: the workers and peasants had finished with the autocracy and engaged in combat against it; the political parties became clearer in their ideas and the working class turned to the party of their class. Serge considered the defeat a victory for the proletariat in this sense, that it rose to its feet and resumed its actions while the bourgeoisie continued to be divided, weak and indecisive. Lenin wrote of the lessons of 1905–06 and underscored the importance of the soviets as organs of direct mass struggle which were transformed into 'organs of an uprising' (Lenin 1962:156, 1965:124–5).

WHITHER THE SOVIETS?

The promise of the soviets was the promise of socialism – a *genuine* democracy in which workers were the masters of their destiny, a society in which people organised collectively, at every level from bottom to top, to become the masters of their work, their lives and their fate. The Russian Revolution held out the promise of socialism, but it was doomed by its isolation and dashed by the rise of Stalin. Subsequent revolutionary struggles were judged politically healthy by contemporary leftists if the key marker was present – the existence of soviets.

Despite its later degeneration and demise, the Russian Revolution was the first socialist revolution and it became the model for revolution. Crucial to its victory were the soviets, yet they did not survive the civil war as institutions of democratic governance. Nonetheless, the revolution triumphed in no small part because of the presence of the soviets, dual power and a party of capable leaders who understood the historical moment, could 'see reality, grasp possibility, and conceive the action which [would be] the link between the real and the possible' (Serge 1992:58). As the Bolsheviks became the party of the proletariat and the majority in the soviets, what happened to the independence of the soviets? How did the Bolsheviks see their role?

Looking at what happened to the soviets is not to play into the post-soviet fashion of seeing the October Revolution as but a Bolshevik *coup d'état*, the work of a small conspiracy which intended to establish a monopoly of power from the outset. Nor is it to abstract the relationship between the party and the soviets from the objective circumstances of the time, which were dire. Lenin and Trotsky always emphasised that it was easier to come to power in Russia than to move towards socialism. Simply put, the drive toward authoritarian centralism couldn't be avoided. Victor Serge's *Year One of the Russian Revolution* makes the case that the early drive toward a dictatorial one-party state was not the result of ideological ardour, though party patriotism played its part, but rather was the outcome of improvised emergency measures in response to a crisis situation. The Bolsheviks themselves were aware of the contradictions between their democratic goals and their authoritarian practices, which they justified by the danger of reaction. They couldn't surmount the contradictions, but it seems they suppressed them through demagoguery. They were sincere in their goal, yet they also had an underdeveloped commitment to soviet democracy.

While this period must be studied within its historical context, the keynote is the universality of the issues facing the young revolution and Bolshevik party. Unfortunately, as mentioned above, the success of the Russian Revolution led to it becoming a model, sometimes crudely imitated by subsequent revolutionary movements, along with a cavalier attitude to democratic institutions in much more favourable conditions than faced the Bolsheviks. The Stalinoid left has either neglected or dismissed the question of democratic forms of socialism, and the Trotskyist left has always counterposed the higher form of soviet or council democracy to the bourgeois democratic parliamentary forms.

The Bolsheviks' attitude to the role of the soviets cannot be separated from the specific conditions which led to the suspension of democratic freedoms. History forced them into a dilemma that couldn't be resolved: yet it is useful to explore how they viewed the distinction between the soviets as a tool of revolution, and/or representing the future form of governance. Lenin stressed that the soviet was an 'organ of insurrection', or as Trotsky put it, a tool of working-class power, but subsequent generations emphasise the soviet as the highest form of democratic self-organisation and governance. Trotsky saw the soviet as the organisation *of the proletariat*, created for the purpose of coordinating their actions, aimed at the struggle for revolutionary power (Trotsky 1971:266; see also Trotsky 1970:60). After the experience of the Russian Revolution, could the soviet deepen democracy in a post-revolutionary environment, indeed, could it become the *form* of democratic governance in post-revolutionary society?

THE MYSTIQUE OF DEMOCRACY?

The Bolsheviks regarded the soviets and soviet democracy as a superior form to parliamentary democracy. Even so, Trotsky admitted as he wrote about 1905 that his work 'lacks clarity on the question of formal democracy, as did the whole movement it describes' (Trotsky 1971:10).

He added that even ten years later, in 1917, they were not operating under the 'mystique of democracy', and in fact never envisaged the revolution putting into practice 'certain absolute democratic norms'. They saw the progress of the revolution not in terms of *democracy* but 'as a war between classes, which for their temporary needs, had to make use of the slogans and the institutions of democracy' (Trotsky 1971:11). Certainly the Bolsheviks' demands from the 1905 revolution amounted to an advanced political democracy with universal suffrage, a representative republic, right of instant recall, etc., but Trotsky considered this a phase in the development of the workers' struggle until they were able to liberate themselves from 'the prejudices of political democracy' in the revolution itself (Trotsky 1971:11).

The dissolution of the Constituent Assembly in 1918 brought the contradictions between democracy and revolutionary dictatorship to a head, posed in legal terms which Trotsky conceded 'crudely' fulfilled a revolutionary aim, but could alternatively have been postponed. Lenin admitted that the Constituent Assembly was the legitimate, highest expression of democracy realised in a bourgeois republic, but the soviets were a form of higher democracy, the only form ensuring an uninterrupted transition to socialism (Serge 1992:126).

Clearly the question of democracy revealed an early contradiction that was not resolved. The soviets died in the civil war and were never revived. What survived were moribund institutions that served the party's empty rhetoric and dead slogans. Lenin and Trotsky were attacked from the beginning for advocating democratic control from below but actually controlling from above. As is usually the case, the reality was more complex.

There is both tragedy and irony in heralding the soviet as a superior form of democratic governance from below – a tool in the revolutionary arsenal that the Russian proletariat gave to the international working class – even as it could not itself survive the aftermath of the Russian Revolution. The world political reality the Bolsheviks operated in further complicated the economic crisis, civil war conditions, internal counter-revolution, and the failure of the revolution to spread, to strangle the feasibility of socialist democracy. No alternative existed to the emergent Bolshevik dictatorship, other than chaos or worse. The soviets became auxiliary organs of the party, de facto party committees. The leadership in these circumstances was not committed to the 'democratic self-governance of the working class' – the working class barely survived the civil war. The country was exhausted and the notion of 'power to the soviets' was truly an empty one given the overall situation.

Eviscerated during the civil war, the soviets became rubber-stamp organs of the party and later the state. This wasn't the doing of the party per se, but of the transformed composition of the soviets as the Bolsheviks became the majority force within them, outnumbering the Mensheviks and SRs. Political power resided in the Bolshevik Party. In a one-party state, soviet governance is easily co-opted, corrupted, de-fanged or simply sidelined by the party of power. In the Stalin years the soviets stopped holding meetings altogether, even for ceremonial purposes (Urban 1990:3). Existing in form only, the soviets were lifeless assemblies that could hardly even be called governmental institutions. They had no real role in political life in the Soviet Union. Power was administrated by higher-ups in the party–state hierarchy – the secret police, state ministries and party apparatus. During the Gorbachev period the demand for 'more power to the soviets' was resurrected, but not as a form of direct democracy and workers' power.

While recognising the key role of the soviets in the revolutions of 1905 and 1917, the Bolsheviks in power in the 1920s were less concerned with soviet democracy than with the danger of capitalist restoration. Even Preobrazhensky and Trotsky of the Left Opposition, whose programme was a principled critique of bureaucratisation and the stifling of democracy in the party, rarely addressed the issue of democracy in the society as a whole. Socialism *is* control from below and soviets in theory are the instrument. The situation by the 1920s had deteriorated to the extent that discussions about democracy were about *inner-party* democracy, not multi-party democracy, nor about reviving the soviets. Serge raised the issue of revitalising political parties and political life, stating that 'socialism and workers' democracy cannot be born out of pronunciamentos' (Serge 1996:151–2n.), yet even while demanding democracy both in and out of the party, Serge admitted that after 1921 'everybody that aspires to socialism is inside the party; what remains outside isn't worth much for the social transformation' (Serge 1939:54). This explains the concentration on inner-party democracy rather than on revitalising democratic institutions for the society at large. Serge wrote that the chief omission in Bolshevik discussion in this period was the problem of liberty, which with democracy and political pluralism was drowned in the avalanche of the civil war. And Serge recognised that 'the socialist revolution which unfolded in Russia could never be considered apart from the international labor movement' (Serge 1996:147–8).

Herein lay another contradiction for the Bolsheviks, who recognised that the soviets were both the tool of the proletariat and the form of transition to socialism: internationalism was more important to them than ensuring the survival of democracy. The revolution was under siege: the SRs took up arms against the Bolsheviks, and the suppression of the Kronstadt revolt was the last straw for the anarchists, whose support had waned during the civil war. The Bolsheviks hadn't intended to rule alone, but they only trusted themselves to understand the nature of the struggle for socialism in the world – no other political party saw the importance of the extension of the revolution as the only way they could survive, so Lenin and Trotsky didn't trust the others to rule with them. With the Bolsheviks representing the majority in the soviets, the locus of activity shifted to what they saw as the more important political arena of the party. So the contradictions residing in creating vibrant revolutionary institutions of democratic control from below were evident from the outset. Trotsky's comments (above) show he was aware of this problem.

In retrospect it can be said that Lenin's crucial failure while in power was that he paid too little attention to the creation of democratic institutions, soviet or otherwise, and to the democratic rights and liberties of individuals, which were later thoroughly trampled by Stalin, never to be restored. On the other hand Lenin and Trotsky recognised that the transition to socialism wasn't possible in a beleaguered, backward and isolated country. Had they held on to the soviets as the socio-economic form of genuine control from below, they might have inspired revolutions in the West.

When the Soviet Union collapsed the model for electoral democracy later adopted most closely resembles the shallow democracy of the United States. Some call it 'illiberal democracy'. Elections, campaign rules, the corrupting influence of money, media restrictions, voting procedures, everything is fudged. This is relevant because the struggle for governance from below means engaging in a struggle for 'genuine democracy', i.e. putting democratic content into the hollow forms.

The model of the soviet has failed and this raises the issue of whether it can be resurrected and whether it can be viable. Can governance from below survive the heady days of revolution, and if so what form must it take? As we have seen, the Bolsheviks themselves were unclear on this critical point.

DEFEAT AND RENEWAL

In several of the essays Serge wrote in the last years of his life,[2] he looked forward from the defeats inflicted by Stalinism and fascism and called for a renewal of socialism. The call remains unanswered 60 years later. As the post cold-war era struggles for definition and the world faces a bleak landscape of competing religious nationalisms, the renewal of socialism seems more urgent than ever.

Reviewing the issues that preoccupied Serge's thinking in these dark years yields much to salvage for the present day, even though the context of his time is radically different from the 'present' we inhabit. Serge was writing during the Second World War and the immediate post-war environment, in which the outlines of the cold war were emerging. He was frightened by what he saw – efficient bureaucratic machines with collectivist tendencies that completely choked democratic participation from below.[3] His writings about these developments no longer pertain, nor do they reflect the reality of world development: how could Serge have imagined the end of the Soviet Union, the decline of social democracy and the neoliberal model so prevalent today? Yet the tendencies he noted and the questions he asked are surely relevant. On this note Serge proved prescient: if a historically conscious collectivism did not successfully challenge the totalitarian collectivism of Stalinism and fascism, it would mean the end of socialism for a whole era.

Serge held that the axioms from the Russian Revolution were no longer adequate. Writing in 1943, he observed that everything had changed – science, production, social movements and intellectual currents. History only permitted apparent stability to religious

2. Serge died in Mexico in 1947.
3. A fuller evaluation of Serge's thought in his final years can be found in Weissman (2001).

dogma. An intellectual rearmament was necessary and for that a creative investigatory effort was required. As Serge noted,

the poverty of traditional socialism coincides...with the immense revolutionary crisis of the modern world that unavoidably puts on the order of the day... – independently of the action of socialism – the problem of a social reorganization oriented toward the rational and the just. (Serge 1943)

Serge couldn't emphasise strongly enough that the socialist movement had to break free from its fossilised thinking, and that the terrible new conditions demanded new thinking – dialectical thought combined with political action, a form of active humanism. Serge was fully justified in warning that the consequences of sticking to the old patterns and formulas would be grave for the socialist movement. Sadly, he was proved right.

Much had changed in the years since 1917. The actuality of the revolution emboldened workers in the West, radicalised by war, revolution and the deepening capitalist crisis. Labour movements in the West were active and communist parties grew in membership, supported financially by the USSR. In the inter-war period the threat to capitalism's very survival was so great that Germany and Italy resorted to fascism. The New Deal in the United States was capitalism's response to a militant labour movement, using concessions to incorporate rather than crush the working class – though fascism and social democratic reforms had the same goal: to stave off revolution. After the Second World War the welfarist reforms, including capitalist nationalisation of key sectors of industry, were accommodations to the threat represented by a radicalised working class and the continued existence of the Soviet Union.

Serge's thinking about post-Second World War economic and political development was shaped by the terrible experience of the twin totalitarianisms of fascism and Stalinism. The condition of humanity had been worsened by these regimes: the working-class movement was deeply damaged by fascism, and Stalinism threatened the fate of socialism everywhere. Neither labour militancy in the West nor the colonial revolution in the East buoyed his spirits so long as the Soviet Union was in a position to crush revolutionary movements to its left and channel the others into anti-imperialist national liberation struggles that would lead to an extension of Soviet totalitarianism, a far cry from socialism (Serge 1985:181).

Stalinism – in the guise of Russian socialism – was degenerate, intolerant and insufficiently dialectical, according to Serge. European socialists, tainted by Stalinism, could not see the roots of racism and anti-Semitism, nor the appeal of fascist reactionary nationalism – and they were weakened by their inattention to the changes to the state and the economy brought about by technological innovation (Serge 1946:12–14). It was undeniable that the Soviet regime, fascism, Nazism, and the New Deal shared common traits which as Trotsky too had noted in 1939, derived from the collectivist tendencies of the modern economy. The socialist movement needed intellectual rigour, an understanding of political economy, a living philosophy – which could find a way for workers to achieve democratic control of society, organise a rational economy and realise a higher dignity (Serge 1972).

In essence, socialist thought needed updating to keep current with developments in the economy, discoveries in science, and advances in the understanding of human psychology. Stalinism had retarded intellectual development with its state dogma, directed thought and 'ownership' of philosophical truth. As a consequence, Marxist method of analysis and interpretation of history had been degraded. Even on its own terra firma of political economy European socialists had ignored the changes brought about by advances in technology which increased productivity but reduced the importance of manual labour. The developments in industry upset traditional proportions and relations of classes, giving increased importance to governing bureaucracies as well as to intermediary layers of administrators, technicians, managers, and an intelligentsia of sociologists, economists and psychologists. The existing analysis of the class struggle was too schematic, Serge wrote, taking account neither of the role of the shareholders and tycoons, nor of the civil employees of the totalitarian state (Serge 1943:18).

Serge was grappling with new uncertainties, frustrated by the inability of socialists to think creatively to deal with the new world conjuncture. He characterised the war as one of social transformation taking place in a transitional epoch that would usher in new social formations, distinguished by a tendency toward totalitarian collectivist command economies (Serge et al. 1944:11–41).

Serge was convinced that the new social layers comprising a technical intelligentsia in the totalitarian societies (in the civil service or governing bureaucracies) played an important new role, even more important than the working class. Moreover, these new collectivist bureaucracies, whether soviet or fascist, operated in societies that were thoroughly anti-democratic and allowed virtually no civil liberties. This made the question of democracy and freedom even more important.

The USSR represented a new force in the world that was neither capitalist nor socialist, but altered the nature of class struggle in the world. It was now an obstacle to socialism, exerting a negative influence on all current struggles. We have yet to recover from its damage.

It was sobering to realise that collectivism was not synonymous with socialism (as Serge and his comrades had previously thought) and could in fact be anti-socialist, demonstrating new forms of exploitation. For Serge this revealed the extreme weakness of socialist movements and socialist thought. The defeats suffered in Europe were partly due to this theoretical as well as organisational debility. Lacking energy and foresight, the European socialists were not clearly aware of the dangers they faced nor of the opportunities offered to them. Likewise, the Bolsheviks were responsible in part for the march toward totalitarianism in the Soviet Union: Serge blamed their psychology, their ignorance of democratic values and the methods they employed. The Bolsheviks compensated for their ideological insufficiency with will and authority – and also terror (Serge 1946:12–14).

American socialists (Sidney Hook, Dwight Macdonald, James Burnham and others) and liberals were more concerned with freedom and liberty than their European counterparts, but Serge noted that their ideas were based on the ideals of bourgeois liberal humanism and the traditions of parliamentary democracy. Honourable but out of date, Serge warned, because the role of the state increased in the era of nationalised economies. In totalitarian states the coercive function increased, while in democratic states the organising role increased. The extended functions of the modern state, Serge believed, made obsolete the notion of the abolition of the state. The libertarian commune state of the Bolsheviks in 1917 went bankrupt and the withering away of the state died during Lenin's lifetime (Serge 1946).

The world had changed, and the old theories could not take into account the age of finance capital nor the role of Stalinist expansion. Stalin drowned socialism in blood, creating a terrible system that became equated with Marxism. Theoretical accounts are still being settled with this black heritage that confused working people everywhere. Marxism was turned on its head by this anti-socialist, exploitative system which was contemptuous of humanity.

There were grounds for optimism: the rebuilding of Europe after the war would strengthen the working class, and the interdependence of nations could result in an internationalisation of societies that Serge believed would promote the growth of socialist struggle. At the same time, the totalitarian regimes produced vigorous and deep anti-totalitarian reaction, though the younger generation was confused in its aspirations. They were nonetheless receptive to freedom and liberty and no matter how tragically difficult the immediate situation was, socialism had a great future in front of it. The intellectual weakness of the socialist movement (sapped by the formidable Stalinist machine) could only be remedied by an 'epoch of uprising' (Serge 1946).

In the Europe of today, 100 years after 1905, unemployed immigrant youth rise in confusion, anger and frustration, bereft of the intellectual armour required, yet an epoch of uprising is ostensibly upon us.

Serge misjudged the tendencies he noted, believing the world was in transition away from capitalism, influenced by the Soviet Union. Unlike other thinkers of the time, Serge did not proclaim socialism a failure, but called for its rebirth. He insisted the aims must be for a society that guarantees human freedom – in the interests of more than just the working masses, for all of humanity. Democracy must mean democracy of work; liberty must mean personal and political freedom.

For the down at heart then and now, it is salient to recall the situation of left oppositionists like Serge, who survived the 1930s when they were hounded by the NKVD and the Gestapo, who rejected both Stalinism and the cold-war liberalism of capitalism. In a letter to Macdonald in 1945, Serge cautioned that negativism is an attitude, not a solution. Emotional reactions to the horrors of mid century were understandable but characteristically renounce investigatory thought and clear-sighted analysis. All we have left is intelligence, that is, knowledge and technique, and an inner impulse for a more dignified life. In response to the many socialists, including Charles Plisnier and A.J. Muste, who reverted to Christian mysticism, or to those who retreated to individual acts of conscience, Serge noted that scruples and courage of conscience are absolute necessities, but have no social value unless joined to action that is perseverant, general and draws in the greatest numbers. A progressive movement is needed (Serge 1945).

FROM SERGE'S 'PRESENT' TO OURS – AND THE FUTURE

Reconsidering the question of 'formal democracy' as well as the form of democracy represented by the soviet 100 years after its appearance is a bit eerie given all that happened in the years of Soviet rule, when democracy was crushed in every important way. We live in a time of disintegrating democracy, where democratic forms and institutions are but empty shells robbed of democratic content, corrupted by the direct or indirect influence of money. What can we take from that revolutionary year to be of use for the struggles we surely face?

The soviet failed as did the extension of the socialist revolution to advanced capitalist countries, but the question of democracy persists.

In fact, the influence of the revolution's promise was felt in the industrialised capitalist democracies. Important elements of a more advanced political democracy, such as the universal franchise, representative democracy, free speech and other basic rights, were won and conceded to in response to the existence of the Soviet Union and to contain radicalism at home. These were demands advanced in the revolution of 1905.

After 1918 and again after 1945 the radicalised working class demanded and gained social protections and democratic advances. The concessions provided a springboard for more demands. The democratic gains of the second half of the twentieth century, brought by the civil rights movement, the women's movement and other sectors, significantly deepened democracy without appreciably deepening the struggle for 'economic democracy' or further specific workers' rights (see Lichtenstein 2002:ch.5). Workers' individual rights have improved, winning protection from discrimination at work, but at the expense of union rights and protections – which have been eroded and often exist in name only.

These reforms strengthened democracy, but cut into the profitability of capitalism. With the disintegration of the Soviet Union and Eastern Europe, the social democratic concessions were less necessary, and increasingly difficult to deliver in the age of finance capital. Perhaps it is no surprise then that the collapse of the Soviet Union hastened the decline of social democracy. At the same time, we are seeing the hollowing out of bourgeois democracy, perhaps nowhere more pronouncedly than in the United States itself. It is caricatured in the so-called new democracies of the former Soviet bloc and now in occupied Iraq. The promise of democracy is potent and even risky, as more and more people demand the genuine article, not managed electoral shams.

The twenty-first century began with the pessimism of TINA (there is no alternative), while the clarion call of the anti-globalisation activists is that 'another world is possible'. Was the notion that the working class could emancipate itself an anarchist dream?

The disintegration of the Soviet Union left in its wake revulsion and rejection of statist solutions and a resurgence of a kind of pro-anarchist sentiment, evident in social movements left and right. The reaction in the former Soviet Union (FSU) was hardly surprising given the power of its state over every aspect of people's lives. Anarchism appeals to youth who are disenchanted with 'globalisation', just as it attracted a section of mainly young workers in the former Soviet Union. The rise of anarchist sentiment has more to do with the rejection of the present than a real theoretical allegiance to anarchism, which properly belongs to a pre-industrial age. It rose among peasants and artisans, but with the rise of industrial capitalism anarchism gave way to anarcho-syndicalism and socialism. The anti-statist sentiment of the present time is contradictory, reflected in the romanticised notions about anarchist and anarcho-syndicalist ideas. While rejecting the coercive and intrusive functions of the state, radicalised sectors still look to the state to protect what is left of the safety-net.

The intellectual rearmament Serge called for has not occurred. If anything, more confusion reigns today, in a period of generalised attack on democratic rights and living standards. Reaction to these class-based policies has created a strange nostalgia for the nation state, as if it were a benign structure the forces of globalisation are undermining. As workers vainly look to the nation state for protection against the forces of globalising capital, they are demanding that the state maintain the social democratic benefits won through years of struggle. But social democracy in effect was capitalism's response to the Russian Revolution, and when the USSR imploded the falling trajectory of social democracy was delineated.

In the United States the libertarian right is 'anarchistic'. This was on full display in New Orleans in the wake of hurricane Katrina, when the message was 'you're on your own' for survival, but a full-scale military presence appeared in response to individual 'looting'. Left on their own, with no state in view, ordinary working people in the Cajun community of Ville Platte acted heroically, pulling together and cooperating, democratically organising rescue missions, shelters, distribution of food, water and healthcare. It was a vindication of grassroots and participatory democracy. When asked who was making the decisions, a Creole community leader said 'We don't have leadership, we don't have decision-making, we just know how to cooperate.'[4] It is this kind of solidarity and spontaneous democratic organisation that reminds us of the old Industrial Workers of the World (the Wobblies), organising workers since 1905 without condescending leaders. The Cajun community of Ville Platte organising their own relief gives us a glimpse that control from below is possible.

The decline of bourgeois democracy is directly tied to the weakened labour and socialist movements. Parliamentary democracy is still quite young – if we count its beginning with universal franchise – and many of the advances in political democracy were won through the efforts of socialists in the labour movement. Even in its current state of decay, there are scores of examples like Ville Platte that show the unevenness of democratic decline which could be quickly turned around, even though the crisis of democracy is well advanced. Money buys media access and corrupts politicians and the electoral process. Politicians resort to false promises or xenophobia to curry favour – or to wedge issues like abortion and homosexuality which distract workers from voting in their economic interests. Everywhere non-profits and NGOs – single issue organisations – have sprouted to meet the needs that political parties and politicians ignore from constituencies that can't afford to buy access and representation.

The fine principles of liberal democracy are not enough – their forms of democratic governance do not solve economic crisis, nor can elections halt the slide in the standard of living, much less empower workers. Increasingly larger voter blocs lose confidence in the process and ignore elections. Nonetheless, glimmers of hope abound: the internet and blogosphere decentralise the dissemination of information and allow for a wide spectrum of political views and debate, beyond the control of the state. Where politicians fail, community organisations and churches take up the slack to help meet basic needs.

Authentic democracy – control from below – requires a sufficient level of understanding and education, and is impossible if money

4. Interview with Mike Davis upon his return from New Orleans. He recounted his conversation with Jennifer Vedreen, black Creole community leader in Ville Platte, Louisiana (26 September 2005).

has influence in the process. In many ways the struggle for this bottom-up democracy is a revolutionary struggle that involves coming up with better forms than the soviets promised: getting real democracy means getting revolutionary. We can't presume in advance what forms the working class will take when it acts for itself. The political form will be determined by the struggle itself, though without control from below in a society that eliminates the division of labour and has a high level of education and participation, we can't get to substantive democracy. We have gone full circle: the future depends on our discarding all the remnants of Stalinism, rejecting the corrupting divisions of capitalism, and recapturing the daring and imagination of Wobblies and Bolsheviks in 1905. To do so we must pay heed to Serge's concerns – more than ever we must see clearly, work courageously and be socially effective. And we must never lose sight of the human impulse for freedom, dignity and self-organisation that emerges over and over again – and is cause for great hope.

REFERENCES

Haro, L. (2005), 'The Threat of "Red Rosa": Luxemburg, the Mass Strike and the 1905–06 Revolution', *Against the Current*, 118, (September–October).

Lenin, V. I. (1962 [1905–6]) *Collected Works*, x (Moscow: Foreign Language Publishing House).

—— (1965 [1906–7]) *Collected Works*, xi (Moscow: Progress Publishers).

Lichtenstein, N. (2002) *State of the Union: A Century of American Labor* (Princeton: Princeton University Press).

Serge, V. (1939) 'Reply to Ciliga', *New International* (February).

—— (1943) 'Necesidad de una renovación del Socialismo', *Mundo, Libertad y Socialismo*, Mexico, (June).

—— (1945) to Dwight Macdonald, 8 October 1945, Macdonald Papers, Yale University Library.

—— (1946) 'Pour un Renouvellement du Socialisme', *Masses/Socialisme et Liberté* (June).

—— (1972) 'L'URSS a-t-elle une régime socialiste?' *Spartacus*, B/50 (October–November).

—— (1985) *Carnets* (Arles: Actes Sud).

—— (1992 [1930]) *Year One of the Russian Revolution* (New York: Writers and Readers).

—— (1996 [1937]) *Russia Twenty Years After* (Atlantic Highlands: Humanities Press).

—— (2002 [1951]) *Memoirs of a Revolutionary* (Iowa: University of Iowa Press).

—— Gorkín, J., Pivert, M. and Chevalier, P. (1944) *Los Problemas del socialismo en nuestro tiempo* (Mexico City: Ediciones Ibero-Americanas).

Trotsky, L. (1970 [1930/1906]) *The Permanent Revolution* and *Results and Prospects* (New York: Pathfinder Press).

—— (1971 [1922]) *1905* (England: Penguin Books).

Urban, M. (1990) *More Power to the Soviets* (Aldershot: Edward Elgar).

Weissman, S. (2001) *Victor Serge: The Course Is Set on Hope* (London and New York: Verso).

12

Trotsky's Omission: Labour's Role in Combined and Uneven Development

Andrew Herod

Leon Trotsky's 1906 *Results and Prospects,* and his defence of this work in *The Permanent Revolution,* are centrally concerned with the nature of political revolution. But they are also unquestionably concerned with geography or, more precisely, with how the geography of capitalism and the geography of revolution are imbricated, the one with the other. Although little developed by Trotsky himself, there is a clear spatial sensibility which runs through these works, as Trotsky (1970:43) talks of how Russia's 'enormous distances... had been overcome by the telegraph, which imparts confidence to the actions of the administration and gives relative uniformity and rapidity to its proceedings (in the matter of repressions)', of how the Tsarist 'autocratic government made the European Stock Exchange its exchequer, and the Russian taxpayer thus became a hopeless tributary of this European Stock Exchange' (ibid.), and of how, in the nineteenth century, the railroads had facilitated urbanisation and industrialisation by so 'widen[ing] the sources of supply for the town as to make it possible to concentrate [there] such large masses of people' (p. 48). Indeed, much of the imagery invoked by Trotsky – that of new telecommunications technologies overcoming geography, of a 'less developed' country serving as a geographical destination for capital from the metropoles, and of new modes of transportation allowing for the sourcing of raw materials from broader expanses of the economic landscape – are strangely reminiscent (perhaps 'prescient' is a better word) of the language used to describe the contemporary spatial transformation of early twenty-first century capitalism, with its 'shrinking globe', its new international division of labour, and the global sourcing practised by transnational corporations and facilitated by modern jet aircraft.

Equally, the basic political lesson of Trotsky's work is also spatial, namely that socialist revolution cannot be confined, *à la* Stalin, within particular absolute spaces – that is, nation states – but must, rather, transcend these spaces and spread across the global political terrain. For Trotsky, proletarian internationalism is necessarily 'a political reflection...of the world development of productive forces and the world scale of the class struggle' (1970:133), so that the character of the permanent revolution is shaped by the unevenly developed geography of capitalism. Given that, by the early twentieth century, 'capitalism ha[d] converted the whole world into a single economic and political organism' (p. 107) marked by the scars of global uneven geographical development, for Trotsky socialist revolution would have to be spread globally if it were to be successful.

As is well known, the central aspect of Trotsky's theoretical exegesis of how capitalism operates – and hence of the possibilities for socialist revolution – is the notion of combined and uneven development, by which Trotsky means that the geography of capitalism is both necessarily unevenly developed and that what happens in one part of the globe is related to what happens elsewhere. Such ideas present capitalist development in processual terms, seeing uneven development as not simply the result of the impossibility of 'even' development but, rather, as fundamental to the accumulation process which, over time, draws under its sway ever greater swaths of the Earth's surface. Significantly, however, Trotsky views the motor driving such combined and uneven development as being that of the internal contradictions of the accumulation process, such that

[i]n the process of its development, and consequently in the struggle with its internal contradictions, every national capitalism turns in an ever-increasing degree to the reserves of the 'external market,' that is, the reserves of [the] world economy...[with the result that the]...uncontrollable expansion growing out of the permanent internal crises of capitalism constitutes a progressive force up to the time when it turns into a force fatal to capitalism. (1970:153)

Somewhat surprisingly, given his politics, such an explanatory framework – that combined and uneven development results from the internal contradictions of capitalism – omits the one social entity that is, presumably, the principal object of Trotsky's emancipatory theorising: labour.

In evaluating what Trotsky's analysis of the laws of combined and uneven development mean for understanding contemporary capitalism, then, in this chapter I want to do three interrelated things. First, I will briefly make the case for understanding how the operation of capitalism is fundamentally intertwined with the making of geographical landscapes, that is to say, how the production of capitalism's geography is central to how the accumulation process works. Second, I want to argue that workers play important roles in the processes of combined and uneven development which Trotsky theorises and thus that they are central actors in making the geography of global capitalism. Finally, I will engage with some of the recent literature concerning how geographical scale is theorised, to show that Trotsky's arguments about the impossibility of socialist revolution within a single country incorporate a particular spatial imaginary regarding how the world is scaled hierarchically – that is to say, they incorporate a particular view of what exactly geographical scale is and of the relationship between the various spatial scales (local, regional, national and global) at which capitalism is seen to be organised.

ON THE GEOGRAPHY OF CAPITALIST DEVELOPMENT

Until the 1970s, much neo-Marxist theorising paid scant attention to issues of geography. Although Marx himself had made some passing allusions to the geographical organisation of capitalism – most famously in his observations in *Grundrisse* (1973:539) concerning how the building of the railroads in Victorian Britain was leading to the 'annihilation of space by time' and in the final chapter of volume one of *Capital*, in which he talked about how European colonies could serve as geographical 'safety-valves' for surplus capital and labour – most orthodox Marxists had had a very superficial understanding of space and the geography of capitalism (for a more detailed argument of this claim, see Herod 2001:ch.2). For their part, most academic geographers – at least in the Anglo-American academy – had not particularly engaged with Marxism. However, with the Marxification of academic geography in response to events such as the Vietnam War, the civil rights movement, and concerns about imperialism and environmental degradation (see Peet 1998 for more details), a number of theorists began to explore how the capitalist mode of production generates particular economic geographies. For example, writers such as Manuel Castells (1977, 1978) and David Harvey (1973, 1978) attempted to understand the logic of urbanisation under capitalism, whilst others such as Doreen Massey (1984) argued that capitalist accumulation generated particular 'spatial divisions of labour', such that a place's economic character is the result of how it has been integrated into the broader geographical organisation of capitalism historically and how this has shaped flows of capital investment between and to various places. In the francophone world, Marxist geographer Henri Lefebvre (1976:21, emphasis in original) outlined how 'capitalism has found itself able to attenuate (if not resolve) its internal contradictions for a century...*by occupying space, by producing a space*', contending that capital's ability to 'produce space' in particular ways was a central, rather than contingent, aspect of capitalist social relations (see also Lefebvre 1991).

During the 1980s Marxist geographers increasingly considered how the spatial patterning of the economic landscape was 'not just an outcome...[of capitalist social relations but] part of the explanation' of how capitalism functions (Massey 1984:4). Two in particular – David Harvey and Neil Smith – demonstrated how the spatially uneven development of the economic landscape was a necessary, rather than accidental or merely contingent, aspect of the dynamics of capitalist accumulation. For Harvey (1982), the way to connect the geography of capitalism with its internal workings was through the notion of what he called the 'spatial fix', by which he meant the ways in which capitalists must structure the economic landscape so as to enable accumulation to take place. Thus, Harvey argued, capitalists must ensure, either individually or collectively, that transportation links are constructed so that workers and raw materials can be brought together in particular geographical locations for purposes of commodity production, that finished goods can be distributed to points of sale and that workers have places to live so that they can reproduce themselves on a daily and generational basis, all of which requires a certain spatial arrangement of investments in the built environment. In considering how capitalists must structure the economic landscape so as to facilitate accumulation, Harvey (1978:124) noted, though, that the spatial fix which facilitates accumulation at one moment in time might not do so in another, such that whilst 'capital builds a physical landscape appropriate to its own condition at a particular moment in time' it may 'have to destroy it, usually in the course of a crisis, at a subsequent point in time'. In summarising how the geography of capitalism takes on particular spatial forms at particular historical junctures, then, Harvey (1982:416–17, emphasis added) argued that the key to understanding how the geography of capitalism is made is to appreciate that 'the territorial and regional coherence that...is at least partially discernible within capitalism is *actively produced rather than passively received* as a concession to "nature" or "history"'.

For his part, Neil Smith (1990) has made the case that contradictory spatial tendencies within capital have fuelled capitalism's uneven geographical development. Thus, Smith shows, capital must both be physically fixed in the landscape so that accumulation may occur and yet also seeks to maintain sufficient mobility so as to take advantage of new investment opportunities which might arise at any time elsewhere. Geographically uneven development under capitalism, then, is not simply the result of the impossibility of even development nor merely the product of Nature endowing particular places with raw materials or favourable climates but is, rather, actively produced by the working out geographically of these spatial tensions – it is 'the systematic geographical expression of the contradictions inherent in the very constitution and structure of capital', such that uneven development is the very 'hallmark of the geography of capitalism' (Smith 1990: p. xiii).[1]

This brief outline of how the geography of capitalism is neither simply a reflection of the workings of the accumulation process nor is contingent to it but is, instead, central to how capitalism operates as an economic system takes us back to Trotsky, for in his theory of combined and uneven development Trotsky clearly understands that capitalism creates particular types of economic landscapes, even if he does not develop a formal conceptual outline in the way in which more contemporary writers such as Harvey and Smith have done. Thus, for Trotsky, the spread of capitalism throughout the world market is marked by a number of geographical relationships and patterns of uneven development related to the activities of capital – the falling of the countryside 'into economic enslavement to [urban] capital' (1970:73), the creation by capital of a new 'international division of labour and the world market' (p. 146), the 'uneven development of different branches of economy, different classes, different social institutions, different fields of culture' which give form to the 'peculiarit[ies] of...national social type[s]' (p. 148), the exploitative relationships between imperial nations such as Britain

1. Smith argues that whereas under pre-capitalist modes of production Nature had a great influence upon patterns of uneven development – such that wealthy agricultural regions were largely the outcome of naturally-given weather or soils – as the means of production under capitalism have developed, technology and new forms of social organisation have increasingly been able to overcome Nature's constraints. Thus, irrigation schemes make the desert bloom whilst the application of capital (in the form of greenhouses) has allowed Iceland to become a producer of bananas!

and colonies like India, such that 'if Britain were subjected...to an economic blockade, it would perish sooner than would India under a similar blockade' (pp. 152–3), and the geographical spread of capitalist social relations out from Europe to the world economy's 'periphery' as a result of the 'permanent internal crises of capitalism' which cause 'every national capitalism [to] tur[n] in an ever-increasing degree to the reserves of the "external market"' (p. 153), to highlight just a few. Significantly, however, both Trotsky's understanding of how the spatially unevenly developed economic landscape of capitalism comes about and that of much Marxist-inspired writing by economic geographers rely for their explanation of such combined and uneven development upon understanding the contradictions within capital and the actions of capitalists. This is, perhaps, not surprising, given that Marx – who was, after all, the inspiration for both Trotsky and Marxist economic geographers – was himself concerned with examining the processes of capitalist accumulation so as to develop a critique of bourgeois political economy as constructed from the viewpoint of capital. However, it does mean that labour's active roles in shaping patterns of combined and uneven development have remained rather marginalised conceptually. It is to this issue that I now turn.

LABOUR AND THE GEOGRAPHY OF CAPITALISM

In much the same way that capital must create particular configurations of the economic landscape so that accumulation and its self-reproduction as capital may proceed – ensuring that the landscape is one of profitability rather than unprofitability, for instance – so, too, must labour assure that the economic landscape is made in particular ways so that workers may reproduce themselves on a daily and generational basis – ensuring that the landscape is one of employment rather than unemployment, for instance. It is, of course, a truism to say that the process of labour's self-reproduction (both biological and social), by necessity, takes place in particular geographical locations, for social life is spatially embedded. Consequently, workers must secure access to places of work and rest, they must make certain that their children have access to schools, and they must be able to purchase or produce the food and other commodities necessary for them to sustain themselves, which requires access to either shops or fields. Certainly, these are all questions of social access but they are also questions of spatial access. Hence, as Hanson and Pratt

(1995) have shown, women's spatial embeddedness in particular places (the result of their domestic responsibilities such as child rearing and home maintenance) means that they are limited in the distances they can travel to locations of paid work, and certainly more spatially limited than are their husbands who frequently do not have such domestic responsibilities. Likewise, urban workers' inability to access spatially jobs in the suburbs or rural areas because they have no means of travelling from where they live to where new labour markets are opening up may result in a spatial paradox – jobs go unfilled in one place whilst workers remain unemployed in another, a 'spatial mismatch' which might be solved, for instance, by government provision of public transport allowing geographic entrance to suburban labour markets (see Kain 1968; Peck 1996).

Of course, just as capital is not free to construct economic landscapes as it pleases, neither is labour. Rather, the production of economic landscapes is the result of political conflict, between labour and capital and between different segments of labour and of capital who might have quite different visions for how the landscape should be structured – white suburban workers, for example, might object vociferously to public transport which brings non-white urban workers into 'their' neighbourhoods, as might urban-based employers who worry that the provision of such spatial accessibility to suburban labour markets could encourage their own workers to leave for higher-paying suburban work opportunities. Equally, just as the landscapes which capitalists seek to construct at particular historical moments may later prove limiting to their abilities to accumulate, so may workers find that the landscapes which facilitated their social and biological reproduction in earlier times are no longer suitable for doing so, and thus they may struggle to transform them so that they are more appropriate for their contemporary needs. The fact, then, that workers clearly have a vested interest in making the geography of capitalism in some ways and not in others is important for considering the combined and uneven development which characterises the spatiality of capitalism.

Just as capital must continuously negotiate the tensions between the desire for spatial mobility and fixity, so, too, must workers. Thus, whereas on some occasions workers may be relatively free to migrate from place to place or may be able to overcome the spatial distances which separate them – such as through various forms of international solidarity, some forms of which the telecommunications revolution is transforming (see Lee 1997) – on others they are not. Hence, workers may be tied to particular places through kinship or work attachments (such as the difficulty of finding employment elsewhere given their age or skill set) and/or financial constraints, such as the inability to sell their houses in economically depressed regions due to a lack of newcomers to the area. Whatever the reason, many workers find themselves spatially embedded in place, an embeddedness which impacts their political consciousness and the praxis in which they choose to engage. Two examples are pertinent for considering labour's role in combined and uneven development.

First, workers' spatial embeddedness may encourage many to believe that their best chance for ensuring their own self-reproduction – either on a daily or a generational basis – is to engage in various kinds of local boosterist campaigns designed to attract circulating investment into 'their' communities, in the hope that this will support continued employment opportunities. Whilst such involvement in local boosterist campaigns is often portrayed as simply a bad dose of false consciousness in which workers defend spatial interests over class ones and so help to sustain local capitals, in fact most workers would probably see retaining and attracting capital investment in/to their particular communities as integral to their ability to sustain themselves. Rather than acting as class dupes, their spatial embeddedness and inability to move elsewhere makes this participation a rational economic decision for such workers. Importantly, for my argument here, in engaging in these types of local growth coalitions workers shape how capital investment flows across the economic landscape and so play active roles in structuring the geography of capitalism, such that uneven development can be seen to result not just from capital's activities but also from those of workers. Certainly, workers' interests may change, depending upon the specific conditions being experienced in various places (conditions which may themselves alter as communities' places within the broader spatial division of labour are transformed by processes such as globalisation) – hence, for example, steelworkers in the north of Britain organised across space and along class lines to resist steel-mill closures in the early 1980s but by the mid-1980s had largely resorted to a strategy of using boosterism to defend their communities' places within the broader industry in the face of rationalisation by the Thatcher government (Hudson and Sadler 1986). But the fact that they can play significant roles in such defence of particular spaces of the economic landscape and that they may choose to emphasise class or spatial interests at different times means that we must consider workers' praxis as having an important impact upon the processes of spatially uneven development which characterise capitalism.

Second, in contradistinction to the rhetoric of contemporary neoliberals, who see the spread of capitalism globally as being the result of the expansionary nature of capital, it must be recognised that workers, too, have played roles in spreading capitalist social relations and in integrating the capitalist world economy. During the nineteenth and twentieth centuries workers from the imperialist nations often worked hand in hand with their nation's capitalists to ensure that sources of raw materials and markets overseas were secured so that industrial production – and thus employment for themselves – could be maintained in places like the textile mills of Manchester (see Thomson and Larson 1978). Thus, the US labour movement (in the form of the American Federation of Labor and, later, the AFL–CIO) has played a significant role in supporting US capital to secure markets and sources of raw materials in Latin America and the Caribbean by undermining anti-US and anti-capitalist trade unions and political parties in the region (Herod 1997). As part of this strategy, during the 1960s and 1970s the AFL–CIO actively engaged in the process of 'development' – admittedly, a highly selective form thereof – by building housing and engaging in various infrastructure improvement programmes under the auspices of the American Institute for Free Labor Development. These projects were designed to show that workers who supported US interests in their countries could expect material benefits for so doing. In the process, AIFLD dramatically shaped patterns of economic development throughout the hemisphere (see Herod 2001:ch.7 for more details).

Likewise, through their international solidarity activities workers shape global flows of capital, thereby moulding the geography of combined and uneven development. Hence, successful proletarian solidarity to increase the wages of workers in developing countries will have the effect of improving the economic position of such workers and thus will fashion geographies of future development. Equally, an unwillingness to engage in such solidarity will influence capital flows and patterns of development in quite different ways – perhaps ensuring that workers in developing countries remain lowly paid and thus more likely to continue producing cheap consumer goods to satisfy consumers in the global north. In discussing how proletarian internationalism – or the lack thereof – shapes patterns of global development, however, it is important to appreciate that not all instances of internationalism are designed to put common class interests ahead of the particular spatial interests – defending 'their' community's position in the broader spatial division of labour – of those initiating such actions. Thus, whereas solidarity actions are often designed to help workers overseas regardless of the impacts on those engaged in these actions, such that helping workers overseas might result in real economic costs for those doing the helping, sometimes they are entered into by workers in the privileged spaces of the global economy as a way of protecting those spaces – by helping workers overseas to improve their lot, such workers become less attractive to relocating capital. This kind of solidarity – what Rebecca Johns (1998) has called 'accommodationist solidarity' because it seeks to accommodate rather than transform capitalist social relations – effectively divides workers spatially whilst giving the impression of uniting them across space. In the process, of course, it helps sculpt the geography of global combined and uneven development.

THE NATION STATE AS A RECEPTACLE OF POLITICAL PRAXIS

Such discussion of the impact upon the geography of capitalism of workers' political praxis and of the need, according to Trotsky, to spread political revolution beyond the boundaries of the nation state raises one further geographical question, namely how Trotsky (and others subsequently) conceived of the nation state as a spatial entity and understood how it was intertwined with other spatial scales of political and economic organisation such as 'the local', 'the regional' and 'the global'. Most particularly, it is fairly clear from the way in which Trotsky's argument (1970:133, emphasis added) about how socialism 'cannot be completed *within* [national] foundations...[and that t]he maintenance of the proletarian revolution *within* a national framework can only be a provisional state of affairs' that he viewed the nation state as, to all intents and purposes, a spatial 'receptacle' of social life. Such a conceptualisation understands the world as being ordered at a number of discrete geographical scales, with each such scale serving as a geographical delimiter of particular absolute spaces. For sure, Trotsky does suggest (ibid.) that 'a national revolution is not a self-contained whole [but] is a link in the international chain', but this suggestion does not relate so much to the nature of the nation state as a scalar entity itself as it does to the national scale's position within the broader scalar hierarchy that connects the national with the supranational.

Certainly, Trotsky's thinking in such areal/topographical terms is not an unusual way of conceptualising how social life is scaled. Hence, analysts have frequently visualised the scaling of social life using metaphors which represent scales as circumscribers of particular discrete spatial units – as a ladder, wherein each scale is viewed as a separate rung so that one 'climbs up' from the local scale through the others to reach the global, or as a series of ever-larger concentric circles, with the local scale at the centre such that one moves 'outwards' from this scale to the others (see Herod 2003 for a more detailed accounting). Despite differences in such conceptualisations – the ladder metaphor obviously is a more vertically framed view of scale whereas the concentric circle metaphor is more horizontal in its formulation – the one thing that they share in common is that they regard scales as discrete spatial 'arenas' within which economic and political activities take place, and that going beyond one scale to act at another – such as moving beyond the national scale to act at the 'international' or 'global' scale – requires crossing from one scalar realm into another.

Such a representation of scale – as a spatial arena for social action – is, however, but one view. Hence, as Bruno Latour (1996:370) has argued, rather than thinking of the world in terms of discrete levels or layers, it is also possible to view the global economy's structure in terms of it being 'fibrous, thread-like, wiry, stringy, ropy, [and] capillary'. Thus, drawing upon Latour, a different metaphor for understanding the relationship between the local, the regional, the national and the global might be that of a tree root fanning out in the earth or perhaps a series of earthworm burrows or a spider's web, with the local and the global representing not discrete arenas of social life but, rather, various 'points of view on networks that are by nature neither local or global, but are more or less long and more or less connected' (Latour, 1993:122). This Latourian perspective represents a topological – rather than a topographical – way of thinking (Castree et al. 2006), one which views 'the local' and 'the global' not as opposite ends of a scalar spectrum with other scales positioned between these two extremities, but as a terminology for contrasting shorter and less-connected networks with longer and more-connected networks.

Three things are important to consider in this regard. First, neither perspective – topological versus topographical – is necessarily more 'correct' in some absolute sense. Rather, each simply represents a different conceptualisation of how the world is structured. Second, although changing the metaphors by which we understand the world's scaled nature does not change the way the world is actually constituted materially, it does change the ways in which we engage with it (Herod 2003). But third, and arguably most significant with regard to matters of political praxis, such a discussion of how geographical scales are understood has vital implications for considering Trotsky's primary political enunciation, namely that anti-capitalist revolutions must transcend 'national foundations' and become international in nature. Specifically, it is evident that Trotsky's political prescriptions only make sense if one adopts an areal view of scale, one in which the scales we use analytically to represent the spatial order of the world economy are understood as circumscribers of particular absolute spaces. In such a representation, proletarian internationalism involves making the scalar jump out of the spatial confines of the nation state and into 'international space', which is viewed either as 'above' all other absolute spaces (à la the ladder metaphor) or as 'encompassing' all other spaces (à la the concentric circles metaphor). However, if a networked view of scale is adopted, then any political praxis is simultaneously multi-scaled, at once 'local' and 'global' (and 'regional' and 'national'). To 'act nationally', then, is concurrently to be connected into and affect a wide-ranging panoply of 'global', 'local' and 'regional' processes, whilst 'acting globally' is always grounded in particular 'local', 'regional' and 'national' places. The shift from a topographical/areal view of the relationship between the national scale and the supranational scale to a topological/networked one dramatically changes the political calculus for worker praxis from a question of how to 'jump' from the one to the other scale – in effect how to go beyond the bounds of one discrete absolute space (the nation) so as to operate in and across the larger discrete absolute space which contains all such national spaces (that is, global space) – to a question of how to diffuse anti-capitalist activities throughout the economic and political networks which link various parts of the global economy to each other. This changed calculus, I would argue, is something with which an emancipatory anti-capitalist politics must engage.

CONCLUDING COMMENTS

In this chapter I have looked at Trotsky's arguments from a geographical perspective to explore some of the lacunae and implications which arise from the way in which Trotsky structured his claims. Whereas Trotsky does show a degree of spatial sensibility concerning the notion of combined and uneven development, he fails to adequately understand how the geography of capitalism is produced out of struggle between and amongst competing factions of both capital and labour. Rather, his is a somewhat one-dimensional consideration, namely that the geography of capitalism reflects the unfolding of the logic of capitalist accumulation. However, conceptualising the production of the unevenly developed economic geography of capitalism as the outcome of conflicts over competing spatial visions amongst groups of capitalists and workers, together with understanding how social actors' spatial embeddedness and contexts shape their possibilities for political praxis, provides for a richer understanding of how processes of combined and uneven development play out. Equally, whilst Trotsky's implicit view of what spatial scale is – namely, a technology for bounding particular absolute spaces such as the nation – leads him to have a distinct view of what workers' praxis might involve ('breaking out' from the national scale of anti-capitalist political engagement so as to be able to operate in the larger global arena), conceptions of how the world is scaled which view the national and the global scale not as clearly distinguishable and discrete arenas of political praxis but as, instead, different 'takes' on the networked geography of capitalism change considerably our notions of what it means to engage in proletarian internationalism. Engaging with such geographical concepts as spatial scale and how the conflicts between different actors to implement in the economic landscape what they consider to be the most appropriate spatial fixes for their current needs, then, is important if the potential to construct truly emancipatory landscapes is to be realised.

REFERENCES

Castells, M. (1977) *The Urban Question: A Marxist Approach* (London: Edward Arnold).
—— (1978) *City, Class and Power* (London: Macmillan).
Castree, N., Featherstone, D. and Herod, A. (2006) 'Contrapuntal geographies: The politics of organising across socio-spatial difference', in K. Cox, M. Low and J. Robinson (eds) *Handbook of Political Geography* (London: Sage).
Hanson, S. and Pratt, G. (1995) *Gender, Work, and Space* (New York: Routledge).
Harvey, D. (1973) *Social Justice and the City* (London: Edward Arnold).
—— (1978) 'The urban process under capitalism: A framework for analysis', *International Journal of Urban and Regional Research*, 2:101–31.
—— (1982) *The Limits to Capital* (Oxford: Blackwell).

Herod, A. (1997) 'Labor as an agent of globalization and as a global agent', in K. Cox (ed.) *Spaces of Globalization: Reasserting the Power of the Local* (New York: Guilford), 167–200.

—— (2001) *Labor Geographies: Workers and the Landscapes of Capitalism* (New York: Guilford).

—— (2003) 'Scale: The local and the global', in S. Holloway, S. Rice and G. Valentine (eds) *Key Concepts in Geography* (London: Sage), 229–47.

Hudson, R. and Sadler, D. (1986) 'Contesting work closures in Western Europe's old industrial regions: Defending place or betraying class?' in A. Scott and M. Storper (eds) *Production, Work, Territory: The Geographical Anatomy of Industrial Capitalism* (Boston: Allen and Unwin), 172–94.

Johns, R. (1998) 'Bridging the gap between class and space: US worker solidarity with Guatemala', *Economic Geography*, 74/3:252–71.

Kain, J. (1968) 'Housing segregation, Negro employment, and metropolitan decentralization', *Quarterly Journal of Economics*, 82:175–97.

Latour, B. (1993) *We Have Never Been Modern* (Cambridge, Mass.: Harvard University Press).

—— (1996) 'On actor-network theory: A few clarifications', *Soziale Welt*, 47:369–81.

Lee, E. (1997) *The Labour Movement and the Internet: The New Internationalism* (London: Pluto Press).

Lefebvre, H. (1976) *The Survival of Capitalism: Reproduction of the Relations of Production* (London: St Martin's Press; originally published in French in 1973).

—— (1991) *The Production of Space* (Oxford: Blackwell; originally published in French in 1974).

Marx, K. (1973 [1857–58]) *Grundrisse: Foundations of the Critique of Political Economy* (New York: Random House).

Massey, D. (1984) *Spatial Divisions of Labour: Social Structures and the Geography of Production* (London: Macmillan).

Peck, J. (1996) *Work-Place: The Social Regulation of Labor Markets* (New York: Guilford).

Peet, R. (1998) *Modern Geographical Thought* (Oxford: Blackwell).

Smith, N. (1990) *Uneven Development: Nature, Capital and the Production of Space* (Oxford: Blackwell).

Thomson, D. and Larson, R. (1978) *Where Were You, Brother? An Account of Trade Union Imperialism* (London: War on Want).

Trotsky, L. (1970 [1930/1906]) *The Permanent Revolution* and *Results and Prospects* (New York: Pathfinder Press).

13

Combined and Uneven Development as a Strategic Concept[1]

Bill Dunn

In this chapter, I argue that the particular importance of the concept of combined and uneven development lies in its ability to inform socialist strategy. One important aspect of this involves a dynamic understanding of the relationship between social processes in different places and of different forms. This allows a strategic prioritisation of key bases for action, which underlies the familiar connection with the idea of permanent revolution, the 'growing over' of more limited struggles. In particular, it provides the basis for moving beyond contemporary debates around 'globalisation', which tend to pose internationalism against local and national action and the political and economic as exclusionary alternatives.

I emphasise two aspects of combination and unevenness. Firstly, debates elsewhere in this volume notwithstanding, there is a familiar geographical sense. Trotsky understood the Russian Revolution as a world event, in both its causes and its consequences. Today too, capitalist development should be understood as a whole. No one can stand 'outside' and act independently. For example, we feel the effects of rising oil prices or dollar devaluation, consume goods from far away and feel the effects of distant political and ideological changes. Place-specific events or actions 'reach out' and affect the whole. Secondly, I want to discuss how the concept of combined and uneven development relies upon but also helps to articulate the interdependence of politics and economics. The two arenas influence, even constitute, each other, without being identical or either being wholly determining. Despite much controversy, this is an ancient truth acknowledged by writers from very different traditions (see, for example, Lawson 1997). Thus, for example, it is not mere coincidence that parliamentary democracy develops under capitalism, rather than under feudalism or amongst prehistoric

1. Thanks to Hugo Radice and Carmen Couceiro Vicos for their comments on an earlier version of this chapter.

troglodytes. But, as socialists know through bitter experience, similar economic conditions can exist alongside very different forms or levels of struggle or organisation. Political action, to use another familiar if contested phrase, is 'relatively autonomous'.

Interdependencies of geographic scale and of political economy may appear self-evident. Unfortunately, this is apparently not so. It is easy, for example, to find claims of the homogenising effects of contemporary economic globalisation supposedly eliminating any room for political manoeuvre. In contrast, various postmodernisms suggest something closer to absolute political and ideological autonomy. Against such interpretations, it may be worth restating these obvious interdependencies.

However, there is a danger of simply asserting a truism that everything influences everything else and reproducing a rather vacuous sociology of reciprocal interaction. While there is nothing original or uniquely Marxist in recognising an 'asymmetrical interdependence' (Keohane and Nye 1977), bourgeois social science often avoids suggesting any primacy, particularly one that might condemn capitalism as an economic system. However, some variables may be more important than others. Interdependencies of scale are seldom egalitarian. National economies influence each other but some are bigger and more powerful than others. The importance of dollar or oil prices varies according to who and where we are, to 'exposure' to a particular currency or commodity. Events in one place are transformed and reinterpreted as they 'arrive' elsewhere. Sometimes we win international solidarity, sometimes we remain isolated. Similarly, in political economy, interrelation need not imply equivalence. However, disentangling the complexity and identifying key determinants are often difficult. Sometimes a theoretical prejudice for giving a certain priority to 'the economic', seeing work in particular as the most basic of distinctly human activities, can help. Metaphors of base and superstructure convey this, but do so rather mechanically, losing the sense of reciprocal interaction. At least at certain times, political action is decisive.

It is here that the strategic nature of the concept of combined and uneven development is important. The expression 'concept of strategy' comes from Nicos Poulantzas (1978) but other writers have expressed similar thoughts, from Marx's (1975) *Theses on Feuerbach* to Robert Cox's (1981) contemporary international political economy. Asking what an analysis implies for strategy directs us towards questions of priority. If we intend to act, we need to start somewhere, to act in a particular way, albeit on the basis of knowledge we know to be imperfect. As Trotsky wrote in a different context: 'There are seven keys in the musical scale. The question as to which of these keys is "better" – do, re, or sol – is a nonsensical question. But the musician must know when to strike and what keys to strike' (1971:136). Strategic analyses attempt to orchestrate something more coherent and discriminate than mere interdependence. But to add a caveat to which I will return at the end, these are only confirmed or confounded by action. We can imagine ourselves so many Beethovens, until we perform.

In 1906, Trotsky wrote *Results and Prospects* not merely as a social and historical analysis but in order that Russian Marxists should understand the revolution differently, and therefore collectively act differently. Despite occasionally describing the revolutionary process as inevitable, he explicitly saw permanent revolution instead as a question of 'tactics' (1962:163). It was an argument for breaking down the barriers between programmes for limited democratic reforms and the struggle for workers' power.

At the risk of jumping too rapidly from the sublime to the ridiculous, I want to discuss many social scientists' recent preoccupation with questions of 'globalisation' and 'state retreat'. The antagonists can marshal swaths of data with little sign of resolution. Asking what the evidence means for socialist or labour strategy cuts through much of this. How do contemporary 'global' connections change the basis and the prospects for organisation? Does 'state retreat' mean workers should no longer attempt to win or defend reforms at national level? The pertinent questions then shift from whether 'globalisation' is happening in some spurious 'objective' sense to how or whether the concept can inform strategy.

TROTSKY'S STRATEGIC LINKING OF COMBINATION AND UNEVENNESS

Development is combined *and* uneven. Appropriately, however, the relative strategic importance of combination and unevenness may vary. It is uneven.

Results and Prospects restates a vital Marxist axiom that analysis begins with the whole. Marx saw the world market as 'the prerequisite and condition of capitalist production' (1981). It was the world's workers who needed to unite. The phrases were much repeated. But much practice and analysis subsequently shifted to an orientation on established nation states. Trotsky rejected this. Russian development had to be understood not through crude national historical analogies or typologies of revolutionary stages but in its specificity, within the context of a world capitalist system. This created particular conditions, which made a workers-led revolution possible. Other countries, including the most advanced, Britain, were also reckoned too deeply enmeshed in the web of global capitalist relations to achieve socialism alone. Nevertheless, initially, it was strategically less important to stress such links and unnecessary to establish the possibility of workers' revolution in an advanced country – something that most Marxists took for granted. Trotsky was particularly concerned with Russian results and prospects and emphasised its specificity, its unevenness.

Again, politics and economics are not really separable, yet their combination may be uneven. There is no simple formula or transhistorical rule. Trotsky roots his analysis in one of capitalism as an economic system but challenges any crude reductionism to develop a more 'politicist' reading of Russian prospects than that found in the orthodoxies of Second International Marxism. He describes how the state in Russia was much more directly involved in economic development than it had been in the early stages of Western capitalism. He identifies, amongst other things, how the West influenced Russian development through the intermediary of the state, and later how foreign capital established its presence more directly (1962:168–82). This meant that Russia never experienced the gradual development of independent, artisan, capitalist production, but also left the state relatively isolated and more vulnerable. This greater and peculiar state role then had implications for political strategy, rendering it more susceptible to workers' revolution – as confirmed in 1917.

Later, in *Permanent Revolution*, Trotsky writes of rescuing the notion of uneven development from 'the tender theoretical embraces of Stalin' (1962:131). By the mid-1920s, Stalin argued two mutually incompatible things about Russia's particularity. Post-revolutionary Russia was socialist – or was moving towards socialism – and to deny this by recalling its backwardness was to deny the revolution's achievements. However, these were not reproducible. Workers in other 'backward' countries like China could not make a revolution. The material conditions were not ripe and the Menshevik strategy of support for national economic development was now combined with the slogan of 'democratic dictatorship of the proletariat and peasantry', abandoned by Lenin and the Bolsheviks in 1917.

These arguments would not be logically contradictory (rather than simply wrong) were they based on specific analyses of the particular countries. However, beyond a cursory gloss, that was never attempted. Rather, these formulae supported a general line that workers and communist parties should become adjuncts of 'progressive' anti-imperialist forces like the Chinese Guomindang. Trotsky therefore reasserts the combined nature of development. Unevenness remains important. Indeed, even in the classic formulation in the *History of the Russian Revolution* (1980) he describes combination as derived from unevenness rather than the reverse. Nevertheless, this different context and strategic task helps explain Trotsky's generalisation of the theory and the greater emphasis on economic and geographical combination. It had become vital to reiterate the impossibilities of sustaining socialism in one country. It was less crucial to highlight Russian exceptionalism, to combat the too rigid typologies of Second International Marxism. It was more important to emphasise that workers in many countries found themselves in similar situations and could learn from the Russian experience.

Trotsky's generalisations were perhaps too sweeping, allowing later interpretations of the theory as a universal proclamation of the impossibility of anything but proletarian revolution. In fact his argument was qualified, stating only that in the absence of proletarian leadership, democratic, national liberation struggles would produce at best very partial results, whose content would be 'directed against the working masses' (1962:132). Despite any over-optimism, combined and uneven development was not a universal formula, but a concept which socialists might use to develop appropriate specific analyses and tactics. Nevertheless, attempts to generalise beyond the Russian experiences were less conspicuously successful. Elsewhere, particularly in the post-war period, states in the South proved more vulnerable to non-proletarian and nationally contained revolution than Trotskyists anticipated. At the same time, Northern states proved resilient. Accordingly, state-centred interpretations of politics again became the norm. For much of the last century, Marxists have battled against these. Any state autonomy was only relative, limited by powerful international political but particularly economic forces, by the dictates of capital accumulation. Socialism could not succeed in one country, impervious to external economic relations.

We still fight on similar intellectual fronts. Firstly, the national level is sometimes so elevated that 'politics' becomes synonymous with the affairs of national governments, national economies are conceived as singular entities and considerations of external constraint are minimised. Against this, some academic Marxism has the great merit of emphasising the 'world system' but in doing so downplays any room for manoeuvre within this. Perhaps more importantly, the general brouhaha around 'globalisation' makes it hard not to conceive national or local political economy in its interconnections with the rest of the world. Marxists can reckon this a considerable advance; better starting with the whole than emphasising the specific as the basic unit of analysis, whether that specificity is individual utility, as in neoclassical economics, or the nation state, as in much of mainstream political science. Contemporary globalisation apparently confirms Marx's predictions of capitalism's relentless conquest of the world. If nineteenth-century capitalism failed to produce the anticipated world after its own image, now, the suggestion is, it succeeds. However, as the rest of this chapter will argue, such discourses may lose sight of capitalism's enduringly contradictory unevenness, suggesting that local sites of resistance and states and politics are swept aside. This then has important practical consequences.

COMBINED AND UNEVEN DEVELOPMENT TODAY

What is offered here should be understood as a call for, rather than an attempt to provide, a general description of contemporary combined and uneven development. However, it is possible to say a few things to qualify the more glib characterisations of globalisation. In particular, the concept of combined and uneven development provides a basis for overcoming dualist debates around the fate of nation states and the relationship between politics and economics. The task remains to articulate their changing but uneven interconnection.

Arguments against state-centric understandings of politics remain important, the 'progressive nationalism' of 'globalisation sceptics' often being profoundly limited (Radice 2000). Many 'sceptics' see states as 'authors' rather than victims of change, suggesting that, particularly since Thatcher and Reagan, Western states orchestrated much of what is now seen as globalisation. Karl Polanyi's (1957) critique of Marx, which interpreted the great transformation from feudalism to capitalism as a political process driven by the (British) state, has become a fashionable model. Such perspectives entail at worst a crude political reductionism; even at best, they tend to underestimate global economic pressures, and imply that national-level opposition and conventional social-democratic agendas remain sufficient.

However, I believe the greater and more common problem lies in an alternative economic reductionism according to which 'globalisation' is a process 'from above' compelling certain types of behaviour, reducing nation states to mere 'transmission belts' from the global to the local (Cox 1996). Global economic transformation overrides once-appropriate individual, local or national specificity. Analysis flips from stressing individuality and particularity to emphasising instead homogeneity; or at least powerful tendencies towards convergence (Strange 1998). Taken to its determinist conclusions, such a perspective is obviously politically paralysing, as theses of the 'end of history' make explicit. In particular, capital's greater mobility and increasing geographical spread supposedly renders workers powerless.

However, the more grandiose theorising of 'globalisation', in particular any technological determination, appears deeply flawed (Rosenberg 2000). Rather than creating a homogeneous social space, contemporary change remains uneven and contested. It is, at most, likely to create new cleavages, new nodes and interstices of opposition even as (or if) others are foreclosed. Evaluating labour's situation can be informed by theory but must also be an empirical and above all a practical question. Spaces of resistance may have become more precarious but we only know by trying to occupy them.

John Holloway (1995) emphasises capital's inherent mobility. It exploits, chews up, spits out and moves on when it is done. At the same time, capital also relies on at least temporary immobilisation. The actual exploitation must usually happen in particular places utilising relatively place-bound relationships. This produces contradictory logics within capitalism that continuously push workers together and pull them apart. The more careful contemporary accounts capture some of this tension in formulations like 'glocalisation' (Ruigrok and van Tulder 1995; van Tulder and Ruigrok 1996) or by depicting concurrent centrifugal and centripetal forces (Gehrig 1998). However, without addition, this does not describe when and why capital moves, how its mobility varies or whether something fundamental might have changed in the last 20 or 30 years. Outcomes are the result of complex dynamics of accumulation but also of social struggles. As such, they are inherently 'messy', politically organised rather than driven by strict capital logics. Overall trends are likely to be contradictory and ambiguous, varying according to the scale at which we look, the activity or industry we study, and over time. There might, however, be phases in which a tendency towards dispersal predominates, others of (re-)concentration.

A tendency to increase the extraction of what Marx called absolute surplus value making workers work longer, harder or for less pay may augur moves to low-wage locations. Some industries – garments and textiles and toys are the classic examples but also some heavy industries like steel – have utilised this and greatly increased their geographical spread in the latter half of the twentieth century. Some formerly prosperous areas declined, such as the 'rust belts' in Northern Europe and North America. Over a somewhat longer period, and less emphatically, some once-rich countries like Britain and Australia have fallen down the pecking order. Other, once-poorer places have grown faster, for example, the 'Asian tigers', but also areas of the US or European south and more recently of China. Levels of trade and foreign investment have grown to unprecedented levels. While still often predominantly concentrated amongst rich countries they have incorporated many new areas into a worldwide capitalist system.

There may then be a sense in which the world has become more globalised. This has certainly been a common perception amongst the self-consciously internationalist anti-globalisation or anti-capitalist resistance that has developed in recent years. Here the idea that labour's retreat is simply inscribed by the structures of global capitalism is challenged. However, those who see the world as substantially globalised usually conclude that action must be 'upscaled' to the global if it is to have any chance of success. This general perspective stands in welcome contrast to a conservative (sometimes even racist and fascist) parochialism that has been a widespread, alternative response to globalisation. Of course, in practice proposals vary from revolutionary internationalism through an extension of official trade unionism to very modest agendas for international institutional reform. However, the common danger is that in seeing the world as globalised, labour supporters downplay the possibilities of 'lower' scales of action, effectively accepting their opponents' exaggeration of the difficulties. It is easy to see how 'globalisation' can work as ideology, continually telling workers that resistance is futile, denying spaces of resistance to capital's relentless march. Sometimes this is quite overt as firms bully workers with threats of relocation. Of course, there are real 'external' pressures on nation states and workers. This was Trotsky's point 100 years ago. Even then, socialism could only succeed on a world scale. However, achieving international revolution involved processes of 'growing over' of particular, limited struggles. Such prospects now seem to be denied.

Qualifications are therefore needed. Processes of globalisation were not universal. If they were assisted by increased capital mobility in the late twentieth century, this too has to be understood as uneven, and socially constructed, rather than simply technologically determined. Furthermore, investment and technological innovation in production may produce counter-tendencies towards spatial fixity. Many industrial sectors remain strongly concentrated, notably even when their products and production processes might be reckoned highly mobile, for example in microelectronics and finance. Meanwhile at a national level, overall the hierarchies of rich and poor countries have remained rather stable over the last 100 years. Thus, capital's mobility may sometimes have increased, strengthening its power over relatively less-mobile workers. However, the evidence of it exercising this, rather than merely threatening it, is limited. New concentrations of workers in many places in the South have not necessarily replaced, or been achieved at the expense of, those in the North (Dunn 2004).

Even where capital's spread has increased, it may confer greater power to local concentrations of workers over extended production chains (Herod 1995, 2001). Some writers also argue that the development of new communications media also increases the prospects for solidarity between distant groups of workers (Lee 1997). However, this raises the question of the extent to which the lack of such links was ever a barrier to international solidarity. It did not preclude some notable examples at least as early as the nineteenth century. Looking outwards, whether at local, national or international levels, was ever likely to strengthen any specific struggle. Therefore, laudable and important as international solidarity may be, it is possible to exaggerate the extent to which it is a novel response to contemporary capital mobility, downplaying the local and the utility of historical lessons in broadening action.

Similarly, many activists are not only anti-statist in a normative sense but also embrace notions of state retreat or transformation (or earlier anarchist ideas) arguing that we can and should sidestep the state and reject 'political' organisation. This, too, misreads contemporary change and does little to inform strategy. At least implicitly, it affirms a deeply problematic separation between politics and economics. Of course, it is because of a partial separation of politics and economics that capitalist internationalisation is possible in the first place;

capital can often go abroad without an accompanying invasion force (Rosenberg 2005). Similarly, this separation is important for workers. It opens spaces, which would be unthinkable in feudalism for example, for organisation and action. Workers seek reforms from the state, as in the crucial demand for the eight-hour day in 1905. In this instance defeated, at other times workers have pursued and more or less successfully secured economic ends in the political arena even against opposition from employers.

However, any room for manoeuvre is, of course, limited and any autonomy is only relative, the separation of politics and economics more apparent than real. Imperatives of accumulation shape state behaviour while capital requires political support, including that of both home and host nation states in its movements around the world. States' actions against labour have themselves been a vital part of contemporary change, whether in pursuit of explicitly economic objectives of privatisation and marketisation or in overt attacks on workers' rights and organisation. The concrete forms of state intervention vary between places and over time but disengagement from 'the political' thus seems singularly inappropriate. If the nature of state intervention is changing it should lead to renewed questions and investigations of how (rather than whether) to act in and against it.

By posing the question around state retreat, both sides of the globalisation debate tend to exaggerate former national autonomy and reformist governments' past effectiveness (Burnham 1997; Callinicos 2001; Callaghan 2002). If sceptics continue to do so, strongly globalist accounts often link the state of social democracy, too casually, to the reforms it can or cannot deliver and 'read back' economic change from the retreat of erstwhile socialists. Successes, as achieved by the post-war Labour government in Britain, no doubt helped secure support. But these were hardly typical and provide insufficient explanation for social democracy's appeal, evidenced prior to taking office and despite so many failures. Not simply the result of successful government, the roots of reformism lie rather in the contradictory experiences of life under capitalism. This is an alienated existence, dominated by money and competition but also characterised by continual collective struggles and resistances, although they are often at a low level, against capital and its political supports. This acceptance/rejection of capitalism finds a more or less appropriate expression in social democracy. Of course, this is not absolute; otherwise we would all be social democrats. However, it is these contradictory experiences and struggles that provide the basis for social democracy but also for more radical organisation and strategies for change. Without a basis in struggle, such strategies, including amongst other things calls for internationalism, have a rather abstract and idealist colour.

In practice much, perhaps most, resistance to capitalism still occurs at, or has a focus on, the national level. The incursions of world and regional institutions notwithstanding, the election of governments, executive decision making, the legal frameworks including those of industrial relations, all remain substantially national. Workers continue to raise demands of the state and many major struggles have been substantially national: general strikes in several countries, and nationally specific campaigns even against similar attacks, for example on pensions. Even in a period of labour's general retreat, such action clearly 'works' to some extent. Struggles against neoliberal reform have halted or ameliorated attacks. The welfare state in most rich countries and workers' rights to organise remain real, if diminished. States' behaviour continues to be shaped by internal as well as external relations.

Rosa Luxemburg (1989) used what has become a well-known metaphor of reformism as a 'labour of Sisyphus', always an uphill struggle against the inexorable pressures of the capitalist system. What I am suggesting is that the slope may have become steeper and the effort required greater. The logic of reformism may be changing, with any gains becoming less stable. But it is hard to know in the absence of determined reformist policy. Only experience confirms the incline and the weight against which we push: it may also seem harder because we are out of condition. Even allowing that the spaces of resistance might become less secure and the need to extend struggles greater and more urgent, there is much to defend. The alternative in any case would appear to be abandoning what was ever an unequal struggle.

None of this denies the importance of identifying commonalities across national boundaries, nor that an orientation on the state might risk fostering various social-democratic illusions. However, although we await a fully adequate description, even the most cursory review confirms capitalism's enduringly dynamic but contradictory and uneven nature. Conflicts between and within states leave us far from the harmonious liberal world of capitalism's apologists and make attempts to manage the system through international coordination and institutions at best fraught with difficulties. They also indicate possible room for manoeuvre, spaces of resistance. Many people within the labour movement, particularly socialists, have attempted to link the general anti-capitalism with specific struggles, particularly against war but also around more local issues. As Herod argues (this volume) it might not even be appropriate to perceive a hierarchy of scales, the task better seen as spreading or diffusing anti-capitalist activities into different arenas. Rather than abandoning the state as one of these, we should re-emphasise the need to go beyond limited national reforms: the process and the tactic of permanent revolution.

A strategic prioritisation of globalisation may fail to make such connections, and thereby reinforce notions of local incapacity. It may also imply the need for a more or less thoroughgoing internationalism prior to any effective action. In so far as this suggests we cannot act effectively until we have changed the way we think, it reverses the Marxist axiom that ideas change in struggle. Of course, there is a danger of stating this too crudely. Successful workers' struggles are often built by politically informed (and internationalist) militants rather than being genuinely 'spontaneous'. However, unless we are to give up on workers' self-emancipation there is a sense in which the act must precede the solidarity. They are linked, but asymmetrically. If, instead, action at lower scales, local and national, remains possible, and if this action can achieve a degree of success (albeit necessarily limited and constrained by the nature of the global system), it may provide the basis of a thoroughgoing internationalism, in thought and deed, rather than vice versa (Budd 1998).

There is a caricature of Trotskyism as demanding simultaneous revolution everywhere. By implication, much of the globalisation literature replicates this. This is just as disabling and denies the idea of permanent revolution quite as much as 'nation-statist' approaches which reckon only on limited place-specific struggles. The whole point is interconnection and the 'growing over' of types and places of action. New spaces of struggle and more or less effective resistance, including opportunities at an international level, develop without necessarily overriding more localised and familiar arenas.

RE-EMPHASISING THE STRATEGIC

Theory and practice are interdependent. We understand the world in order to act to change it. Having acted, we reflect upon theory. Whether an analysis is more or less correct remains untested, and in a sense irrelevant, unless or until it is acted upon. Trotsky's *Results and*

Prospects was a remarkable piece of engaged social theory, substantially verified by the events of 1917.

We cannot rote-learn the lessons of 1917. However, as a way of understanding the world, combined and uneven development has the flexibility to be applied creatively and practically in different situations. Strategic analysis directs us towards particular actions but also indicates their broader connections and thus how they might be generalised and strengthened; developed as ongoing or 'permanent' processes of social transformation.

Such analyses of labour's strengths and weaknesses must, of course, then be tested by organised practice. Unfortunately, historically, the isolation of Trotskyism has limited this. Even the confirmation of 1917 was in a sense accidental, occurring only because Lenin and the Bolshevik party reached similar conclusions and were able to lead the revolution. Yet this hardly invalidates the principle. Any movement towards strategic agitation implies identifying actions most likely to succeed and how they can be broadened and deepened. An analysis of the combined and uneven development of contemporary capitalism is needed to inform this.

REFERENCES

Budd, A. (1998) '*Workers in a Lean World. Unions in the International Economy* – reviewed', *Historical Materialism*, 3.

Burnham, P. (1997) 'Globalisation: states, markets and class relations', *Historical Materialism*, 1.

Callaghan, J. (2002) 'Social democracy and globalisation: the limits of social democracy in historical perspective', *British Journal of Politics and International Relations*, 4/3.

Callinicos, A. (2001) *Against the Third Way: An Anti-Capitalist Critique* (Cambridge: Polity).

Cox, R. (1981) 'Social forces, states and world orders: beyond international relations theory', *Millennium*, 10/2.

—— (1996) *Approaches to World Order* (New York: Cambridge University Press).

Dunn, B. (2004) *Global Restructuring and the Power of Labour* (Basingstoke: Palgrave).

Gehrig, T. (1998) 'Cities and the Geography of Financial Centres', Discussion Paper series no. 1894, Centre for Economic Policy Research.

Herod, A. (1995) 'The practice of international solidarity and the geography of the global economy', *Economic Geography*, 71/4.

—— (2001) *Labor Geographies: Workers and the Landscapes of Capitalism* (New York: Guilford Press).

Holloway, J. (1995) 'Capital moves', *Capital and Class*, 57.

Keohane, R. O. and Nye, J. S. (1977) *Power and Interdependence* (Boston: Little, Brown).

Lawson, T. (1997) *Economics and Reality* (London: Routledge).

Lee, E. (1997) *The Labor Movement and the Internet: The New Internationalism* (London: Pluto Press).

Luxemburg, R. (1989 [1900]) *Reform or Revolution* (London: Bookmarks).

Marx, K. (1975 [1843–44]) *Early Writings* (Harmondsworth: Penguin).

—— (1981 [1894]) *Capital*, iii (Harmondsworth: Penguin).

Polanyi, K. (1957 [1944]) *The Great Transformation* (Boston: Beacon).

Poulantzas, N. (1978 [1974]) *Classes in Contemporary Capitalism* (London: Verso).

Radice, H. (2000) 'Responses to globalisation: a critique of progressive nationalism', *New Political Economy*, 5/1.

Rosenberg, J. (2000) *The Follies of Globalisation Theory* (London: Verso).

—— (2005) 'Globalization theory: a post-mortem', *International Politics*, 42/1.

Ruigrok, W. and van Tulder, R. (1995) *The Logic of International Restructuring* (London: Cheltenham).

Strange, S. (1998) 'Globalony?' *Review of International Political Economy*, 5/4.

Trotsky, L. (1962 [1930/1906]) *The Permanent Revolution* and *Results and Prospects* (London: New Park).

—— (1971 [1931]) *The Struggle Against Fascism in Germany* (New York: Pathfinder).

—— (1980 [1932]) *History of the Russian Revolution* (New York: Pathfinder).

Van Tulder, R. and Ruigrok, W. (1996) 'Regionalisation, globalisation or glocalisation', in M. Humbert (ed.) *The Impact of Globalisation on Europe's Firms and Industries* (London: Pinter).

14

The Geography of Uneven Development

Neil Smith

...Marxism is not a schoolmaster's pointer rising above history, but a social analysis of the ways and means of the historic process which is really going on.

Leon Trotsky

The concept of uneven development is an enigma in Marxist theory. It was most forcefully advanced by Trotsky in relation to permanent revolution but enlisted too by Stalin for quite opposite purposes. Quickly codified as a 'law' in the 1920s, it passed into arcana, only to be cautiously dusted off several decades later. A polemic-stopping retort, 'the law of uneven (and combined) development' was actually subjected to a remarkable lack of serious analysis. While it is important to know this history, it is even more important to develop the theory of uneven development in a way that helps us understand the present world. Insofar as it is barely an exaggeration to say that 'uneven development' came to mean all things to all Marxists, the most urgent task today would seem to be the development of an analytical foundation for the concept. Accordingly, and as a contribution to this collective effort, I want here to try to do several things: first, briefly to discuss how and why the concept of uneven development became arcane; second to broaden the concept from its specifically political origins; and third to consider what a theory of uneven development might look like in the wake of a globalisation of capital that purportedly challenges the coherence of national economies.

THE GOOD, THE BAD AND THE ARCANE

Trotsky's discussion of uneven and combined development grew out of his theory of permanent revolution. The latter theory, pestled in the crucible of the Russian revolutions of 1905 and 1917, insisted that no strict stage theory of history determined the transition to socialism and that, despite the expectations of many Marxists, an anti-tsarist revolution in Russia, where the proletariat was underdeveloped but the bourgeoisie even more so (and certainly too politically weak to rule), was not condemned to go through some preordained capitalist stage. Instead, a strategic workers' coalition with the peasantry – who dominated numerically, whose grievances were powerful and at boiling point, but whose inveterate fragmentation, Trotsky argued, prevented them from leading the revolution – could carry the day. Contrary to most expectations, revolution would not necessarily erupt first among the most developed working classes of Western Europe and North America, but might, as Lenin later put it, strike the weakest link first. The development of socialism was uneven, Trotsky insisted, with respect to a certain historical evolutionism that permeated much Marxist theory at the time (Stalin's accusation was precisely that Trotsky was trying to 'jump over necessary stages of history').

Rather than proceeding by relatively discrete stages, the revolution could be more of a rolling affair, Trotsky maintained, from social democratic control of an initially bourgeois polity to a dictatorship of the proletariat, allied with the peasantry. Political development, was not simply uneven, therefore, but 'combined', in the sense that no country, and certainly not 'backward' Russia, could implant socialism on its own. Uneven development, he later summarised, 'reveals itself most sharply and complexly in the destiny of the backward countries' which, under 'the whip of external necessity', are 'compelled to make leaps'. Uneven development therefore engenders a further law, 'which for the lack of a better name, we can call the law of *combined* development...' (Trotsky 1977:27). As a bulwark against Stalin's theory of 'socialism in one country' (Trotsky 1962), the theory of uneven and combined development thereby became a vital underpinning to the very theory that had spawned it in the first place – the theory of permanent revolution.

Uneven (and combined) development began, above all, as a political concept deployed to analyse and evaluate the possibilities and trajectories of revolution. It was ground out in the political battles of revolutionary socialism in the first three decades of the twentieth century and the specific history of Russia and the USSR. It is curious, given the reversal of conceptual priority between permanent revolution and uneven development, that in Trotskyist circles, the former theory survived as perhaps his most fundamental contribution to Marxist theory, while its fundamental underpinning, the notion of uneven development, faded into relative obscurity. It only reappeared as an object of analytical interest several decades later, by which time there was little if any dissent across the spectrum of Marxist thought that 'uneven development' represented a universal 'law'. 'The law of uneven development', according to Ernest Mandel, 'which some have wished to restrict to the history of capitalism alone, or even merely to the imperialist phase of capitalism, is...a universal law of human history' (1962:91). Louis Althusser ratchets up the universalist ante when he informs us, with almost cosmic exuberance, that the 'law of uneven development...contrary to what is sometimes thought ...does not concern Imperialism alone, but absolutely "everything in the world"' (Althusser 1975:200–1). The 'great law of unevenness suffers no exceptions...because it is not itself an exception' but rather 'a primitive law, with priority over...peculiar cases'. Uneven development 'exists in the essence of contradiction itself' (Althusser 1975:212–13). For Mao, on whom Althusser draws here, the law of uneven development is essential because 'Nothing in this world develops absolutely evenly' (Mao 1971:117).

Uneven development, first conceived by Trotsky as an empirical condition in Russia that necessitated the theory of permanent revolution, had been trans-substantiated by mid-century into a universal law to rationalise any or all political positions. Stalin led the way in voiding 'uneven development' of any content, and Trotsky's political defeat and Stalin's brutal consolidation of power, the subsequent world war, and eventually the cold war, all helped marginalise any broader analytical or political concern with the concept. Yet Trotsky was not blameless either. He too appealed to 'the universal law of unevenness', as 'the most general law of the historic process' (Trotsky 1977:27). But Stalinism's effect was more decisive and more personal: Mandel records somewhere that several early 1920s manuscripts on uneven development were destroyed by Stalin, never to be found, and their authors were victims of his early purges. The suppression of such ideas set Marxist theory back many decades.

The purported universalism of the concept was crucial in the undoing of uneven development as a coherent theory during much of the twentieth century, and quite frankly it came to represent a theoretical and conceptual embarrassment in the Marxist tradition. A law that explains absolutely 'everything in the world' explains nothing, and the fact that 'nothing develops evenly', used as a philosophical justification for such a law, reduces it to triviality. Dressed in such pretence, it tells us absolutely nothing specific about capitalism, imperialism, or the present moment of capitalist restructuring. Historically, 'uneven development' became arcane precisely because whatever polemical heat it both generated and sustained, it had no real explanatory utility. The point here is not to bash past political or scholarly figures, even less to dwell on past debates, but to learn from the degeneration of the concept, pick up on more recent work that is far more promising, and most importantly to use this diagnosis to devise alternatives.

A revival of uneven development theory took place in the 1970s and 1980s. Some of this work continued the political debates of the earlier period (Löwy 1981; Molyneux 1981), but some, while mindful of 1968 and the various national liberation revolts around the world, yet recognising that the revolutionary situation of the early twentieth century was not on the agenda in its latter decades, shifted focus toward the political economics of uneven development. Not surprisingly, the resulting work was eclectic, ranging from dependency theory in Latin America to theories of unequal development in Africa and Europe (Frank 1967; Emmanuel 1972; Amin 1976) to political and economic geographies of uneven development (Smith 1984). That the latter theories were not tied to the precise problematic of the Russian Revolution six or seven decades earlier, but drew their energy from contemporary anti-imperialist struggles and a thirst to know the specific dynamics of uneven capitalist development, was all for the better. They were sufficiently successful that, as many Marxists and theorists, radicalised in the 1960s and 1970s, regrouped in academia during this period, the rubric of uneven development became not just familiar again, but almost fashionable. A powerful Marxist tradition in geography since the 1970s has been especially successful in re-centring questions of uneven development such that the concept is common parlance in that discipline. A price was certainly paid for the academic rediscovery of uneven development insofar as in some circles it also involved a greater or lesser detachment from any kind of Marxist politics. Yet the gains within Marxist theory included, centrally, a distance from the polemical cul-de-sac of the early 1920s and, more positively, a glimpse into the processes that created the uneven economic and geographical politics with which Trotsky's theory of permanent revolution had to grapple. There were hints of such a broadened conception of uneven development in the various pre- and peri-revolutionary writings of Lenin (1975, 1977) and Luxemburg (1968) concerning imperialism and the necessity of colonies, and for all that he saw uneven development as a universal law, Mandel (1962, 1975) early on began to talk directly as no one else had done about the broader economic and geographical dimensions of uneven development. The blossoming of uneven development theory, even in more academic garb, presents a *political* opportunity.

POLITICS AND SPACE: BEYOND MARX'S FOOTNOTE

In a famous footnote in *Capital*, i Marx says the following:

In order to examine the object of our investigation in its integrity, free from all disturbing subsidiary circumstances, we must treat the whole world as one nation, and assume that capitalist production is everywhere established and has possessed itself of every branch of industry. (1967:581)

This abstraction from the differences between different places and experiences was vital insofar as Marx's broad goal was an analytical critique of the contradictions of capitalism in its essence; the power of his analysis would have been impossible otherwise. It is not accidental, therefore, that in an era of so-called globalisation nearly a century and a half later, Wall Streeters stumble back to Marx (Cassidy 1997) as the premier diagnostician of the system that provides their mansions, yachts and political power. But Marx's abstraction also limited the applicability of the theory. In particular it both despatialised and detemporalised the development of capitalism, and provided few theoretical signposts for dealing with social, political and economic differences across space. Yet conceptions of spatiality, or their apparent absence, can have profound political implications. Put bluntly, a theory that uncloaks the inner workings of capitalism is a sine qua non of political analysis, but without appropriate and nuanced elaboration it may be a fairly blunt weapon for evaluating the contemporary workings of capitalism or for deciding what is to be done – whether in 1905 or a century later.

Significant historico-geographical differences in kinds and levels of capitalist development produced precisely the conundrums that Trotsky, Lenin, Luxemburg and many others found themselves having to deal with in their discussions of imperialism, colonialism and uneven development. For Luxemburg, it was impossible to understand the reproduction of capitalism without positing an 'outside' to capitalism, a non-capitalist source of labour, as much as markets: 'the accumulation of capital becomes impossible in all points without non-capitalist surroundings' (Luxemburg 1968:365). Lenin was more circumspect, thinking capitalism not quite such a zero-sum geographical game. The fruition of European colonialism, which 'has *completed* the seizure of the unoccupied territories on our planet' (Lenin 1975:90), did not necessarily imply the end of capitalism, he insisted, but was likely to lead to an internal 'redivision' and restructuring of colonial power. For Lenin, in other words, there already was no 'outside' to capitalism. Rather, the power of internal reorganisation became of paramount significance.

This is of no mere academic concern. Hardt and Negri (2000) have recently claimed to discover this loss of an 'outside' in the contemporary era. In a similar vein, if from a diametrically opposed political location, Ellen Meiksins Wood (2003:127) argues that 'we have yet to see a systematic theory of imperialism designed for a world in which all international relations are internal to capitalism and governed by capitalist imperatives'. But some seven or eight decades ago Lenin already had such a prospect in sight, and Trotsky's admittedly politically inspired discussion of uneven development was on the same track. (This was the entire point of his insistence on *combined* as well as uneven development – a qualification that is no longer necessary today insofar as it is implicit, taken for granted.) Moreover, bourgeois geographers, from the British liberal imperialist, Halford Mackinder to the American Isaiah Bowman to the German Alexander Supan (whom Lenin quotes), were all explicit that the territorial expansion of capitalism had come to an end and the world was faced with a 'closed political system', as Mackinder put it. Writing months before the 1905 revolution and Trotsky's *Results and Prospects*, Mackinder (1904) grasped the consequences in a famous passage: 'Every explosion of social forces, instead of being dissipated in a surrounding circuit of unknown space and barbaric chaos, will be sharply re-echoed from the far side of the globe...'[1]

This period, say from 1898 to 1917, witnessed the birth of uneven development proper in the global political economy. No longer could geographical unevenness be passed off as an accident of historical geography, the result of being outside the project of civilisation, a matter simply of having been left behind by 'modern' capitalism. The dynamics of unevenness were now increasingly recognised as internal to the dynamics of capitalism itself; the very language of civilisation and backwardness began to fade into its own arcana, not because of any new-found political morality among the European ruling classes but in the forced recognition from revolts around the

1. Mackinder was hardly one of socialist sympathies. An avid anti-communist, he worked inside Russia for British intelligence against the Bolsheviks in 1919.

world that the distinction itself was obsolete. Whatever historical remnants of pre-capitalist societies survived – and they manifestly did survive in large swaths across the globe as well as in smaller enclaves – were now enveloped, appropriated and soldered into a larger global capitalism. Unevenness now primarily emanated from the laws of capital themselves rather than from the archaeology of past social and geographical difference. Mao's insistence that 'nothing develops evenly' represented, in its day, a desperate abstraction against a reality that even his own peasant-based revolution was eventually unable to staunch.

That the historic break point in the history of capitalism reached in this period is largely missed – due not simply to the fate of the theory of uneven development as a casualty of Stalinism, and its absurd universalisation on various sides, but also to the political geographical sensibility that tied together such unlikely figures as Lenin and Mackinder, and indeed Cecil Rhodes (with his famous tying of London East End poverty to the necessity of imperialism) – was also lost, or rather submerged. This 'lost geography' has complex causes (Smith 2003:ch. 1), but it remains very much alive today in the formulations of Hardt and Negri and of Wood, among many others. The loss of geographical sensibility was simultaneously a loss of political sensibility; despatialisation facilitated a certain depoliticisation insofar as the source of local as much as global power, the political target of socialist revolution, lost any spatial definition. The proposal of 'socialism in one country' was part of this process. It took the Russian Revolution, which was transnational, and the largely urban-scale 1919 uprisings that erupted in its wake – from Berlin, Munich and Budapest to Seattle, Winnipeg and Amritsar, India – and collapsed them into a one dimensional national imaginary of future possibilities. The language of 1930s geopolitics and the binary geographies of the cold war further flattened the prevailing comprehension of uneven development and any geographical sense of politics into a nationally based board-game mentality.

Giovanni Arrighi (1994), by contrast, has recognised just such a historical break in terms of a shift from a British to a US-centred globalism, and this is surely correct. But the shift may be broader even than that. The power of European-centred imperialism certainly involved military might on the high seas – the control of trade – but it increasingly depended on the control of colonial territory. The US-centred imperialism that succeeded it in the twentieth century was by and large not colonial, far less territorial and more market based.

The victory of geo-economic over geopolitical power never became absolute, of course, as today's proliferating war in the Middle East certainly attests, but the US ruling class began to realise quickly after 1898 that geographical expansion was no longer a guaranteed or even plausible means to economic expansion. Geopolitical calculation was never renounced but it was significantly marginalised in favour of the economic calculus that has come to rule a neoliberalism dominated by US power.

If despatialisation engenders a certain depoliticisation, the corollary also holds, and a theory of uneven development appropriate for the twenty-first century needs to take this to heart. The world is very different from what it was a century ago and the assumption that national economies and nation states are the be-all and end-all of uneven development needs to be radically revised. The argument here is not at all that globalisation has rendered nation states obsolete; such a conclusion is absurd. But it does suggest that whatever the vagaries of national-scale power today we are no longer in a period of blanket ascendancy of national power. On the one hand, the economic power of nation states is vastly different from their political power, and on the other the bullying hegemony of the US state is a quite different beast from the power of Botswana or Scotland. New forms of global restructuring during this latest neoliberal moment of US global ambition have dramatically altered the relationship between the different scales at which power is exercised – global, national, regional, urban, and so forth.

The question of scale is therefore especially important here (Smith 1995; Herod and Wright 2002; Swyngedouw 2004). There is nothing given about the scale of power; rather insofar as the scales at which power manifests itself are themselves the outcome of political struggle, the making of scale is highly political. The scale of the nation state itself is historically highly contingent and the outcome of multifaceted struggles. The discussions of uneven development from the first decades of the twentieth century, not unreasonably, took for granted that the national state represented the necessary if not the only possible scale of analysis. This despite the emphasis on an *urban* proletariat, at least for Trotsky. Today, however, any theory of uneven development has no such luxury and has to cover not only national-scale political economies but processes of economic restructuring, political movements and cultural revolts at sub-national scales – the urban, the regional, and (as feminism has surely taught us by now) the scale of the household – and simultaneously the international scale. For all that nation states retain massive political, cultural, and in some cases military power, they are no longer unchallenged as the building blocks of a global social and political economy. We live today in a world of incipient global governance (IMF, World Bank, UN, WTO, etc.), organised international blocs (EU, Mercosur, Asean, NAFTA) and, conversely, the increasing devolution of social reproductive functions, among others, to the urban scale. All of these developments have become targets of political struggle, from Porto Alegre to East Timor, Chiapas to the anti-globalisation movement. A contemporary theory of uneven development needs to have the political economic theory to take these and many other struggles into account.

THE POLITICAL ECONOMY OF UNEVEN DEVELOPMENT

A contemporary theory of uneven development finds its starting point in Marx, not in some obscure undiscovered writings but in the very text that apparently abstracted from spatial and temporal difference in the first place – *Capital* – and in the straightforward distinction between the value and use value of commodities, especially the commodity of labour power. The argument that follows is somewhat abstract and schematic, but unavoidable.[2]

Capitalism distinguishes itself from other modes of production in many ways for Marx, but central is the incessant differentiation and redifferentiation of concrete labour driven forward by the systemic requirements of capital accumulation. At the same time capitalism is characterised by the avaricious conversion of use values, through the application of wage labour, into value, and this in turn provides a metric for comparing, on the market, commodities with different physical and qualitative characteristics – shoes versus steel versus advertising copy versus lorry deliveries to market. This drives what Marx called the 'universalizing tendency of capital'. The law of value under capitalism is therefore built on an essential contradiction between on the one hand a constant tendency for differentiation rooted in the division of labour and an opposite tendency toward universalisation that finds its apotheosis in the tendency toward an equalisation of the profit rate. The differentiation of labour is of course challenged by an integral deskilling, and the equalisation of profit rates is just as surely challenged by innovative practices designed

2. For a more elaborated version of this argument, see Smith (1984).

to escape the downward equalisation of profits. Marx emphasises the inherent lack of equilibrium that inheres in capitalist societies as a result of this contradiction and, temporalising from this result, derives (in however unfinished a fashion) a multifaceted theory of capitalist crisis.

But what if, instead of temporalising this result, we spatialise it? What if, in addition to Marx's temporalisation, yet consonant with it, we weave through it a spatialisation of the critical dynamics of capital? The division of labour is a highly spatial question. Capital moves to specific places where economic advantages can be gleaned and higher profits made. Even were capital to have encountered a completely homogeneous world – the flat plain of economic opportunity so beloved of neoclassical economic theorists that finds a parallel in Marx's footnote abstracting from national differences – the rigid requirements of accumulation would quickly lead to a development of certain specialties and conditions of labour, different wage rates, different resources and different technologies in some places at the expense of others. In search of profit and driven to compete, capital concentrates and centralises not just in the pockets of some over the pockets of others but in the places of some over the places of others. Integral to the spatial differentiation of rents, wages, production costs and so forth are differentiated systems of financial circulation and of social reproduction, and all are built in various ways into the geography of capitalism. Of course, capitalism did not sprout on an undifferentiated plain, but the larger point is that the physical geographical calculus of Ricardo's hallowed law of comparative advantage, which surely had some historical basis in differential physical and climatic conditions, is largely displaced as capitalism expands its sway across the face of the earth. The differentiation of places, one from the other, is less and less a question of locational and natural endowment and increasingly the product of a spatial logic as inherent to this mode of production as Marx's temporal theory of capitalist crisis. (It is worth noting that this is not simply a historical detail. IMF consultant and critic Jeffery Sachs attributes underdevelopment to 'a case of bad latitude', and such warmed up geographical determinism has become a virtual cottage industry: see Sachs 2001, 2005; Diamond 2005; Kaplan 1997).

On the other hand, the tendency toward an equalisation of conditions of labour exploitation, facilitated first and foremost through the financial system which of course circulates value in its most abstract form, is just as real. 'Capital is by nature a leveller',

Marx argues, for it 'exacts in every sphere of production equality in the conditions of the exploitation of labour' (Marx 1967:397). Indeed, capital's universalising tendency, which distinguishes mature capitalism from all other modes of production, tends toward 'the annihilation of space by time' (Marx 1973:539–40).

So how are we to resolve this apparent theoretical contradiction between opposed tendencies toward radical differentiation on the one side and a similarly ruthless, competitive equalisation of conditions of social production and reproduction on the other? In practice, this contradiction, internal to the logic of capital accumulation, finds its resolution precisely in uneven geographical development, which establishes discrete places differentiated from each other and at the same time pressures these places, across borders, into a single mould. Uneven development represents a forced yet contested, momentarily fixed yet always fluid resolution to this central contradiction of capitalism. The levelling tendency of capitalism continually gnaws at the radical differentiation of the conditions of exploitation of labour, and yet the corrosive differentiation of labour also eternally frustrates this 'annihilation of space by time'. The question of scale becomes absolutely vital here, because without a sense of the making of scale, it is impossible to grasp the expansion from Marx's largely temporal logic to the geographical logic inherent in uneven development. Put differently, if we can understand the inherent tendency to differentiate places one from the other, as an impulse of capitalism per se, what precisely constitutes a coherent place?

At the turn of the twentieth century, it was simply assumed that the unevenness of development by and large concerned the scale of the nation state. This was not an unreasonable assumption given that the period witnessed a crescendo of nation state formation in the global political economy. But there is nothing inherently privileged about the national scale as a spatial unit of political organisation. Earlier centuries saw a greater dominance of city states and kingdoms, duchies and provinces, shires and cantons, and the like, and in fact the national division of the globe is very much the twin of capitalism's globalising (universalising) ambition. The nation state, in fact, performed a crucial yet very specific function in the evolution of capitalism. In the bluntest terms, as the scale of capital accumulation expanded dramatically the inherited political and territorial units of social, cultural and military organisation were no longer capable of administering economies that had outstripped old boundaries. The expanded scale of economic power required expanded polities for helping to organise the process of capital accumulation, and it fell to emergent national states to create a new geography of more or less homogeneous conditions internally – labour and tax laws, transportation systems, media, systems of social reproduction, state subsidy of capital, etc. The national state effectively organised a solution to the inherent contradiction between the need for socio-economic cooperation on the one side and economic competition, now implanted at the centre of the global economy, on the other. The global system of nation states thus represented a territorial solution to a vital political economic contradiction thrown up by the universalisation of capital; this system organised political economic differentiation into a global system that was more unified than ever before. Luxemburg was entirely correct that capitalism needed its constitutive 'outside', but the system of nation states provided the basis for creating such an outside *within global capitalism.*

Although the making of the national scale thus played a pivotal role in the early evolution of capitalism, it is not unique in proffering territorial solutions to the political economic contradictions between competition and cooperation, differentiation and equalisation, in capitalist societies. Parallel processes operate at other scales, equally if differently embedded in and transformed by the needs of capital accumulation. Across history, the urban scale has provided various social functions, centralising not just economic but military, religious, cultural and political power. Focussing on the economic, Marx once held that the 'foundation of every division of labour that is well developed, and brought about by the age of commodities, is the separation between town and country' (Marx 1967:352). For a long time, this spatial distinction was broadly synonymous with the general division of labour between agriculture and industry, but in the age of industrialised agriculture and global eco-tourism that functional boundary is blurred. Still, whereas wage rates and a broad array of other costs of production are crucial for determining the unevenness of development at the national scale, the power of ground rent becomes vital at the urban scale. Any metropolitan area and its hinterland is a single geographical (if not social) labour market, and so the organisation of activities within urban areas is regulated more according to rent than wage rates. Other geographical scales – whether the household, the sub-national region, or the multinational region – are similarly the product of specific social, economic and political relations. In short, we witness under capitalism a scaffolding of geographical scales which to a greater or lesser extent organises the essential territorial differentiation of capital accumulation – the means of delineating, at various scales, the construction of capital's 'outside' *within* – and the flow of capital across boundaries.

We can therefore conceive of a spatial correlate of Marx's derivation of capitalist cycles of expansion and crisis. Capitalism not only generates temporal cycles of expansion and crisis but spatial cycles of development at one pole and underdevelopment at another. The dynamism of capital accumulation converts this logic into something of a 'see-saw' model of capitalist expansion (Smith 1984). Insofar as development in one region, nation, urban area or district creates underdevelopment – higher unemployment, lower rents, under-investment, etc. – it simultaneously creates the conditions for a new wave of expansion in precisely those areas that were underdeveloped; conversely, developed areas become susceptible to underdevelopment in the face of competition from lower cost areas. This dynamic can best be seen at local scales where political impediments to the flow of capital are weakest. Thus the development of suburbs deprived cities of much-needed capital, but the consequent cheapening of the cities and the ageing of capital devoted to the suburbs created the opportunity for the gentrification of the city. The intensive and vicious underdevelopment of Ireland under the auspices of British imperialism has similarly been reversed as that country has become one of the most prosperous regions of Europe, recently outstripping its old ruler in terms of per capita income. East Asia, which emerged from the Second World War as an indisputably 'Third World' region, is now increasingly integrated into the circuits of global capital, production and (in some cases) consumption. Taiwan, Hong Kong and more recently China are emblematic of this shift as are Singapore and India to the south. That this development is highly uneven within these economies is precisely the point and certainly draws comparison with the earlier, and in many ways more limited, industrial revolutions of Europe. South Korea may be the emblematic case: a picture-scape of war-torn paddy fields in the 1950s, it now boasts the eleventh largest gross domestic product of any country in the world.

The logic of capital accumulation is spatial as much as it is temporal, and uneven development is its quite precise if not always predictable result. The revolutionary socialists of the early twentieth century glimpsed this only partially. Trotsky (1962:169–82) indicted the adverse geographical situation of Russia, its sparse population and pre-capitalist 'natural economic development', its climate as much as its transport system, and its absolutist state, as factors in its 'backwardness'. Whatever progressive impulse was implied in early theories of uneven development was abruptly truncated by Stalinism and by the self-interest of capitalist elites which kept the ideological focus on a puerile equation of spatial difference with narrowly national-scale presumptions, even when, as with Trotsky, the political point was resolutely internationalist. Just as Marxists today should have little truck with the kind of iron 'laws of history' that marked an earlier era, it is vital at the same time to recover a sense of the ordered if always malleable geography of capital accumulation at multiple scales. Or as Trotsky (1962:130–1) put it, the force of 'the law of uneven development...operates not only in the relations of countries to each other, but also in the various processes within one and the same country', and yet the 'reconciliation of the uneven processes of economics and politics can be attained only on a world scale'.

That capitalism does not operate on a level plain, and that therefore the see-saw logic of capitalist geographic expansion does not occur in any pure form, no less condemns this theory of uneven development than the unreality of Marx's one-nation assumption dooms his analysis of capitalism. The point, as ever, is to use the theory to understand the geo-historical processes as they are 'really going on'.

CONCLUSION

Just as the form of bourgeois rule differs between and among 'advanced' and 'backward' countries, Trotsky once wrote, 'the dictatorship of the proletariat also will have a highly varied character in terms of the social basis, the political forms, the immediate tasks and the tempo of work in the various capitalist countries' (Trotsky 1962:129). Throughout most of the world today, we are not living in a revolutionary moment or even in a peri-revolutionary moment. Indeed Perry Anderson (2000:17) suggests he can find 'no significant opposition' to capitalism in 'the West'. However that may be, the transition to socialism, which preoccupied revolutionary socialists a century ago, is certainly not the dominant context today, and our comprehension of uneven development needs to be filled out accordingly. A theory of uneven development appropriate for the present conjuncture needs to understand the capitalist logic that underlies the 'varied character' of places, their 'social bases' and 'political forms'.

In search of solutions to internal contradictions, capitalist societies create specific geographies, yet these geographies themselves become the prison-house of social, economic and especially political possibilities. The geographies of uneven capitalist development quite literally *contain* struggle, whether in colonies or ghettoes, empires or suburbs. The theories of uneven development that formed in the first quarter of the twentieth century glimpsed these possibilities as uneven development proper emerged as the hallmark of the geography of capitalism. As the history of revolutions and national liberation struggles in the twentieth century amply attest, there is no necessary one-to-one mapping between levels and types of capitalist development in a particular place and the propensity for revolution, but an astute analysis of political possibilities in the future *is* dependent on a developed theory of uneven development.

REFERENCES

Althusser, L. (1975 [1965]) *For Marx* (London: New Left Books).

Amin, S. (1976) *Unequal Development: An Essay on the Social Formations of Peripheral Capitalism* (New York: Monthly Review).

Anderson, P. (2000) 'Renewals', *New Left Review*, 1:5–24.

Arrighi, G. (1994) *The Long Twentieth Century* (London: Verso).

Cassidy, J. (1997) 'The Return of Marx', *New Yorker*, October 20–7.

Diamond, J. (2005) *Collapse: How Societies Choose to Fail or Succeed* (New York: Viking).

Emmanuel, A. (1972) *Unequal Exchange* (New York: Monthly Review).

Frank, A. G. (1967) *Capitalism and Underdevelopment in Latin America* (New York: Monthly Review).

Hardt, M. and Negri, A. (2000) *Empire* (Cambridge, Mass.: Harvard University Press).

Herod, A. and M. W. Wright (eds) (2002) *Geographies of Power: Placing Scale* (Oxford: Blackwell Publishing).

Kaplan, R. (1997) *The Ends of the Earth* (New York: Vintage).

Lenin, V. I. (1975 [1917]) *Imperialism, The Highest Stage of Capitalism* (Moscow: Progress Publishers).

—— (1977 [1899]) *The Development of Capitalism in Russia* (Moscow: Progress Publishers).

Löwy, M. (1981) *The Politics of Combined and Uneven Development* (London: Verso).

Luxemburg, R. (1968 [1913]) *The Accumulation of Capital* (New York: Monthly Review).

Mackinder, H. J. (1904) 'The Geographical Pivot of History', *Geographical Journal*, 23.

Mandel, E. (1962) *Marxist Economic Theory* (London: Merlin Press).

—— (1975) *Late Capitalism* (London: New Left Books).

Mao, Z. (1971) 'On Contradiction', in *Selected Readings From the Works of Mao Tsetung* (Beijing: Foreign Language Press).

Marx, K. (1967 [1867]) *Capital,* i (Moscow: International Publishers).

—— (1973 [1857–58]) *Grundrisse* (New York: Random House).

Molyneux, J. (1981) *Leon Trotsky's Theory of Revolution* (New York: St Martin's Press).

Sachs, J. (2001) 'A Case of Bad Latitude: Why Geography Causes Poverty', *Foreign Policy,* 122.

—— (2005) *The End of Poverty: Economic Possibilities For Our Time* (New York: Penguin).

Smith, N. (1984) *Uneven Development: Nature, Capital and the Production of Space* (Oxford: Basil Blackwell).

—— (1995) 'Remaking Scale: Competition and Cooperation in Prenational and Postnational Europe', in H. Eskelinen and F. Snickars (eds) *Competitive European Peripheries* (Berlin: Springer Verlag).

—— (2003) *American Empire: Roosevelt's Geographer and the Prelude to Globalization* (Berkeley: University of California Press).

Swyngedouw, E. (2004) 'Scaled Geographies: Nature, Place, and the Politics of Scale', in E. Sheppard and R. McMaster (eds) *Scale and Geographic Inquiry* (Oxford: Blackwell Publishing).

Trotsky, L. (1962 [1930/1906]) *The Permanent Revolution* and *Results and Prospects* (London: New Park).

—— (1977 [1930]) *The History of the Russian Revolution* (London: Pluto Press).

Wood, E. M. (2003) *Empire of Capital* (London and New York: Verso).

15

The Reinvention of Populism: Islamist Responses to Capitalist Development in the Contemporary Maghreb[1]

Alejandro Colás

Like many other parts of the erstwhile Third World, the Maghreb region of north-west Africa has lived under a general socio-economic and political crisis since the early 1980s. The three major states of the westernmost reaches of the Arab world – Algeria, Morocco and Tunisia – have witnessed profound socio-economic and political upheavals (in Algeria amounting to a civil war in all but name), which have tested the resolve of both state and society for over a generation. One of the most powerful responses to this general crisis has come in the guise of Islamism.[2] I will argue in this chapter that such reactions can be interpreted within the framework of Leon Trotsky's notion of combined and uneven development. For Islamic revivalism in the Maghreb is the particular expression of universal forces dominating our world: it results from the peculiar insertion of the region into global capitalist relations, and from a specific combination of local and universal political idioms. In this respect, I invert somewhat Trotsky's original focus on the state as the cause and effect of combined and uneven development by looking more narrowly at civil society as a site where the articulation of the particular and the general delivers unique forms of political contestation.

Such political forces, like that of Islamism in the Maghreb, are specific in that they invoke an undifferentiated political subject – 'the

1. This is a highly abridged and revised version of a paper first published in *Historical Materialism: Research in Critical Marxist Theory*, Vol. 12, No. 4, 2004, pp. 231–60. I am grateful for the publishers E.J. Brill for permission to reproduce sections of that article.
2. An abbreviated and generic term covering a variegated phenomenon, which nonetheless encapsulates the appropriation of the precepts and civilisational markers of Islam for the purposes of political action and mobilisation.

people' (*al-sha'ab* in Arabic) – in the context of an internationally mediated collapse of state legitimacy and social cohesion. Whilst by no means absent in the advanced capitalist world, such responses are also peculiar in that they emerge within social formations which experienced the subordinate insertion into the world capitalist market – in the Maghreb, through forceful imperialist penetration (which incidentally Trotsky had relatively little to say about) – and have since then suffered the structural consequences of this specific articulation with global capitalism. The socio-political struggles which accompanied this history have also engendered specific forms of mass mobilisation which (re)combined long-standing 'vertical' allegiances to kin, trade, ethnicity or creed with budding 'horizontal' allegiances of class (Thompson 1974). In the course of this history, class-based political movements have, with a few notable exceptions, fared less well than rival organisations built around specific conceptions of the 'the people'. The Islamist programme in particular draws on (and thus 'reinvents') a long-standing populist tradition of anti-imperialism in the region in ways that are radically antithetical to communist alternatives (Black 1991).

MARXISM AND POPULISM: A QUESTION OF CATEGORY

Like their bourgeois counterparts, Marxist theorists of populism (particularly those of the Americas) have grappled with the expansive and elusive nature of the term and its concrete socio-political expressions from the beginning. Indeed, Trotsky's twin texts, *Results and Prospects* and *Permanent Revolution* are excellent illustrations of the problems faced by concrete Marxist analyses of kinds of politics thrown up by the combination of uneven geopolitical forces and divergent historical trajectories. Three key aspects of historical materialist approaches to populism were first broached in Marx's own 'Eighteenth Brumaire of Louis Bonaparte'. There, Marx emphasised, firstly, the contingency associated with modern politics and its relative autonomy from class relations; secondly, the centrality of conflicting historical temporalities and the accompanying sense of socio-economic and political crisis in fostering populism; and thirdly, the role of 'residual', pre-capitalist classes such as peasants, aristocrats, lumpenproletariats or petty bourgeois in the unfolding of modern history, especially in the context of sharp urban–rural divides. To this we must add a fourth concern of Marxist theories of populism which only emerged after the Second World War, namely the 'overdeveloped' nature of the post-colonial state (Alavi 1972).

Populism, then, can be seen variously as a form of rule, a political movement, an ideology and a strategy for socio-economic development. Critics of the concept point to such capaciousness as a demonstration of its analytical vacuity. But such versatility can also be interpreted as a virtue, for it allows us to engage with a form of politics which, as one observer has noted, is chameleon-like: constantly adapting its political hue to specific environments (Taggart 2000). Thus, invocations of 'the people' by a charismatic leader of a mass party can adopt both right- and left-wing programmes, mobilise subordinate classes against dominant ones, town against country, pit one region against the other, and veer toward opposing extremes of fascism and communism. It is this inherent flexibility and opportunism which distinguishes populism from other modern social movements and ideologies: unlike fascism, populism is not ideologically committed to subjecting local and foreign populations to rule by a militarised state; in contrast to communism, it does not aim to politically mobilise the working class in the transcendence of capitalist social relations. Rather, populism deliberately limits its message to a named 'people', claims to empower this generic political subject (not subordinate it) and is studiously evasive about socio-economic cleavages among 'the people', preferring instead to target an elusive and equally malleable 'power elite' or 'political class'.

All of this poses great conceptual (and political) difficulties for Marxist explanations, as Trotsky himself was painfully aware at the start of the twentieth century. For populism appears, so we have seen, as an eminently *residual* category: it encompasses all those socio-economic and political phenomena – charismatic authority, cross-class allegiances, rural–urban divides – 'left over' from previous historical epochs and modes of production which capitalist development is meant to undermine and eventually eradicate. It places at the forefront classes and social forces which do not fit neatly into the logic of expanded capitalist reproduction. But what if populism is not so exceptional as a political response to the global reproduction of capitalism? What if it describes not a marginal or backward phenomenon, but one central to the political lives of many modern societies across the world?

There is, to be sure, much of the Marxist tradition which, being consonant with crude modernisation theory, reproduces the absolute historical opposition between 'advanced' and 'backward'; modern and traditional. The *Communist Manifesto*, the famous 1859 'Preface' to the *Critique of Political Economy*, and most of Second International Marxism present this kind of dogmatic, 'stagist' view of historical evolution. But there is also a strong legacy of both theoretical and concrete Marxist analysis which highlights the uneven and contradictory patterns of historical evolution, especially when transferred onto a world scale. Marx's famous correspondence with Vera Zasulich (Shanin 1983) in many respects serves as a reference point for a whole range of Marxist engagements with the 'simultaneity of the unsimultaneous' – of which Trotsky's own musings on 'combined and uneven development' are a primary example.

This dialectical, dynamic understanding of historical change also challenges claims that categories such as 'class', 'value' or 'labour' are ossified in the Marxist analysis of living societies. By insisting that say, an ideal–typical, homogeneous proleteriat cannot readily be identified empirically in many parts of the Third World, many critics of Marxism miss the crucial distinction between the structural logic of capital and its accompanying abstractions, with their concrete expression in actual societies. Once we respect the distinction between abstractions such as class, value or free labour, which are all structural properties of the capitalist mode of production, and their concrete manifestation as specific social movements, forms of property or modes of exploitation within particular social formations, it is perfectly feasible to accommodate conflicting socio-political phenomena such as those which fall under the rubric of 'populism'.

In such instances, it is not the abstractions of *Capital* and the *Grundrisse*, with their emphasis on the structural anatomy of capitalism, that are of greatest value, but rather the more incisive, local explorations of the *Eighteenth Brumaire*, or *The Civil Wars in France* which serve as principal inspiration. For it is in the latter that we find how the abstract logic of capitalist society and politics unfolds in concrete social formations through contingent political antagonisms, contradictory historical temporalities and the persistence of pre-capitalist forms of social oppression. On this reading, for instance, the process of African proletarianisation is identified as an inescapable, structural property of capitalist development in that part of the world, which nonetheless manifests itself in diverse concrete forms – underemployment, petty-commodity production, the 'informal' economy.

These latter phenomena cannot be reduced to some ideal–typical proletarianisation which everywhere and always creates an industrial, salaried 'free' worker (although it certainly does do this too); but neither can such realities be explained *without* reference to the dynamics of capitalist reproduction. Something similar happens with populism – although it cannot be read off as mechanically corresponding to the political representation of a particular class, it cannot equally be read *without* reference to specific class antagonisms generated through capitalist development. Here, populism appears not to be *of* capitalism, but it certainly is *in* capitalism, and as such must be explained with reference to forms of crisis, socio-political mobilisation and socio-economic cleavages which are unique to this mode of social reproduction.

In the particular case of the Maghreb, a key factor in explaining the rise and persistence of populism is the experience of capitalist imperialism. What has marked the modern history of this region (admittedly in an uneven fashion) is the perverse unity of 'free' capitalist exploitation and coercive, pre-capitalist forms of oppression in the single colonial moment (Bennoune 1986; Sammut 1983; Stewart 1964).

Whilst private property, the commodification of labour and the extension of market dependence all accompanied the European colonial penetration of the Maghreb, this process was also executed through the racialised, militarised and often arbitrary power of the colonial state. The attempt by French (and to a much lesser extent Spanish) imperialism to reproduce consensual, rule-based capitalist social relations in the area was compromised by indigenous resistance and the racist ideology of the European colonisers. This combination produced not a pristine capitalist civil society of free markets and the corresponding form of modern sovereignty, but rather a racialised, coercive market for labour and a colonial state which accommodated pre-existing forms of political rule premised on kinship, religious authority or ethnic affiliation. It is precisely this contradictory and uneven reproduction of capitalism in the region that delivered a correspondingly amorphous and chameleon-like populist politics which thrives in moments of crisis by eschewing mediated, representative politics and instead mobilising 'the people' through a direct, unmediated identification with a single, charismatic leader representing a given 'communal heartland' (Taggart 2000).

The contemporary revival of populism in the Maghreb, I have thus far argued, is an expression of exactly this kind of contingency, contradiction and uneven historical fissure. It is, however, a populism inflected with a particular religious discourse – we are therefore speaking of *Islamist* populism rather than simply populism, and one among various other expressions of populism in the region.

This underlines the synchronic dimensions of any historical change mentioned earlier and indeed emphasises how '[t]radition from all the dead generations weighs like a nightmare on the brain of the living' (Marx 2002:1). Before delving into the actual detail of political Islam in the contemporary Maghreb, a few words are therefore in order about the specifically Islamist nature of this form of populism, and how it relates to other historical manifestations of this political style.

'Islamism' or 'political Islam' should first of all be distinguished from the precepts of the religion followed by Muslims. It is a political phenomenon which expressly seeks to secularise these precepts, i.e. to bring them into the realm of human socio-political agency and voluntarism, charge them with political meaning and power, and thereby distance them from mere scholastic or theological interpretation aimed simply at injecting morality and spirituality into people's everyday lives. Contemporary Maghrebi Islamism, like its *salafi* precursors of the early twentieth century or the Islamic reformers such as Ben Badis' Association of Algerian Muslim Ulema, has sought to re-appropriate and adjust the major sources of Islamic authority (*sunna, hadith, shari'a* and the Koran itself) so that they respond to contemporary socio-economic and political challenges (Al-Azmeh 1993; Hourani 1983; Rahnema 1994). It has done so by way of applying age-old concepts and practices drawn from Islamic history to the contemporary world, thus attempting to replace 'foreign' imports such as the state, secularism, democracy or progress with their more 'authentic' counterparts such as *umma* (community of believers), *jahiliyya* (pagan ignorance), *majlis al-shura* (consultative council), *jihad* (struggle). To this extent, contemporary Maghrebi Islamism encompasses socio-political movements and ideologies plainly inspired by Islam, but developed in secular political contexts and, significantly, generally deployed by men with very little, if any, formal religious training.

Islamism, then, is not a purely atavistic phenomenon which wishes to recreate a seventh century Arabian utopia in the twenty-first century, but rather a thoroughly modern political tendency fuelled, as Erevand Abrahamian has so convincingly demonstrated in the case of Iran, by all the mechanisms of modern political agitation (political rallies, marches, strikes, local party branches or cells) and much of the political idiom of other modern ideologies (Abrahamian 1990). In order to maintain this perception of Islamism as a modern ideological movement, and crucially, in an attempt to retain the comparative dimension of this phenomenon, I shall be insisting below that Islamism is a specific, religiously inspired brand of populism.

It is, however, also important to note that the Islamist movements discussed in this chapter form part of a broader tradition of populism in the Maghreb. Indeed, with the possible exception of Morocco, populism has been the dominant political style in the region since at least independence, chiefly as a result of the imperialist nature of capitalist penetration in the region (Addi 1990; Harbi 1975; Roberts 2003). For this subordinated and forceful insertion into the world capitalist market created a variety of disarticulated political subjectivities in the Maghreb, none of which became hegemonic until after independence.

Initially, anti-imperialist resistance was mediated through pre-modern forms of tribal or messianic mobilisation, in very much the same shape that previous Ottoman (and indeed Arab) invasions had encountered. The turn of the twentieth century witnessed the rise of liberal and religious–reformist politics among the urban elite, which was accompanied by the emergence of nationalist, populist and socialist politics articulated around mass political organisations during the inter-war and post-war years. In all three major Maghrebi countries, but especially in Morocco and Tunisia where imperial occupation was less comprehensive and pre-existing sources of political authority survived intact, networks of *sufi* brotherhoods (*turuq*), tribal confederations and aristocratic elites also served to crystallise both urban and rural resistance. Overlap and competition among these various movements created a variegated and dynamic political landscape, but it could not deliver what by the end of the Second World War had become the most strident and unanimous popular demand: national liberation.

The specific combination of capitalist exploitation and national oppression which had for decades blocked such an objective now required a political force that might unify the 'social question' and 'national question' in a single mass movement. That force was to become populism. Only in Morocco did the struggle for national liberation deliver a fractured polity where royal authority, and the two rival populisms of Allal al-Fasis's conservative Istiqlal and Mehdi Ben Barka's progressive UNFP competed to represent the 'people's will'. In Tunisia, and even more forcefully in Algeria, cross-class, formally secular (though not anti-religious) mass movements – the Neo-Destour in the first case, the FLN in the second – emerged from the wars of liberation as single, unified depositories of popular sovereignty. Populism thus became the dominant expression of national politics in Tunisia and Algeria because it simultaneously created the modern, sovereign subject of 'the people' and realised their liberation from imperialism through national independence.

THE THREE AXES OF ISLAMIST POPULISM:
CRISIS, CORRUPTION AND ANTI-IMPERIALISM

It is against this backdrop, then, that we should understand the Islamist resurgence of the last three decades as a 'reinvention' of populism. For the Islamists have, as we shall see in more detail shortly, drawn extensively from the imagery, language, programme, idiom, organisation and indeed cadres of the national liberation movements. The one crucial ingredient they have added to the populist legacy is the seeming incorruptibility and authenticity of 'Islam'. Whilst the populism of the national liberation movements was transformed into state power, in the process acquiring all the secular, this-worldly trappings of such forms of political rule, Islamist populism allowed itself, in the main, to resist the world of '*le pouvoir*' and instead built (and billed) itself as an opposition, grassroots movement guided by other-worldly piety. As the legitimacy of post-colonial states collapsed in tandem with that of secular Arab ideologies, the social base of populism remained relatively unaltered. But its ideological axis was realigned towards the only worldview which remained seemingly untarnished: that of political Islam. Three broad political issues in particular have sustained this realignment.

The first of these was a sense of crisis. Contemporary Islamism has succeeded above all as a *conjunctural* protest movement capable of channelling multiple sources of popular discontent through a generic and therefore broadly appealing idiom of 'corruption', 'power', 'degradation', 'the people' and so forth. In the specific case of North African Islamism, because the sources of social malaise are generally associated with 'modernity' and 'modernism' (secularism, materialism, rationalism, humanism), it is also accurate to speak of a *reactionary* (i.e. an anti-modern) form of populism. In short, Islamism emerged in the region initially as a political form that was *against* the existing order. Insofar as Islamist organisations presented positive policy alternatives, they were once again generic ones: the application of sharia law, the shift towards a 'Muslim' or 'Islamic' society, the jihad against corruption, all of which were neatly summarised in one of the preferred slogans of the Algerian FIS: 'Islam is the solution.'

One reason for the use of such highly generic rhetoric is of course the calculation that everyone is 'against corruption' or 'against oppression': the broader the category the more likely it is to capture the allegiance of an otherwise highly differentiated constituency that is 'the people'. A more profound reason, however, lies in the genuinely contradictory nature of Maghrebi Islamist populism, or what Angus Stewart once called the 'Janus quality' of populism:

It is their character as responses to development 'crises' which gives populist movements [this quality]... At the time of the emergence of the populist movement the traditional culture will frequently have been exposed to considerable disruption and the framers of the populistic ideology will often be arbitrary and opportunistic in their selection of this 'traditional' culture. It is the fact that the synthesis seeks to integrate around traditional values as society *exposed* but not necessarily *part of* social change... (Stewart 1969:187)

If we replace (however problematically) 'traditional' with 'Islamic' in the above passage, Stewart's description readily fits the Maghrebi expressions of populism. Thus, the use of generic rhetoric is explained not by the absence of political sophistication, but by quite the opposite, namely the calculated use of the most common of political denominators – an attack on those in power with recourse to a politically undefined but commonly shared idiom: in the Maghrebi case, 'Islam' – for the purpose of crystallising a highly diversified, often incompatible set of classes into a single constituency. More importantly, Stewart's emphasis on the 'combined and uneven' ('exposed/not part of') context responsible for the rise of populism resonates with the recent general crisis of the Maghreb outlined above. For as most studies on the social origins of Maghrebi Islamism have concluded, it is those groups most affected by the crisis – students, state employees (particularly teachers) and petty bourgeois merchants – which constitute a disproportionate number of Islamist cadres. North African Islamist movements cut across the social cleavages of class, gender, ethnicity and geographical location precisely because they have been able to capture a generalised sense of social crisis; that is, a widespread breakdown of the quotidian parameters of legitimacy, be these economic, political, social or cultural.

For instance, Islamists associate the modern assault on the 'role of the traditional family mother' with the violation of an 'authentic' identity (Lazreg 1994; Lloyd 1999; Moghadam 2004). Like other forms of populism, mothers and housewives are presented as depositories of that 'communal heartland' which existed prior to the externally imposed forms of modernity: the equilibrium sustained by the traditional sexual division of labour is upset, according to most Islamist thinking, by the insistence on the public equality between men and women. They also draw on agents of 'civil society' in the reconstruction of that elusive constituency that is 'the people'. The political success of Islamism must be judged not so much on its capacity or otherwise to acquire state power, but rather in its conquest of those expanding arenas of the public sphere – education, social security, health, culture – from where the state has retreated. Like other expressions of populism, North African Islamism takes over where the legitimate authority of the state has collapsed, thereby reconstituting 'the people' in its own image. By mobilising and providing for those social sectors most affected by the state's retreat from its welfare obligations, Islamist organisations have effectively established parallel forms of popular sovereignty through their work in charitable foundations, mosques, professional and recreational associations, or collective health and welfare institutions.

This Islamist colonisation of civil society undeniably linked to the process of 'state restructuring' occasioned by international economic and political pressures. Islamists have, wherever possible, replaced the state's role as provider of social goods during the period of state retreat of the 1980s and 1990s. Yet it is equally important to highlight the self-destructive role state officials in the Maghreb have played in the de-legitimisation of the post-colonial state during the past two decades. Rampant corruption, ostentatious display of wealth, cynical manipulation and naked oppression have characterised much of the ruling classes' political behaviour in the region during this period. Particularly in Algeria, the military regime's obstinate monopoly of economic and political power and its opaque campaign against armed Islamist insurgency after 1991 have severely dented any faith in representative politics as an expression of democracy. Indeed, on several occasions since the country's first multi-party elections in December 1989, the Algerian people have eagerly participated in democratic consultations only to see their collective will – however fractured it may be – squandered by a ruling elite intent only on proverbially 'changing things so that things stay the same'.

It is in this generally repressive and unrepresentative context – replicated with some important qualifications in Tunisia and Morocco – that Islamist forces have developed their successful critique of representative democracy as a Western sham. The political distance generated by a secretive, manipulative yet literally absent state (or present only in its repressive capacity), is easily turned into a geographical distance, where generalised crisis and the specific events that concretise it, are blamed on the nebulous 'Party of France' or *Hizb França*. This transnationalisation of political responsibility allows Islamists at once to denounce the 'neo-colonial' character of existing regimes in the Maghreb, and to further undermine the legitimacy of any mediated or representative politics. On this view, the Western oppression of the North African masses is mediated through corrupt, secular and Francophile dictators in the region; the way forward for Islamists is therefore to break this link by returning to the direct, immediate and authentic politics offered by Islam: *shura*, sharia and *umma*.

The de-legitimisation of the post-colonial state and the rejection of its accompanying forms of politics has, for North African Islamists, been tightly connected to the region's peculiar insertion into the international system. Islamists therefore present and respond to a world-view which is not unlike that offered by the North African nationalists during the last period of colonial rule: one where the region's past – its civilisational achievements and cultural heritage – is actively being destroyed by foreign influences, and where an authentic 'golden age' prior to European conquest serves as a model to combat the region's contemporary general crisis.

The dual emphasis on the inferiority and humiliation of the Maghreb on the one hand, and the possible alternative in the path of Islamic civilisation on the other, echoes forms of Third World anti-imperialism which have characterised the international relations of other Islamist movements across the world. North African Islamists have readily adopted the Iranian revolution's slogan 'Neither East nor West' (*la sharqui, la gharbi*) as a rallying point for their more internationally minded sympathisers. This ideological commitment to an international 'third way', often informed by more classical anti-imperialist language, was not simply rhetorical. North African Islamists have developed an extensive transnational support network with other like-minded Islamists, to form what may loosely be termed an 'Islamist international'. Rachid Ghannoushi's close relationship with the then spiritual leader of Sudan, Hassan al-Turabi, during the early 1990s provided his party, *al-Nahda*, a considerable measure of international standing and no small amount of logistical support. More sinister relationships were established between elements of the Algerian Islamist insurgents and Afghani mujahedin, so that by the mid-1990s many of the former were simply referred to as 'Afghanis'

(Martínez 2000). These anecdotal illustrations clearly cannot replace a systematic and nuanced analysis of 'Islamist internationalism'; yet they do at least point to the impact of 'the international' on North African Islamism at both the ideological and operational levels.

CONCLUSIONS:
POPULISM AS COMBINED AND UNEVEN DEVELOPMENT

Islamist politics have demonstrated different degrees of endurance in the contemporary Maghreb. Whilst in Algeria the armed struggle between the state and insurgent Islamic militants is only now abating after close to two decades of bloodshed, Tunisia and Morocco have thus far proved successful in reining in Islamist protest through a combination of fierce repression and selective improvements in the standard of living for certain sectors of the population. The historical conditions which generated the initial Islamist resurgence of the 1980s, however, have not substantially altered and as one recent observer has suggested it is therefore premature to announce the 'defeat of political Islam', in North Africa or elsewhere (Ismail 2001). Islamic activists, it is true, have been largely unsuccessful in seizing and maintaining state power since the Iranian revolution of 1978–79, but their social and political power within 'civil societies' across the Middle East and beyond should not be underestimated. Indeed, it has been the claim of this chapter that the force of political Islam in North Africa rests largely in the capacity of its representative organisations to channel the discontents of capitalist development in the region into a distinctly populist form of protest. There are at least three theoretical implications that arise from such a conclusion, two more general ones for social analysis, the last more specific to Marxism.

Firstly, whilst it is essential, as this contribution has sought to indicate, to situate the history and development of contemporary Islamism in an international context, it is important not to do so in a purely 'culturalist' fashion that pits the 'West' against 'the Rest' or 'McWorld vs. Jihad'. As I have tried to show, Islamism is certainly an expression of political protest that places great emphasis on the power of local, cultural or civilisational traditions like 'Islam' in combating the negative consequences of a seemingly alien capitalist globalisation. But this form of political protest is both comparable to other forms of populist opposition to globalisation and, more importantly, can, in its ideological content and social base, be traced to the very specific conjuncture of neoliberal reform of the 1980s and 1990s. Thus, it has been argued, recent waves of Islamist politics are best understood as the historically specific expression of the contradictions inherent in the combined and uneven reproduction of global capitalism. Such an understanding of the international dimensions of social-movement activity can, in turn, offer a more dynamic account of the changes in the nature of interstate relations, so that for example, a deeper explanation of contemporary Euro-Maghrebi relations might incorporate the reality and potential of Islamist protest in the Maghreb and its populist counterparts in the northern Mediterranean.

These considerations lead on to a second general theoretical conclusion, namely that such incorporation of the dynamics of 'international civil society' into our understanding of international relations must also be keenly aware, as I think Trotsky was some hundred years ago, of the particular *mediating structures* of political or social authority in the reproduction of the international system. In other words, it is essential to continually probe the interaction between the 'domestic' and 'international' structures and processes, and indeed to constantly re-chart and re-analyse the new forms that arise out of such an interaction. In the specific case of North Africa, what this means is that the international dynamics of the region should not be reduced to an endless struggle between 'collapsed states' and their Islamic populist alternatives. Not only is this no longer the empirical case in a country like Tunisia, but more importantly, such an attitude would overlook the reshaping of both state and society, and the political challenges that are constantly emerging from the social contradictions inherent in these two spheres. What the future forms of political contestation in the Maghreb might look like is, of course, an open question; that they are likely to be shaped by the conflicting interaction between the dynamics of international capitalism and the apparently local political responses, is not.

Accepting some degree of contingency in political outcomes should not, however, be tantamount to forgoing a structural analysis of the current crisis in the Maghreb and elsewhere across the world. And so the third and final implication of the reflections expressed in this chapter is the urgent need for Marxists to extend and strengthen our analyses of what Michael Löwy's classic study labelled 'the politics of combined and uneven development' (Löwy 1981): to examine the socio-political responses to the concrete articulation of global capitalism in different social formations. I have suggested here that it is worthwhile for Marxists to retrieve certain disused categories like 'populism' in this endeavour, not as descriptors of accidental, residual forms of mass political mobilisation, but rather as structural features of societies – like those in North Africa – much more powerfully subject to the vagaries of combined and uneven capitalist development. This in turn involves revisiting classical debates over the relationship between communist and other expressions of democratic politics, and indeed the sources of political allegiance other than class. This is something which of course has been the mainstay of leftist movements across the global South for decades, but which their Northern counterparts have been recently inattentive to. The tallest order for contemporary Marxist analyses of global politics therefore seems to involve identifying how the particularities of regional crises and their accompanying socio-political responses can be harnessed to worldwide struggles for democracy and socialism.

REFERENCES

Abrahamian, E. (1990) *Khomeinism* (London: IB Tauris).

Addi, L. (1990) 'De la permanence du populisme algérien', *Peuples Méditerranéens*, 52–53, (July–December): 37–46.

Alavi, H. (1972) 'The State in Postcolonial Societies: Pakistan and Bangladesh', *New Left Review*, 74:59–81.

Al-Azmeh, A. (1993) *Islam and Modernities* (London: Verso).

Bennoune, M. (1986) *The Making of Contemporary Algeria* (Cambridge: Cambridge University Press).

Black, A. (1991) *The History of Islamic Political Thought* (New York: Routledge).

Harbi, M. (1975) *Aux origins du FLN: le populisme révolutionnaire en Algérie* (Paris: Christian Bourgeois).

Hourani, A. (1983) *Arabic Thought in the Liberal Age, 1798–1939* (Cambridge: Cambridge University Press).

Ismail, S. (2001) 'The Paradox of Islamist Politics', *Middle East Report*, 221:34–9.

Lazreg, M. (1994) *The Eloquence of Silence: Algerian Women in Question* (London and New York: Routledge).

Lloyd, C. (1999) 'Organising Across Borders: Algerian Women's Associations in a Period of Conflict', *Review of African Political Economy*, 26 82:479–90.

Löwy, M. (1981) *The Politics of Combined and Uneven Development: The Theory of Permanent Revolution* (London: Verso).

Martínez, L. (2000) *The Algerian Civil War 1990–1998*, translated by Jonathan Derrick (London: Hurst).

Marx, K. (2002 [1852]) 'The Eighteenth Brumaire of Louis Bonaparte', translated by Terrell Carver, in *Marx's 'Eighteenth Brumaire': (Post)Modern Interpretations* edited by Mark Cowling and James Martin (London and Sterling, Va.: Pluto Press).

Moghadam, V. M. (2004) *Towards Gender Equality in the Arab/Middle East Region: Islam, Culture and Feminist Activism* (New York: Human Development Report Office).

Rahnema, A. (ed.) (1994) *Pioneers of Islamic Revival* (London: Zed Books).

Roberts, H. (2003) *The Battlefield Algeria, 1988–2002: Studies in a Broken Polity* (London and New York: Verso).

Sammut, C. (1983) *L'impérialisme capitaliste français et le nationalisme tunisien (1881–1914)* (Paris: Publisud).

Shanin, T. (1983) *Late Marx and the Russian Road: Marx and the 'Peripheries of Capitalism'* (London, Melbourne and Henley: Routledge & Kegan Paul).

Stewart, A. (1969) 'The Social Roots', in Ghiţă Ionescu and Ernest Gellner (eds) *Populism: Its Meaning and National Characteristics* (London: Macmillan) 180–96.

Stewart, C. (1964) *The Economy of Morocco* (Cambridge, Mass.: Harvard University Press).

Taggart, P. (2000) *Populism* (Buckingham and Philadelphia, Pa.: Open University Press).

Thompson, E. P. (1974) 'Patrician Society, Plebeian Culture', *Journal of Social History*, 2/7:382–405.

16
China:
Unevenness, Combination, Revolution?

Neil Davidson

The pace of change in contemporary China is so intense that discussions of it intended for publication are often overtaken by events before they appear in print – a fate from which contributions to collections of essays are not exempt. It would therefore be futile to try to register every episode down to the one that happens to be current as I write (the impact of Chinese textiles on European markets), the historical significance of which is in any case unlikely to be apparent immediately. I want instead to situate recent Chinese developments, particularly since 1978, within the theoretical framework established earlier in this book. If there is one place in the world where the *process* of uneven and combined development is unmistakable, it is China, but what should the *theory* of uneven and combined development lead us to expect from the process?

THE FIRST PHASE

China was the first country outside Russia for which Trotsky argued that a strategy of permanent revolution was applicable. And, although he did not formulate the law of uneven and combined development until after the revolutionary crisis of the 1920s had ended in disaster for the working class, it clearly lay behind his political conception. As I argued in my earlier chapter, combination emerges from unevenness where a backward country attempts to 'catch up' with the advanced in terms of capitalist development, but is unable to complete the process fully in the way that Scotland did in the eighteenth century or that Japan did in the nineteenth (Davidson 2006). These countries are then in a contradictory position. They may have adopted the most modern forms of technology, industrial organisation and scientific thought in certain areas, but most of society remains at a much lower level. The decisive point, however, is that the archaic and modern do not simply sit side by side, offering a picturesque or appalling contrast according to personal taste, but interpenetrate to produce new hybrid forms of explosive instability. The importance of China in relation to Trotsky's theorisation of the process was that it clarified two important issues which the Russian experience did not.

First, it made clear that the process of uneven and combined development was not confined to countries, like Russia, which were either politically independent of imperialism or themselves imperial powers. The precise forms which combination took in these countries obviously varied depending on whether the country involved was a formal colony controlled by a single imperial power, like India, or one nominally independent, but actually subdivided between several warlords and imperial powers, like China. Clearly there were differences. Unlike Tsarist Russia, neither imperial nor republican China was in a position to stimulate capitalist industrial growth. Where similarities did exist was in the role of foreign capital and imported technology, and in the limited geographical implantation of capitalist industry.

Second, it demonstrates that 'combination' does not necessarily involve two different modes of production. Trotsky was quite insistent – perhaps over-insistent – on which mode dominated the Chinese social formation. He rejected Communist International claims that feudalism predominated in the Chinese economic base and political superstructure: 'Of course, matters would be quite hopeless if feudal survivals did really *dominate* in Chinese economic life', he wrote in 1928: 'But fortunately, survivals in general cannot dominate.' Instead he emphasised the extent of market relations and the influence of different forms of mercantile and banking capital. Rural social relations 'stem in part from the days of feudalism; and in part they constitute a new formation', but within this formation 'it is capitalist relations that *dominate* and not 'feudal' (more correctly, serf and, generally, pre-capitalist) relations. Only thanks to this dominant role of capitalist relations can we speak seriously of the prospects of proletarian hegemony in a national revolution' (Trotsky 1974b:159–60).

Where industrial capitalism was established in China, the changes it involved for the working class were dramatic. After 1918, these workers were mainly former peasants or rural labourers, who were now subject to the very different and unaccustomed rhythms of industrial urban life without any intervening stage. Chesneaux writes that the main characteristics of the Chinese proletariat were 'its youth, its instability, its swollen lower ranks and its lack of a developed labor elite' (Chesneaux 1968:50). And in this the Chinese working class closely resembled its Russian forerunner, not least in the openness to Marxism which these conditions tended to produce.

Combined development was not only experienced in the workplace, of course, but in the entire texture of urban life where capitalism took hold. Shanghai was in the vanguard in terms of both production and consumption. It had textile mills before anywhere in the southern states of the United States and by 1930 was home to the largest mill in the world; the first cinema in Shanghai opened only five years after the first large cinema opened in San Francisco (Pye 1981: p. xv). But, important though it was, Shanghai was not the only site of these transformations. By the 1920s Lanzhou, capital of Gansu province was 'a study in contrasts weighted towards the pre-industrial':

A few official buildings, banks and hospitals in Lanzhou were modern style and of two or three stories. But most residences and shops had dirt floors, mud roofs and old-style paper windows. Self-consciously conservative Lanzhou residents described their community as one in which 'women's feet are small [bound] and heads [hair-styles] are big'. But more recently, the number of women with natural feet and bobbed hair had seemed to increase day by day. (Stroud 2000:102)

The parallels between the 1920s and what is currently happening in China are striking. Isaacs opened his classic account of the Chinese revolution of the former decade with this evocative picture:

On the fringes of big Chinese cities the shadows of lofty factory chimneys fall across fields still tilled with wooden ploughs. On the wharves of seaports modern liners unload goods carried away on the backs of men or shipped inland on primitive barges. In the streets great trucks and jangling trams roar past carts drawn by men harnessed like animals to their loads. Automobiles toot angrily at man-drawn rickshaws and barrows which thread their way through the lanes of traffic. Streets are lined with shops where men and women and children still fashion their wares with bare hands and simple tools. On some of these streets are huge mills run by humming dynamos. Airplanes and railroads cut across vast regions linked otherwise only by footpaths and canals a thousand years old. (Isaacs 1961:1)

Yet a recent account of China found different, but equally evocative, contrasts in the rapidly growing cities of the 1990s:

We find, at one end of the economic scale, international hotels, shopping malls, housing developments, nightclubs, gold shops, modern factories funded largely by foreign investment, Development Zones, new roads and airfields... At the other end of the urban spectrum, we find serious overcrowding in colourful but unmodernised lanes, alleys, sweatshops and back-street factories which are frequently ill-lit and unsafe, an array of small pedlars and street stalls reflecting considerable underemployment, and a new underclass composed of part-time or professional criminals, beggars and even street-children (now estimated to total at least 200,000 throughout China). (Gittings 1997:269–71)

The same process has obviously not persisted uninterruptedly over the intervening period of 80 years. What has happened?

DECADES OF REVERSAL

In effect, the components of the Chinese social formation separated out as the process of combined development went into reverse towards the end of the 1920s. The defeat of the working-class movement by the Guomindang alone would not in itself have achieved this result. More significant was the devastation caused by civil war between the Guomindang and the People's Army, and, overlapping with it, the subsequent national war between the Japanese and both Chinese forces. 'In Shanghai, which had been the centre of the textile industry and of working-class formation, the war essentially wiped out the working class as factories closed and workers retreated to the countryside to survive' (Silver 2003:147). What is interesting is that the process of uneven and combined development did not resume with the advent of the Maoist regime in 1949.

After the Second World War almost every developing nation pursued a strategy of urbanisation, in addition to one of industrialisation, whatever the ostensible nature of the regime. In some cases the cities expanded regardless of whether a conscious strategy of growth had been pursued or not. Many former country dwellers found even the dangerous uncertainties of life in the shanty towns which circle all the great Third World conurbations more attractive than the unchanging, unending toil of peasant life. China was the major exception. From the launch of the first Five-Year Plan in 1952, investment was concentrated into production for heavy industry, not consumption. In this respect the Chinese path resembled that of Russia after 1928 and Eastern Europe after 1948. However, it diverged from them in that the growth of urban population was far more tightly controlled. Labour requirements were met through the 'temporary worker system' which conferred no rights on incomers and was widely criticised when state control temporarily slackened during the Cultural Revolution (Solinger 1999:34, 38–40). It was successful enough, as Wong puts it, to have 'effectively created distinct economic worlds in China's cities and the far vaster countryside' (Wong 1997:67). Consequently, although industrial output grew by a factor of 17 between 1952 and 1978, the urban population in 1978 was only 2.4 times larger than it had been in 1949 (Lei 2003:616–17).

One of the main sites of combined development is the industrial city, the breeding ground in which new mutations are born. The Maoist regime seems to have consciously aimed at preventing China's cities from playing this role. In part, this was because the cities could not have accommodated in-migration from the countryside and any influx would have threatened social order. But the regime had no intention of expanding the urban area to house potential migrants: 'Communist bureaucrats feared urban growth, because they recognised the peril in population concentrations that weighed too heavily on public infrastructures, with some people enjoying secure jobs in state run enterprises and bureaucracies while others scrambled at the margins of society' (Wong 1997:185). The CCP, it seems, was not only opposed to Trotsky, but to the social process which he identified and sought to theorise. In effect, they sought to compartmentalise all sections of Chinese society in a process one is tempted to call 'uneven and separate development':

In the years of 1954–1956, a constellation of policies created a great divide between the state and the collective sectors, between city and the countryside, and between industry and agriculture. These multifaceted processes formalised sectoral divisions, gave local and political sanction to lifetime (and even intergenerational) positions, and permanently froze individuals and households in sectoral job and residential pigeonholes. (Selden 1985:280)

Unevenness remained and grew. Bhalla notes that there was a conflict between the twin strategies of 'self-reliance' and 'balanced regional development':

The strategy of self-reliance and self-sufficiency seems to have reinforced regional inequalities and may in practice have neutralised the egalitarian effects of redistributive measures. The promotion of rural industry, within the framework of a local self-reliant strategy, seems to have widened regional inequalities. (Bhalla 1995:297)

In addition to preventing the social combustion of unfettered development, the regime also tried to bind the new working class materially to the state. Lau has noted that

the workers were tied to the enterprise's exploitative and hierarchical relations by means of a form of lifelong personal (and family) dependence on its leaders who, inter alia, took care of them as a 'parental authority' by means of collectivist practices.

He argues that in the enterprise or 'work unit', 'hierarchical practices were a modified form of the organisation of socio-political life in the traditional village, and recognising the predominant peasant origins of the CCP and the newly created working class'. Exploited though they obviously were, workers were therefore spared full exposure to the accompanying effects of industrialisation and urban modernity (Lau 2001:238).

UNEVEN AND COMBINED DEVELOPMENT RESUMED

It was the break with Maoist economic and social policy initiated in 1978 that allowed the process of uneven and combined development to resume. Harvey has argued that the reforms initiated by Deng (the 'Four Modernisations') have to be seen as an early episode in the global turn to neoliberalism (Harvey 2005:ch.5). The inclusion of China within this trend is apt, perhaps even more so than Harvey supposes. If (as I do) we regard China after 1949 as a form of bureaucratic state capitalism, then events after 1978 are best seen as shifts within an already dominant capitalist mode of production – more extreme than those in the West, of course, because of the almost total level of state ownership and control in China – but essentially of the same type. It is the social impact of neoliberalism, rather than the policies themselves, which distinguish China from the rest of the world, even the rest of the developing world.

The outcome has by no means been entirely negative for the mass of the population. In 2000 over 1.2 billion people in the world were living on less than $1 a day and 2.8 billion on less than $2 a day. The fact that by 2002 the number of those living on $1 a day had fallen from 30 per cent to 23 per cent is almost entirely due to economic growth in one country – China (United Nations Development Programme 2003:40–1). Behind these social changes has been the so-called 'third and fourth waves' of industrialisation. The first fell between the First World War and the Japanese invasion of 1937. The second began with the first Five-Year Plan (1953–57) and collapsed in the chaos of the Cultural Revolution (1965–68). The third resumed with the rural industrialisation projects launched in 1978. But the fourth, from the mid-1980s, has been the most far-reaching and sustained. 'Chinese industrialisation in the last two decades of the century took place at a speed and on a scale unequalled anywhere in the world.' The economy grew by an annual average of 10 per cent and per capita income doubled twice over (Hutchings 2000:229). In 1981 only 53 per cent of Chinese exports were manufactures; by 2001, 90 per cent were (United Nations Development Programme 2003:73). Only the prior experiences of Lowland Scotland (1760–1820) and Stalinist Russia (1928–41) come anywhere near to matching the speed and intensity of Chinese growth.

Internal unevenness has been exacerbated by post-1978 developments:

While China as a whole is in the middle range of human development, by global standards, some individual regions, such as Shanghai and Beijing, score well above that and would separately rank as high as 25th and 27th in the world; while poor and minority nationality regions such as Tibet and Qinghai belong in the lower range of human development and would rank 147th and 135th respectively. (United Nations Development Programme 1999:62)

'First World and Third World coexist in China', write Wang and Hu (1999:13–14), but First and Third Worlds also coexist *within* regions, not only between them. This is important for two reasons.

First, taken as a whole, it is possible to underestimate the extent of Chinese economic achievement. Glyn notes that

China is still as far behind the USA as Korea and Taiwan were before their three decades of rapid catch-up beginning in the late 1960s; its percentage GDP is still well below that from which Japan started its spectacular growth climb in the mid-1950s. (Glyn 2005:17)

But the regional figures give quite a different picture. The most extreme example, Shanghai, has seen the most spectacular growth, with a GDP twice that of the capital Beijing and 5 per cent of the national total. It had an average annual growth of 9.5 per cent over 1999–2000 and attracted 10 per cent of foreign investment in China. The population is over 20 million (although this is still only 1.6 per cent of the national total), but of these, only 13.5 million people are permanent residents, the remainder are temporary workers and their families who join them for at least part of the year. Many earn only a fifth of the average income of employed permanent residents (£2,900), although even that is far greater than they would have been able to earn in the countryside where 60p a day is common (Yusif and Weiping 2002:1233; Watts 2003). In the four years between 1994 and 1997 total office space rose from 500,000 square metres to 3.5 million square metres: 'Shanghai is achieving in one decade what it took Hong Kong the best part of four decades to do' (Henderson 1999:30). As an economic actor Shanghai would outperform many Western national capitals.

Second, the mass of the Chinese are becoming aware of the inequalities associated with unevenness in a way that they were not previously:

Before 1978, China was a closed society. Not only did the country close its doors to the outside world, but localities within the country were also largely cut off from one another... At that time, peasants had little chance of leaving their villages. To them, regional disparities were nothing but differences between production brigades or among different communes. Nor did urban dwellers have much chance of travelling. They knew that there were regional gaps, but without travel and access to television, it was hard for them to imagine how serious regional inequality really was. Quite possibly, perceived regional gaps were smaller than objective ones during the pre-reform years... No longer comparing their localities to neighbouring communities, people may now use what they know of the most advanced regions in the country as the benchmark for comparison. (Wang and Hu 1999:69, 73)

The difference in attitude has been caused by access to media and, more importantly, the freedom – in practice, if not fully in law – to migrate. By the early 1980s there were around 2 million rural migrants, but by the mid 1990s the figure had risen to around 80 million (Lei 2003:618). In the countryside this has led to enormous pressures as the young in particular are drawn to the cities. In part they are pulled by the possibilities of different experiences, new skills and higher incomes. In part they are pushed by the rural economic crisis generated by market Stalinism, in which peasants have high and rising production costs but low and falling sales prices; many of the young are consequently surplus in the sense that their families can no longer afford to keep them. The resulting fault line runs throughout Chinese society. Within the family itself it threatens the collectivist approach to inter-generational division of income which both preceded and continued under the Stalinist regime. Hitherto children had contributed to the familial income according to their abilities and this had been redistributed throughout the family. But with the flight to the cities many children no longer feel the need to assist their siblings who earn less or are simply unable to afford to contribute to the family income because of their own requirements. The regime remains unwilling to encourage permanent urban settlement although it is prepared tacitly to encourage temporary migration as long as conditions are made so bad that workers are unwilling to consider relocating. This seems to correspond to the wishes of many – particularly the less well-educated – of the migrants themselves, the majority of whom retain some links with the countryside and wish to return there someday. On the other hand, the employers of migrant labour are unwilling to train workers only to see them leave and have to be replaced by a new wave of the unskilled (Danyu 2000:181–2, 191–4; Knight et al. 1999:87–99).

It was estimated that in the mid-1990s there were over 70 million farmers 'floating' in cities throughout China. These *hukow* are not permitted household registration and are consequently excluded from access to free education, subsidised housing or pensions. 'Rural to urban migrants could only find housing in the flourishing private-rental sector and it is not unusual to find several rural migrants crowded into one room in the suburban areas of large cities' (Wang and Murie 2000:406). The floating population does not simply apply pressure on the urban infrastructure:

Further spatially detached from their home villages, rural migrants could no longer be directly reached by the rural authority in their places of origin. But at the same time, migrants, considered outsiders by local officials, were not effectively brought within the local control system. (Li 2001:27)

And the comparisons which they draw with their rural situation are exactly those which the regime struggled to deny them the opportunity to make:

The peasants and semi-peasants who winter in the city feel comparatively deprived by the tightly locked city walls. Peasants coming in want to enjoy this fat meat with city people. When in the countryside, they feel that everyone is poor, so [their poverty] can be tolerated. But differences in wealth become obvious after entering the city. (Solinger 1999:247)

Unevenness therefore possesses its own potential for social unrest. But it is the experience of the cities in particular, where we see the particular form taken by *combination*. In 1949 there were only 6 cities with more than 1 million inhabitants; by 2000 there were

23. Yet the greatest growth in both population size and levels of urbanisation has come in the last 20 years: between 1949 and 1978 the number of cities of all sizes only grew from 135 to 192, but by 2000 there were nearly 400 (Hutchings 2000:339–43). There were no cities in the south-western province of Yunnan in 1949 and the urban population was only 5 per cent of the provincial total. By 1989 there were 4 cities with an urban population of 12 per cent, and by 1999 there were 15 cities with an urban population of 45 per cent. In 1994 the urban section of Xuanwei County comprised no more than 7 square kilometres; by 1999 it had nearly doubled to 13 square kilometres. While 'the growing urban population and expanded business activities put increasingly high demands on public sanitation and energy supply' it also led to an increased demand for educational provision which was extracted from the peasants of the rural hinterland through the levy of an 'educational surcharge' to pay for what, in China as in Britain, is referred to as 'modernisation' (Xiaolin 2001:111, 112–13, 117–18, 119–20).

Behind the statistics it is the experience of the city, particularly for the recent rural migrant, which offers new forms of consciousness and perception. Rowe has written of the 'strange new world' effect experienced by migrants to the cities:

...many if not most have practically no prior urban experience, given the persistence and strong enforcement of China's household registration system. Although the effect of this sudden change of living environment is also difficult to gauge fully, it will surely be palpable in the future majority's perception and appreciation of life and the manner in which they lay claim to issues on the national agenda. It was often said of Shanghai during its heyday in the 1930s that it was like no other place in China. The effect of this 'otherworldliness' now seems likely to spread both widely and rapidly and, when it becomes more fully familiar, the impact on Chinese society will likely be considerable. (Rowe 2001:289)

But the city is not only a postmodern wonderland of sensory overload: for the majority of urban Chinese, it is a site of intense social struggle. Neoliberalism has brought with it the inevitable increase in sectional unemployment. The official rate in 1997 was 6 million or 3.2 per cent of the urban labour force, although most sources regard this as a massive underestimate. From 1998 to 2000 21 million workers in state-owned enterprises (SOEs) were sacked, although the regime claims that 13 million of these have since found other jobs. If we add to it perhaps 15 million workers not formally sacked but 'stood down' or suspended from their jobs and the 'floating' population, the true level of unemployment may be nearer 20 per cent or 150 million people (Henderson 1999:39; Cook and Maurer-Fazio 1999:1; Lau 2001:241).

Even those who are still in work are faced with attacks on their living conditions while they see vast and ostentatious displays of wealth by the 'little princes and princesses', the offspring of the bureaucracy and – increasingly – the bourgeoisie proper:

Today one senses the presence of the new rich throughout the coastal region and larger cities. One not only notes the prevalence of luxury vehicles, four and five star hotels, golf course, exclusive gyms and clubs, but in many places (such as Shanghai) there are even posh housing complexes that rival the residences of top government officials, surrounded by forbidding gates and separated from ordinary society ...this middle class makes up less than 1 per cent of the population, but controls at least half of the gross national income. (Wang 2003:591)

The balance of employment is shifting from the state sector to that of new private capital. Between 1995 and 1997 the number of workers in the industrial state sectors fell by 4 million and those in the private sector rose by 10 million. The latter figure clearly does not merely represent transfers from one sector to the other but involves the proletarianisation of new generations of workers. As Henderson writes, 'The benefits of the iron rice bowl were psychological as much as they were real.' For 100 million state workers, 'the smashing of the iron rice bowl is a deeply traumatic message, as well as representing a threat to their financial well-being':

Difficult working conditions which were taken for granted in the past when Chinese society was in fact relatively egalitarian (in its misery if nothing else!), are now less tolerated in a time when the official mantra is 'to get rich is glorious'. The perception of widening income gaps reminds the 'proletariat' first and foremost of their stifling working conditions on the factory floor, where advantage is gained by whom one knows rather than what. (Henderson 1999:258, 50, 47)

The differences between workers in the SOEs and those set up by foreign private capitalists are extreme. And it is not only in terms of wages that the divisions are enormous. Workers in the Reebok factories are expected to work an average of 86 hours a month compulsory overtime. They receive no compensation for dismissal and are 'represented' by business unions whose officials are appointed by the factory management. The workforces are almost exclusively female because of the assumption that they will be more docile than ones that are male (China Labour Watch 2002).

TOWARDS THE NEXT CHINESE REVOLUTION?

The resistance to restructuring has been spectacular. Between 1992 and 1997 an estimated 1.26 million workers were involved in disputes with the figure rising to 3.6 million in 1998 alone (Feng 2003:239). In one centre for foreign capitalists, Xiamen, incomplete strike figures show that there were 50 disputes in 1991, rising to 450 by 1993 (Solinger 1999:284). Yet it was only in spring of 2002 that what Leung calls the 'third wave' of post-Mao labour movements began to emerge. The first coalesced around the Worker's Autonomous Federations which were set up during the democracy movement of 1989, initially to support the students, who were also allowed to join. After Tiananmen Square and the repression (in which working-class spokesmen for the movement were treated with particular brutality), the second movement took shape between 1990 and 1994 as a series of mostly short-lived underground organisations, like the League for the Rights of the Working Peoples, which were often led by intellectuals and not necessarily involved with the actual, but inchoate struggles taking place against liberalisation. Nevertheless, these were focussed on particular issues of concern to the working class, rather than democracy in general. The third wave emerged in the north-west of China in the provinces of Daqing and Liaoyang, where between 80,000 and 100,000 workers, mainly from the oil and metal industries, were involved in strikes, occupations, demonstrations and road blockades against retrenchment, the absence of social security and official corruption. The name of one organisation, The Daqing Provisional Union of Retrenched Workers, gives some idea of the defensive nature of the movement. Nevertheless, the demands made by workers show an opposition to the bureaucracy which is based on its failure to be sufficiently socialist and supportive of the working class. As Leung writes:

The 2002 spring protests are still a far cry from mass strikes waged by hundreds of thousands of dock and railway workers in Canton, Shanghai and Beijing in the 1920s and 1930s, which delivered the first Chinese labour movement. But these early labour struggles of the 20th century were primarily nationalist struggles. The 21st century labour movement takes shape as a defensive and class-specific struggle. In their struggle for the rights to defend their work and livelihoods in the face of privatization and globalization, the Chinese labour movement has at last found common ground with the democratic labour movements around the world. (Leung 2003)

It would not be the first time in history that an attack on established terms and conditions of skilled workers has detonated a more general struggle, spreading out beyond the groups initially involved. The most immediate comparison here is the generalised assault on skilled metalworkers across Europe during the First World War (Gluckstein 1985:51–5; Wrigley 1993:5–7, 15–16). What will be crucial in China is the link between threatened and displaced workers from the SOEs and the new workers in the foreign and privately owned enterprises, and beyond them, with the vast incendiary countryside (Yang 2005). As one reformist intellectual, Li Minqi, said in a recent round table discussion:

The situation will be different [from 1989] in years to come. For the first time in Chinese history the modern working class will soon make up a majority of the population. This is going to make a decisive contribution to the victory of democracy in the future... In the West, the historic strength of the labour movement forced the bourgeoisie to make major concessions to the working class, including political democracy and the welfare state. ... But in the case of China, where capitalism depends so much on the abundance of cheap labour, is there any comparable room for the Chinese bourgeoisie to make similar concessions – to grant political democracy or social welfare – and at the same time maintain competitiveness in the world market and a rapid rate of accumulation? It seems rather questionable. (Wang et al. 2003:321–2)

As Li suggests, the so-called 'Fourth Generation' leaders [i.e. since the Revolution of 1949] have no intention of moving towards bourgeois democracy:

They want to soften authoritarian rule, make it more responsive, and use the media and some political institutions, such as elections and courts, as tools to discipline the lower bureaucracy. But they think their society is too complex and turbulent to be truly governable by a truly open, competitive form of democracy. (Nathan and Gilley 2002:235)

Leaving aside appearances, the current discontent has been met by ferocious levels of repression. An internal investigation report on Lu Gan, the Politburo member responsible for law and order, notes that more than 60,000 people were either executed or killed by the police between 1998 and 2001 – an unsurprising result given that China currently has 68 capital offences on the statute book including 'bribery, pimping, selling harmful foodstuffs and stealing gasoline'. If these figures are correct – and they are far higher than the Amnesty International estimates – then in 2002 the Chinese state was responsible for approximately 97 per cent of all executions committed in the world (Nathan and Gilley 2002:191–2). This is slaughter on a truly eighteenth-century British scale, what Linebaugh once called 'capital punishment as the punishment of capital'. Despite hypocritical protestations from Western governments and media, they – epitomised by Rupert Murdoch in this respect as in many others – have no real objection to the repression:

They need the authoritarian rule of the Party to safeguard their billions of dollars of investments, and for this reason are prepared to shut their eyes to any number of crimes it may commit against its own people, first delinking human-rights violations from trade and now keeping silent about the numerous bans on critical works and the suppression of the Fa Lun Gong. (Yang 2005:139)

In fact the CCP today plays a similar role to that previously played by the Russian Tsar or the Chinese Emperor as bearers of pure parental authority, no matter what the crimes and corruptions of its representatives in the factory:

Despite widespread corruption, among both SOE leaders and government officials, and notwithstanding the victimisation of workers in the state's drive towards reforms, one should not underestimate the extent to which the populace in general, and workers in particular, remain attached to the CCP in the absence of an alternative. (Lau 2001:240)

Feng has argued that there are parallels here with the moral economy displayed by eighteenth-century British crowds in protecting traditions or established practices and norms in the face of encroaching market relations (Feng 2003:256–7).

It is in response to this that we can see aspects of the downside of uneven and combined development, the 'debasing of achievements' of which Trotsky spoke in the *History of the Russian Revolution* (Trotsky 1977:27). In particular, the resumption of the process has left social movements in China at an ideological level below that of the 1920s. Given the way in which the exploitation of the Chinese workers and peasants has been carried out under the banner of Marxism, it is unsurprising that historical materialism has not instantly become the theoretical guide to forces seeking to challenge the regime. Instead many have turned to religion. 'The desire for a better life has also seen a religious revival in the country, and for most Chinese the desire for property and material things is complemented by an appeal to the supernatural for aid in that quest' (Guldin 2001:189). For a large minority this had led to support for the Fa Lun Gong, certainly the best known of Chinese religious movements, but it is not alone.

Balong is a hamlet of 90 households in the village of Landu in the – to Western ears – evocatively named county of Shangri-La. The population were originally Muslims, but increasing religious repression after 1949, climaxing during the Cultural Revolution, led to a situation where virtually no one even recalled what their belief system had involved, except for the prohibition on eating pork. However, during the period of market reforms the hamlet experienced a resurgence of Islamic belief:

Balong's story is not atypical in contemporary China. Across the country there is an increasing number of examples of rural communities that are inventing a heritage, be it through religion or lineage, to promote group identity, rebuild solidarity and safeguard the interests of the community. (Hillman 2004:73)

Or take Sipsongpanna, the south-western border region of Yunnan, where 'hills have been levelled to make way for new roads, power lines have replaced the canopy of the rain forest, and new migrants from the coast are building cities in place of villages'. The Buddhist religion practised by the Tai population has been repressed since 1953, but has recently experienced a revival as monks operating across the national borders of Thailand, Laos, Burma and China have attempted to revive the classical Tai 'though today they carry it not on palm leaves but on floppy disks, videos and CDs'. As Davis says: 'Thus we should attend not just to the video itself but to the person who carries the video, who puts it in the machine and presses "play", who explains the images that appear in terms a village teenager can understand' (Davis 1997:177, 199). Religion represents a consolation or defence against the intrusion of capitalist modernity, but religion is also communicated and celebrated using the techniques and technologies that capitalist modernity has provided. State repression of religion may in time drive its adherents to more secular ideologies of resistance, but the possibility is made more likely by the spectacular levels of resistance to neoliberal restructuring that is already taking place.

Rosen has argued that 'as the economy continues to grow at a reasonably high rate, the state and society is not likely to produce an unmanageable crisis for the regime in the near term' (2004:51). But this assumes that a crisis will only emerge as the result of economic downturn. However, this survey suggests that it is the very success of the Chinese economy which has produced the internal strains and tensions which threaten to explode. From Tocqueville on, serious students and practitioners of revolution, of whom Trotsky himself was perhaps the most eminent, have argued that revolutions are more likely to occur when social classes see the possibility of improving conditions, rather than when they are in the depths of economic depression or the grip of political repression (Tocqueville 1966:196; Trotsky 1974a:82). In China, conditions for many have improved, and repression is not consistently applied. At Nanchong in Sechuan province 20,000 workers besieged the town hall for 30 hours demanding unpaid wages until officials were forced to organise loans and partial back payments (Henderson 1999:53). As one commentator has noted:

Workers may soon begin to demand more of the benefits that market globalization is bringing to some Chinese. Like workers elsewhere, Chinese labourers may not be satisfied with the line that their wages and benefits must be kept low so as to maintain Chinese 'competitiveness' in a global market. In Sekou we saw a rise in worker solidarity as factory labourers described workmates as their closest friends, even across regional and linguistic lines. If these feelings become more widespread, they may give workers the social cohesion to challenge the state and system more forthrightly. (Guldin 2001:269–70)

The competitive struggle within the world system led the Chinese ruling class to unleash social forces which for 30 years they had, more or less successfully, prevented from forming. To say, therefore, that China is entering a revolutionary situation, is not to utter a truism about the general objective readiness of the world for socialist revolution, it is to say that quite specific conditions are pushing China in that direction. Although China develops more dramatically than any of the countries, like India, with which it is usually bracketed, it is unlikely on any remotely foreseeable scenario, to 'catch up' with the West in any overall sense. The tensions which uneven and combined development have brought therefore remain, awaiting release. It may be, therefore, that China does indeed show us the future, but not in the way that those who look to it to save the world capitalist system quite imagine.

REFERENCES

Bhalla, A. S. (1995) *Uneven Development in the Third World: a Study of China and India*, 2nd revised edn. (London: Macmillan).

Chesneaux, J. (1968) *The Chinese Labor Movement, 1919–1927* (Stanford: Stanford University Press).

China Labour Watch (2002) 'Reebok Human Rights Standard and Chinese Workers' Working Conditions', <http://www.chinalaborwatch.org/index.htm?http://www.chinalaborwatch.org/reports/reebok.htm>.

Cook, S. and Maurer-Fazio, M. (1999) 'Introduction', *Journal of Development Studies*, 35/3, special issue, *The Worker's State Meets the Market: Labour in China's Transition*.

Danyu, W. (2000) 'Stepping on Two Boats: Urban Strategies of Chinese Peasants and Their Children', *International Review of Social History*, 45, supplement 8, *Household Strategies for Survival 1600–2000: Fission, Faction and Cooperation*, edited by L. Fontaine and J. Schlumbohm.

Davidson, N. (2006) 'From Uneven to Combined Development', this volume.

Davis, D. (1997) 'Social Transformations of Metropolitan China Since 1949', in J. Gugler (ed.) *Cities in the Developing World: Issues, Theory and Policy* (Oxford: Oxford University Press).

Feng, C. (2003) 'Industry, Restructuring and Workers' Resistance in China', *Modern China*, 29/2.

Gittings, J. (1997) *Real China: From Cannibalism to Karaoke* (London: Simon & Schuster).

Gluckstein, D. (1985) *The Western Soviets: Workers' Councils Versus Parliament, 1915–20* (London: Bookmarks).

Glyn, A. (2005) 'Global Imbalances', *New Left Review*, 1/34 (July–August).

Guldin, G. (2001) *What's a Peasant to Do? Village Becoming Town in Southern China* (Boulder: Westview Press).

Harvey, D. (2005) *A Short History of Neoliberalism* (Oxford: Oxford University Press).

Henderson, C. (1999) *China on the Brink* (New York: McGraw-Hill).

Hillman, B. (2004) 'The Rise of the Community in Rural China: Village Politics, Cultural Identity and Religious Revival in a Hui Village', *China Journal*, 51.

Hutchings, G. (2000) *Modern China* (Harmondsworth: Penguin Books).

Isaacs, H. (1961 [1938]) *The Tragedy of the Chinese Revolution*, 2nd revised edn. (Stanford: Stanford University Press).

Knight, J., Lina, S. and Jia, H. (1999) 'Chinese Rural Migrants in Urban Enterprises: Three Perspectives', *Journal of Development Studies*, 35/3, special issue, *The Worker's State Meets the Market: Labour in China's Transition*.

Lau, R. (2001) 'Economic Determination in the Last Instance: China's Political–Economic Development under the Impact of the Asian Financial Crisis', *Historical Materialism*, 8.

Lei, G. (2003) 'Rural Taste, Urban Fashions: the Cultural Politics of Rural/Urban Difference in Contemporary China', *Positions*, 11/3, special issue, *Intellectuals and Social Movements*, part 1.

Leung, T. (2003) 'The Third Wave of the Chinese Labour Movement in the Post-Mao Era', <http://www.hartford-hwp.com/archives/55/297.html>.

Li, Z. (2001) *Strangers in the City: Reconfigurations of Space, Power and Social Networks Within China's Floating Population* (Stanford: Stanford University Press).

Nathan, A. and B. Gilley (eds) (2002) *China's New Rulers* (London: Granta).

Pye, L. (1981) 'Foreword', in C. Howe (ed.) *Shanghai: Revolution and Development in an Asian Metropolis* (Cambridge: Cambridge University Press).

Rosen, S. (2004) 'The Victory of Materialism: Aspirations to Join China's Urban Moneyed Classes and the Commercialisation of Education', *China Journal*, 51.

Rowe, P. (2001) 'Conclusion', in Lu Junhua, P. G. Rowe and Zanf Jie (eds) *Modern Urban Housing in China, 1840–2000* (Munich, London and New York: Prestel).

Selden, M. (1985) 'State, Market and Sectoral Inequality in Contemporary China', in P. Evans, D. Rueschemeyer and E. H. Stephens (eds) *States Versus Markets in the World System* (Beverley Hills: Sage).

Silver, B. (2003) *Forces of Labour: Workers' Movements and Globalisation Since 1870* (Cambridge: Cambridge University Press).

Solinger, D. (1999) *Contesting Citizenship in Urban China: Peasant Migrants, the State, and the Logic of the Market* (Berkeley: University of California Press).

Stroud, D. (2000) '"A High Place is No Better than a Low Place": the City in the Making of Modern China', in Wen-Hsin Yeh (ed.) *Becoming Chinese: Passages to Modernity and Beyond* (Berkeley: University of California Press).

Tocqueville, A. de (1966 [1856]) *The Ancien Regime and the French Revolution* (London: Fontana).

Trotsky, L. (1974a [1921]) 'Flood-Tide', in *The First Five Years of the Communist International*, ii (London: New Park Publications).

—— (1974b [1928]) 'The Draft Programme of the Communist International: A Criticism of Fundamentals', in *The Third International after Lenin* (London: New Park Publications).

—— (1977 [1931–33]) *The History of the Russian Revolution* (London: Pluto Press).

United Nations Development Programme (1999) *China Human Development Report 1999: Transition and the State* (Oxford: Oxford University Press).

—— (2003) *Human Development Report 2003: Millennium Development Goals Among Nations to End Poverty* (New York: Oxford University Press).

Wang, D., Li, M. and Wang, C. (2003) 'A Dialogue on the Future of China', in C. Wang (ed.) *One China, Many Paths* (London and New York: Verso).

Wang, S. and Hu, A. (1999) *The Political Economy of Uneven Development: The Case of China* (New York).

Wang, X. (2003) 'China on the Brink of a "Momentous Era"', *Positions*, 11/3, special issue, *Intellectuals and Social Movements*, part 1.

Wang, Y. P. and Murie, A. (2000) 'Social and Spatial Implications of Housing Reform in China', *International Journal of Urban and Regional Research*, 24/2.

Watts, J. (2003) 'Boom City Struggles to Cope as Millions Move in', *Guardian*, 6 December.

Wong, R. B. (1997) *China Transformed: Historical Change and the Limits of the European Experience* (New York: Cornell University).

Wrigley, C. (1993) 'Introduction', in C. Wrigley (ed.) *Challenges of Labour: Western and Central Europe, 1917–20* (London: Routledge).

Xiaolin, G. (2001) '"Its All a Matter of Hats": Rural Urbanisation in South-West China', *Journal of Peasant Studies*, 29/1.

Yang L. (2005) 'Dark Side of the Chinese Moon', *New Left Review*, 1/32 (March/April).

Yusif, S. and Weiping, W. (2002) 'Pathways to a Global City: Shanghai Rising in an Era of Globalisation', *Urban Studies*, 39/7.

17
Explaining Uneven and Combined Development in South Africa

Patrick Bond and Ashwin Desai

In *Results and Prospects*, Leon Trotsky's notion of permanent revolution represented a profound critique of the Russian bourgeoisie, based on scepticism that genuine democracy and the land question would be solved through their leadership. How well does the argument travel to South Africa a century later, at a time of a marked void in political–economic reasoning by socialists? The theory underlying the permanent revolution, namely uneven and combined development, is entirely appropriate for South Africa. Here, a mix of market and non-market coercion permitted a permanent system of racialised, gendered primitive accumulation to emerge at the very moment Trotsky was analysing Russian social relations. Does a revival of his broader theory and a comparison with a half-century of flawed neo-Marxist intellectual approaches assist in clarifying the character of accumulation and class formation in South Africa? Does it help vanquish both the 'two economies' argument advanced in the African National Congress and the stageist theory so popular in the official centre-left? This chapter makes a preliminary case in the affirmative, without yet attempting to set out the logical political conclusions.

According to George Novack, 'The law of uneven and combined development is a general law of the historical process of which the theory of permanent revolution is a particular expression limited to the period of transition from the capitalist system to socialism' (1970:147). That transition is decades away in South Africa, leaving us with at least the present task of analytical review, for which we will rely extensively on insights associated with uneven and combined development. Even today, the idea of uneven and combined development is still far too risqué for polite political discussion, so instead, South Africans have become distracted by banal notions of 'two economies'.

UNEVEN DEVELOPMENT AND CAPITALIST CRISIS[1]

The intellectual problems associated with these theoretical meanderings compel us to return to root processes. Thus in *Capital*, Marx (1967) cited unevenness as intrinsic to capitalism. But thinking in this manner dates further back, at least to the *Grundrisse* (1857–58), where unevenness represents the condition for a transition from one declining mode of production to another rising, more progressive mode. In the same spirit, Trotsky wrote of countries and institutions as units of analysis in the tracts *Permanent Revolution* and *Results and Prospects*. In Colin Barker's interpretation:

The role of the 'whip of external necessity' in compelling countries to attempt to adopt and assimilate elements of technique, organisation and ideas drawn from their more advanced rivals, and the contradictions of the 'combinations' thus effected, would seem to play a real causal part. (2005)

More generally, though, the concept of uneven development has been deployed to explain more than transitions in modes of production and countries' economic activity. In addition, unevenness applies to the differential growth of sectors, geographical processes, classes and regions at the global, regional, national, sub-national and local levels.

Moreover, the phenomenon of uneven and combined development in specific (peripheral or semi-peripheral) settings was often explained – as in the South African case – as a process of 'articulations of modes of production'. In these analyses, the capitalist mode of production depended upon earlier modes of production for an additional 'super-exploitative' subsidy by virtue of reducing the costs of labour power's reproduction, even if this did not represent a revolutionary or even transitional moment. Evidence for the process of South African apartheid-era super-exploitation – based upon simultaneous class/race/gender/ecological power – is offered below, and represents the crucial *ongoing* (not just initial) role of 'primitive accumulation' within uneven development (see Perelman 2000; Werlhof 2000; Zarembka 2000, 2002). Smith insists, in this respect, that 'it is the logic of uneven development which structures the context for this articulation' of modes of production, rather than the reverse (Smith 1990:123).

1. Partially excerpted from Bond (1999).

Uneven development is, ultimately, 'the geographical contradiction between development and underdevelopment where the overaccumulation of capital at one pole is matched by the overaccumulation of labour at the other', as Smith (1990:148) put it. The condition of over-accumulation crisis heightens the more general process of uneven development caused, in Smith's conception, by

continual, if never permanent, resolution of opposing tendencies toward the geographical equalisation and differentiation of the conditions and levels of production. The search for a spatial fix is continually frustrated, never realised, creating distinct patterns of geographical unevenness through the continued seesaw of capital. (Smith 1989:151)[2]

The search for a temporal fix, likewise, is continually frustrated because although over-accumulation today can be mitigated by credit, this simply puts off the problem until payment is due at some future date, when surplus value must again be extracted. Tendencies towards sectoral unevenness are manifest periodically in financial crisis, when the intrinsic limits of a credit system or speculative market are reached. Uneven development can thus play the roles of both immediate cause and amplified effect of financial turbulence.

These concepts – unevenness as intrinsic to capital accumulation, capitalist crisis tendencies, partial spatial and temporal fixes, amplification of unevenness through the financial system, and 'combined' development in the form of accumulation by dispossession, in a variety of racial, gendered and environmental manifestations – are all vital tools for re-establishing political economic argumentation in South Africa. Because slavery, colonialism, apartheid and their residues evolved within a national state (with crucial regional spillovers), South Africa offers a crucial example of the systematised combination of market and non-market systems of exploitation.

EARLY FORMULATIONS OF UNEVEN DEVELOPMENT

Although, beginning in the 1930s, Johannesburg and Cape Town activist intellectuals established a long tradition of debating the

2. According to available empirical evidence, Smith's 'see-saw' operates very clearly at the urban scale, somewhat actively within sub-national regions, and not yet self-evidently at the global scale, but this is not to say the theory is wrong, simply that it is too early in the cycles of global capitalist expansions and contractions to validate or invalidate the global see-saw effect.

merits of permanent revolution – contrasted to the stageist theory of the Communist Party – it is striking that the many variants of Trotskyist organising never boasted a major analytical statement that advanced our knowledge of uneven development as an interrelated class, racial, gendered, ecological, geographical and geopolitical process.[3] Combining two strands of argument – pro-land reform and democratisation with anti-imperialism – Moshe Noah Averbach, provided a unified *description* (if not theory) of South African social relations in 1936 (Averbach 1993). Meanwhile, amongst urban black African workers, intellectual and political figures, there were exceptional speakers in the revolutionary tradition – e.g., C.B.I. Dladla, Dan Koza, Isaac Bongani Tabata, T.W. Thibedi – whose arguments have only sporadically been recorded, but which contributed to powerful critiques of the Stalinist strategy. However, rather than dwell upon analysis, Trotskyists used their energies to organise and forge links with labour movements in the major centres and establish small political parties, though this work ebbed and flowed depending upon the cycles of repression and nationalist hegemony over the broader progressive movement.

In the void of political economy that resulted, new generations of radical South African scholars applied at least six different branches of Marxian analysis: from 'colonialism-of-a-special-type' theory during the 1960s; to the articulations of 'modes-of-production' argument during the early 1970s; to neo-Poulantzian 'fractions-of-capital' analysis during the late 1970s; to the concept of 'racial capitalism' during the early 1980s; to the social history school of the 1980s; to French regulation theory (and 'racial Fordism') during the late 1980s (for a review see Bond 2000). What is most remarkable about this search for theoretical explanation of race and class, the trajectory of political economy, the macro–micro relations and gender (see O'Meara 1996), among other themes, is that at the point such theory may have been most useful to those engaged in everyday struggle against capitalism during the rise of neoliberalism, it evaporated. The theoretical exercises were, perhaps, so flawed in parts that it became distinctly unfashionable to theorise about political economy. As Fine and Rustomjee cautioned:

3. See the special issue of the journal *Revolutionary History* entitled *Colour and Class: The Origins of South African Trotskyism*, 4, 4, Spring 1993 and the invaluable work of Allison Drew (1996).

The relationship between abstract theory and empirical application is not unique to the study of South Africa. But the virulent form taken by its racism within the bounds of a predominantly capitalist economy has cast considerable doubt on the simple expedient of examining South Africa's development in terms of hypotheses derived from ready-made analytical frameworks. (1996:21)

FROM NEO-MARXISM TO MODERNISATION TO UNEVEN DEVELOPMENT?

Bearing this warning in mind, and in spite of repeated false starts since the 1960s, the analytical frameworks of Trotsky and others who during the 1930s identified the laws of uneven and combined development in South Africa can be re-evaluated in a post-apartheid context. After all, national accumulation processes have, as Trotsky said, nearly universally relied upon 'a combining of separate steps, an amalgam of archaic with more contemporary forms' (1977:27). Today, we are again seeing the interrelationships between processes of sustained inequality in the context of persistent over-accumulation of capital (and unemployed labour) and rising financial volatility, with devastating consequences for low-income people, especially women.

To illustrate the persistence of economic crisis, three currency crashes were witnessed in South Africa during brief periods in February–March 1996, June–July 1998 and December 2001, ranging from 30 to 50 per cent. Each led to massive interest-rate increases, which sapped growth and rewarded speculators. The 2000–04 currency swing was brutal on the way down, and up, as the rand/US$ exchange rate fell from 6 at the beginning to 13.85 in the trough, back to above 6 in mid-2004.[4] Nominal interest rate increases during 2000 were the cause of a great deal of pain, but the over-correction pushed the rand to such heights that the first post-apartheid trade deficit emerged in the first half of 2004 as many South African products became uncompetitive on world markets and imports flooded in to displace local goods. In real (inflation-adjusted) terms, the real prime rate had risen in leaps and bounds from −7 per cent in 1986 to 6 per cent in mid-1994 to 15 per cent in 1998 before stabilising at around 8 per cent in subsequent years – still the highest in modern South African history taken over a decade as a whole.

4. The complex story of the crash, especially over the last three months of 2001, is told in the Afterword to Bond (2003).

Meanwhile, the drivers of capital accumulation were based less upon real 'productive' activity, and increasingly within financial/ speculative functions that are potentially unsustainable and even parasitical. The contribution of manufacturing to GDP fell from 21.2 per cent in 1994 to 18.8 per cent in 2002, while 'financial intermediation' (including insurance and real estate) rose from 16.4 per cent of GDP in 1994 to 19.5 per cent in 2002. Real estate speculation led to housing price increases over the period 1997–2004 of 200 per cent, far higher than other major economies (Ireland was next at 170 per cent with the United States at 60 per cent), according to the International Monetary Fund (IMF 2005). Over-accumulation of capital is evident in the lack of new domestic fixed investment over the past decade, which hovered between 15 and 17 per cent of GDP, far lower than the 1960s (17–25 per cent), the 1970s (25–30 per cent), and even the 1980s (18–25 per cent). The rate at which South African manufacturing plant and equipment were utilised dropped steadily from the early 1980s gold-boom peak of 86 per cent to the late 1990s, when the trough was 79 per cent, followed by a comparatively weak cyclical upturn from 1999 to 2002 (UNDP 2003:Appendix 12).

The capital strike was based upon systemic overproduction for the limited local market, not upon worker militancy. Labour productivity increased steadily after 1994, with productivity increases far outpacing wages after 1998. The real unit cost of post-apartheid labour dropped at around 2 per cent per year (with the exception of 1998) (UNDP 2003:Appendix 12). The number of days lost to strike action fell, the latter in part because of ANC demobilisation of unions and general hostility to national stay-aways for political purposes (e.g. the labour movement's mild-mannered national anti-privatisation strikes) (Altman 2003:174–5).

The results of the system's continuities, not change, are witnessed in resurgent corporate profitability associated with successful crisis displacement. (The basis for crisis – over-accumulation – was not resolved, but corporations used various techniques of crisis displacement to pass the costs elsewhere.) South Africa's pre-tax profit share recovered during the late 1990s to 1960s-era levels associated with apartheid's heyday. From a low of 43 per cent in 1990 and 44 per cent in 1995, the profit share of national income rose to 49 per cent in 2002. Manufacturing profits were relatively weak during the late 1990s, so the most important post-apartheid profit dividends were taken in the two categories of 'commerce' (wholesale and retail trade, catering and accommodation) and 'finance, insurance and real estate' (Nattrass 2003:148).

Meanwhile, most of the largest local companies – Anglo American, DeBeers, Old Mutual, South African Breweries, Didata, Mondi (preceded by Liberty Life and Gencor) – were given permission to delist from the Johannesburg Stock Exchange or relist their primary stock-market residence as London or New York during the late 1990s. Ironically, to encourage businesses to invest, Pretoria had cut primary corporate taxes dramatically (from 48 per cent in 1994 to 30 per cent in 1999, although a dividends tax was added); the 'supply-side' effort was notably unsuccessful. In the first ten years of liberation, Pretoria also offered tax concessions worth R75 billion, mainly to higher-income individual South Africans (offsetting by many times a new capital gains tax). The regressive, controversial Value Added Tax (VAT) – which had catalysed a massive 1991 strike – was also retained in the post-apartheid era, and revenues increased from a value equal to 5.8 per cent of GDP in 2001/02 to 7 per cent of GDP in 2005. Since total tax revenue rose by just 1 per cent of GDP during the early 2000s (from 23.7 per cent to 24.7 per cent), the entire relative increase in social spending was funded by VAT, a tax that hits the poor far harder than it hits the rich. Repeated popular demands for a tiered system to redress inequity in that tax or to zero-rate essential commodities were ignored.

Moreover, another important issue, too often overlooked, is the nature of state capital spending. While updated figures are hard to acquire, the trends from 1994/95 to 2002/03 are disturbing. Disaggregating the state's 'gross fixed investment' in 2002, only 33.4 per cent went to social infrastructure (schools, hospitals and administrative services), down from 38.7 per cent in 1995, while other economic infrastructure (roads, bridges, dams, electricity and water) dropped from 45.8 per cent to 44.1 per cent. In contrast, other 'economic services' – spending by business enterprises not included in the categories above – rose from 15.5 per cent to 22.5 per cent of the total.

Amplified unevenness is also evident in income inequality and poverty data, as when even the state agency Statistics SA confessed that what was amongst the world's worst Gini coefficients actually degenerated after 1994. According to an October 2002 report, in real terms, average black African household income fell 19 per cent from 1995 to 2000 (to the purchasing-power parity level of $3,714/year), while white household income was up 15 per cent (to $22,600/year).

Not just relative but absolute poverty intensified, as households earning less than $90 of real income increased from 20 per cent of the population in 1995 to 28 per cent in 2000. Across the racial divides, the poorest half of all South Africans earned just 9.7 per cent of national income in 2000, down from 11.4 per cent in 1995. The richest 20 per cent earned 65 per cent of all income (Statistics South Africa 2002a; *Business Day*, 22 November 2002).

As a final reflection on the ideological debates surrounding contemporary South African uneven and combined development, these kinds of statistics have been either denied by government officials who claim an offset from the social wage, or explained as the result of 'two economies'. Even President Thabo Mbeki – once a star student of the Lenin Institute in Moscow – divides the South African economy into First World and Third World components. The former

is the modern industrial, mining, agricultural, financial, and services sector of our economy that, everyday, become ever more integrated in the global economy. Many of the major interventions made by our government over the years have sought to address this 'first world economy', to ensure that it develops in the right direction, at the right pace. It is clear that this sector of our economy has responded and continues to respond very well to all these interventions. This is very important because it is this sector of our economy that produces the wealth we need to address the many challenges we face as a country... The successes we have scored with regard to the 'first world economy' also give us the possibility to attend to the problems posed by the 'third world economy', which exists side by side with the modern 'first world economy'... Of central and strategic importance is the fact that they are *structurally disconnected* from our country's 'first world economy'. Accordingly, the interventions we make with regard to this latter economy do not necessarily impact on these areas, the 'third world economy', in a beneficial manner. (Mbeki 2003, emphasis added)

This approach – so reminiscent of modernisation theory – had become the prevailing discourse in government circles by 2005. At times, the idea is presented as a radical divergence from classic neo-liberal or trickle-down economics in that it provides for substantial state intervention. The idea is that the first economy can get on with the business of following the global pattern of integration into the global economy, becoming increasingly capital intensive, with high technology and high skills, while 'the second economy must be targeted by government intervention directly' (Turok 2004:7). These interventions will provide and unlock resources for those stuck in the second economy and perhaps then eventually allow them to enter the first economy either as workers or entrepreneurs.

This two-economy thesis-as-solution has been challenged by researchers and academics. For Andries du Toit, the issue is not that there are 'not enough linkages' but the nature of those linkages, and the extent to which 'they serve either to empower poor people or simply to allow money to be squeezed out of them' (Du Toit 2004a:29–30). Du Toit's research in the Ceres valley, the heart of the Western Cape's wine and food production, illustrates the consequences of new global competitive pressures and the effects of being too well sutured into the first economy. Employers responded by restructuring the labour market to take advantage of a new precariousness which seems to be structured just as effectively as labour control during the apartheid system:

For many, this meant the restructuring of their businesses to reduce their exposure to the risks, costs and administrative burden of employing permanent labour… Temporary and seasonal workers were supplanting permanent workers, and large numbers of farmers…were opting to use third-party labour contractors. In addition, there was a significant move away from the provision of tied housing to farm workers. (Du Toit 2004b:994)

Du Toit argues that labourers on the farms of the Ceres valley

are not people trapped in a second economy, unconnected from the first economy. Farm workers in Ceres, far from being excluded, are thoroughly incorporated into the first economy. Their poverty is produced and created by the normal operations of the market in that economy. This should give us cause to think twice about the simplistic notion that all South Africa needs to end poverty is growth. What matters is the kind of growth and the kinds of power relationships that shape the terms of economic exchange. (Du Toit 2005)

Gill Hart adds another angle to the debate, arguing that Mbeki's shift should be seen as part of

an effort to contain the pressures emanating from the rise of oppositional movements protesting the inadequacies of service provision, the snail's pace of land redistribution, failures to provide anti-retrovirals, and the absence of secure jobs – as well as pressures from within the Alliance… The operative question, then is not whether the First/Second Economy is an accurate portrayal of reality, but rather how it is being constructed and deployed to do political – or perhaps more accurately, depoliticising work. What is significant about this discourse is the way it defines a segment of society that is superfluous to the 'modern' economy, and in need of paternal guidance...they are deserving of a modicum of social security, but on tightly disciplined and conditional terms. (Hart 2005)

The first/second economy thesis in its present incarnation marks a return to liberal modernisation theories of the 1960s. While income and resource transfers to the so-called second economy remain an important and fashionable debating point, at the heart of any discussion on poverty alleviation and at the forefront of most plans for it in South Africa still lies the creation of jobs in the 'first economy'. Falling tariffs on imported industrial machinery meant that the small degree of automation that occurred replaced hundreds of thousands of jobs, while many more tens of thousands in vulnerable industries were eliminated thanks to imported consumer goods from East Asia. During the 1990s, large employment declines occurred in mining (47 per cent), manufacturing (20 per cent), and even the public sector (10 per cent) (Nattrass 2003:142). The country's unemployment rate rose from 16 per cent in 1995 to 31.2 per cent in 2003 (Statistics South Africa 2001, 2003). Adding to that figure the category of 'frustrated job-seekers' (i.e. those who have given up looking for employment) brings the percentage of unemployed people to 42 per cent (rates for whites were 6.3 per cent and for black Africans 50.0 per cent, with women suffering more than 10 per cent higher unemployment than men).[5] The migrant labour system did not end with apartheid, so many of the same processes by which urban capital is subsidised in the reproduction of labour power continue, with only a slightly expanded social wage (a pension and child grant system now reaching into rural areas) providing an even greater social subsidy to employers.

By way of claiming the possibilities of a 'ladder' between the alleged first and second economies, Mbeki and his colleagues made extravagant claims that 2.1 million net new 'jobs' were created between 1994 and 2004. This illustrates some ingenious 'accounting':

Homemakers who help sustain themselves and their families out of backyard vegetable plots or who keep a few chickens are part of the new employed class.

5. A large proportion of these latter people are confined to former Bantustan homeland areas which are generally devoid of both employment opportunities and places to register willingness to work; hence to use the 'narrow' (31 per cent) unemployment rate instead of the broad rate (42 per cent) is to imply that the people who have given up their job search are content – instead of being unable to travel long distances to state offices to register their unemployed status.

In fact, that vast army of the barely hidden jobless who stand forlornly on street corners for hire or who sell coat hangers, rubbish bags or handful of sweets at traffic lights or railway stations in the hope of making a few rand all add to this two million jobs figure. According to the latest statistics, in September 2001, 367,000 workers earned nothing for their labour, while a further 718,000 were paid between R1 and R200 a month. (Bell 2004)

Another key area of disagreement, which flows as much from ideology as from spin-doctoring, is how to understand the informal economy as a provider of sustenance to the unemployed. Are people who sell sweets behind a table or who farm for subsistence even to be considered (self-)employed? There are those who argue that much of what is described as the informal economy consists of very poor and desperate people engaging in essentially survivalist strategies to eke out some sort of existence (NALEDI 2004:61).

Much of that survival strategy is associated with the ongoing reproduction of extremely inexpensive labour power. Colin Bundy made the point that '[d]espite the fact that race and class are the most frequently mentioned lines of inequality, and the urban/rural divide a major structuring factor, there is another basic, ubiquitous, and deeply entrenched vector of historic inequality – and it runs through race, class, and regional imbalances. It is gender' (1993:32–3). As Liesl Orr argues,

Gender issues and household dynamics are almost completely invisible within the current macroeconomic strategy, contributing to the on-going marginalization of women. While the Growth, Employment and Redistribution (GEAR) policy might be called 'gender blind', it is certainly not gender neutral. For example, GEAR calls for greater labour market flexibility in order to attract foreign investment and to improve competitiveness. The implications of this are that the most vulnerable workers (that is, women) will remain unprotected and discriminated against, and where jobs are created they will perpetuate poor working conditions. With greater labour market flexibility the position of women will actually worsen, since this implies decreased benefits (such as maternity benefits) and less working time and parental responsibilities...

Irregular and uncertain working hours have a particular impact for women with respect to safety and secure transport arrangements, and for mothers regarding childcare arrangements, childcare leave, and other household responsibilities. There are also problems with budgeting for household necessities when work is irregular. The fact that casual workers do not have access to benefits, such as maternity pay and leave and unemployment insurance, have a major impact on the impoverishment of women in particular. (2000:11, 12)

More generally, the status of women progressed unevenly after 1994. There were some improvements, especially in reproductive rights, albeit with low levels of access to abortion facilities. Women are certainly empowered through the Constitution and laws such as the Employment Equity Act, as well as institutions including the Gender Management System, the Office of the Status of Women, the Commission on Gender Equality and the Women's Budget Initiative. But substantive, not merely formal equality will require a major upsurge in women's struggles, given the enormous gap between state rhetoric and reality.[6]

Indeed, one of the most striking reflections of backsliding in spite of rhetorical advance was in women's pay. Barely increasing their share of total jobs during the late 1990s, women experienced a massive decline in relative pay, from 78 per cent of male wages in 1995 to just 66 per cent in 1999 (Statistics South Africa 2002b:147). Although subsequent data on gender inequity are mixed, the UNDP's *Human Development Report* does present disturbing information about durable poverty in households characterised as single-parent (6.7 million poor people) and couple-parent (8.5 million poor people):

Relative to the number of poor in each gender category, the proportions of poor males and poor females living in 'Couple with children' families are almost the same, but a significantly larger proportion of poor females live in poor 'Single parent' families (35.3%) compared to males in this category (24.9%). (UNDP 2003:42)

Aside from legalising reproductive rights, the most important post-apartheid gain for mainstreaming gender concerns was probably the women's budget. In February 2004, however, the *Mail and Guardian* newspaper reported:

When former MP Pregs Govender first proposed a gender-responsive budget a decade ago, she warned that without ongoing political commitment to this initiative, it would be wiped out as yet another 'public relations exercise'. Govender's prescience was spot on. Minister of finance Trevor Manuel's Budget speech on Wednesday – although it doesn't spell doomsday for women – spelt the death knell for a women's budget. (*Mail and Guardian*, 20 February 2004)

Finally, in mitigation of the claim that uneven and combined development are worsening, state officials typically claim that they are not pursuing neoliberal policies, as witnessed in the delivery of

6. See the special issue of *Agenda* (40, 1999), on citizenship.

'free basic services' such as water and electricity. But with roughly 1.5 million people disconnected each year because they don't pay their water bills, according to state sources (Muller 2004), and with even higher rates of electricity disconnection, even the state roll-out of basic services fits within the framework of uneven and combined development.

In sum, the contemporary hegemony of neoliberal economic philosophy in South Africa extends even into the realms of social policy, over which so many intense struggles were waged. That process has been quite long in the making, dating to international financial pressure during the mid-1980s, accompanied by the growth of domestic financial liquidity due to the over-accumulation problem, with speculative economic activity rising to unprecedented modern levels. To return to the theoretical processes reviewed at the outset, it is evident that contemporary uneven and combined development has re-emerged in part through classical over-accumulation crisis tendencies, amplified by the ascendance of financial activity. Given South Africa's particular class structure, periodic economic crises have been perhaps most baldly reflected in persistent overcapacity and overproduction of luxury manufactured goods for the white consumer market side by side with growing surpluses of unemployed black workers who suffer from inadequate consumption of basic-needs goods.

What is to be done? The seminal labour/community attempt to strategise a Keynesian-style programmatic reversal of this condition, the 1994 *Reconstruction and Development Programme*, was decisively defeated within the ANC government by 1996, and was replaced by a home-grown neoliberal structural adjustment programme. Instead of the mainly corporatist strategies adopted to date, resistance to uneven and combined development must come increasingly from 'decommodification' social struggles by grassroots social and labour movements, which most of the independent left is now devoting time and energy to advancing (Desai 2002). From the linkage of anti-capitalist organising campaigns for free water, electricity, land, housing anti-retroviral medicines, food, jobs, telecommunications, basic income grants and the like, there is already emerging the basis of a new programme of activism, which in turn might even generate the basis for a working people's political party at some point in the next decade.

REFERENCES

Altman, M. (2003) 'The State of Employment and Unemployment in South Africa', in J. Daniel, A. Habib and R. Southall (eds) *State of the Nation: South Africa 2003–04* (Pretoria: HSRC Press).

Averbach, M. N. (1993 [1936]) 'A Comment on Trotsky's Letter to South Africa', *Revolutionary History*, 4/4:131–3.

Barker, C. (2005) 'Ruminations on Combined and Uneven Development', unpublished paper, Manchester (November).

Bell, T. (2004) 'How "Non-Jobs" come to the Aid of Government Election Propaganda', *Sunday Independent*, 15 February.

Bond, P. (1999) 'Uneven Development,' in P. O'Hara (ed.) *Encyclopaedia of Political Economy* (London: Routledge).

—— (2000) 'From Reconstruction and Development to Neo-Liberal Modernization in South Africa', in H. Othman (ed.) *Reflections on Leadership in Africa: 40 Years after Independence*, essays in honour of Mwalimu Julius K. Nyerere on the occasion of his 75th birthday (Dar es Salaam: University of Dar es Salaam Institute of Development Studies and Brussels: VUB University Press).

—— (2003) *Against Global Apartheid: South Africa Meets the World Bank, IMF and International Finance*, 2nd edn. (London: Zed Books).

Bundy, C. (1993) 'Development and Inequality in Historical Perspective', in R. Schrire (ed.) *Wealth or Poverty? Critical Choices for South Africa* (Oxford: Oxford University Press).

Desai, A. (2002) *We are the Poors* (New York: Monthly Review Press).

Drew, A. (1996) *South Africa's Radical Tradition: A Documentary History* (Cape Town: Bunchu Books).

Du Toit, A. (2004a) 'Why Poor People Stay Poor: The Challenge of Chronic Poverty', *New Agenda*, 16.

—— (2004b) '"Social Exclusion" Discourse and Chronic Poverty: A South African Case Study', *Development and Change*, 35/5.

—— (2005) 'Hungry in the Valley of Plenty', *Mail and Guardian*, 15 April.

Fine, B. and Rustomjee, Z. (1996) *The Political Economy of South Africa* (Johannesburg: University of Witwatersrand Press).

Hart, G. (2005) 'Beyond Neoliberalism? Post-Apartheid Developments in Historical and Comparative Perspective', in V. Padayachee (ed.) *The Development Decade? Social and Economic Change in South Africa 1994–2004* (Pretoria: HSRC Press).

IMF (2005) 'South Africa: Selected Issues', International Monetary Fund, Washington, (September).

Marx, K. (1967) *Capital*, i (New York: International Publishers).

Mbeki, T. (2003) 'Steps to End the Two Nations Divide', *ANC Today*, 3/33: 22 (August) <http://www.anc.org.za>.

Muller, M. (2004) 'Turning on the Taps', *Mail and Guardian*, 25 June.

NALEDI (2004) 'Global Poverty Network Workforce Development Study', National Labour and Economic Development Institute, Johannesburg (March).

Nattrass, N. (2003) 'The State of the Economy', in J. Daniel, A. Habib and R. Southall (eds) *State of the Nation: South Africa 2003–04* (Pretoria: HSRC Press).

Novack, G. (1970) 'The Permanent Revolution in Latin America: Hybrid Socioeconomic Formations and How to Dissect Them', *Intercontinental Press*, November 16.

O'Meara, D. (1996) *Forty Lost Years* (Indiana: Indiana University Press).

Orr, L. (2000) 'Globalising Poverty: The Gender Dimension to Job Losses, Casualisation and Poverty', paper prepared for COSATU Gender Conference, Johannesburg, National Labour and Economic Development Institute.

Perelman, M. (2000) *The Invention of Capitalism: Classical Political Economy and the Secret History of Primitive Accumulation* (Durham, N.C.: Duke University Press).

Smith, N. (1989) 'Uneven Development and Location Theory: Toward a Synthesis', in R. Peet and N. Thrift (eds) *New Models in Geography*, i (London: Unwin Hyman).

—— (1990) *Uneven Development* (Oxford: Basil Blackwell).

Statistics South Africa (2001) *South Africa in Transition* (Pretoria: Statistics South Africa).

—— (2002a) *Earning and Spending in South Africa* (Pretoria: Statistics South Africa).

—— (2002b) *The South African Labour Market* (Pretoria: Statistics South Africa).

—— (2003) *Labour Force Survey, September 2002* (Pretoria: Statistics South Africa).

Trotsky, L. (1977 [1930]) *The History of the Russian Revolution* (London: Pluto Press).

Turok, B. (2004) 'Overcoming Underdevelopment', *New Agenda*, 16/7.

UNDP (2003) *South Africa Human Development Report*, United Nations Development Programme.

Werlhof, C. von (2000) 'Globalisation and the Permanent Process of Primitive Accumulation: The Example of the MAI, the Multilateral Agreement on Investment', *Journal of World Systems Research*, 6/3.

Zarembka, P. (2000) 'Accumulation of Capital, Its Definition: A Century after Lenin and Luxemburg', in P. Zarembka (ed.) *Value, Capitalist Dynamics and Money: Research in Political Economy*, xviii (Stamford and Amsterdam: JAI/Elsevere).

—— (2002) 'Primitive Accumulation in Marxism, Historical or Trans-historical Separation from Means of Production?' *The Commoner* (March), <http://www.thecommoner.org>.

Contributors

Sam Ashman currently teaches political economy at the University of Birmingham and is a member of the editorial boards of *Historical Materialism* and *International Socialism*.

Colin Barker retired in 2002 after 35 years teaching in the Sociology Department at Manchester Metropolitan University. A long-time member of the Socialist Workers Party, he has written on incomes policy, state theory, Solidarity in Poland, social movements and revolution.

Daniel Bensaïd was born in 1946 in Toulouse. A former student of l'Ecole normale supérieure, he is professor of Philosophy at the University Paris 8 de Saint-Denis. He is editor of *ContreTemps*. His books include *Marx for Our Time* (Verso, 2002) and most recently *Une lente impatience* (Stock, 2004) and *Fragments mécréants* (Lignes-Léo Scheer, 2005).

Paul Blackledge is the author of *Reflections on the Marxist Theory of History* (Manchester University Press, 2006), *Perry Anderson, Marxism and the New Left* (Merlin Press, 2004), and co-editor of *Alasdair MacIntyre's Engagement with Marxism* (Brill, 2006), and *Historical Materialism and Social Evolution* (Palgrave, 2002). He teaches politics at Leeds Metropolitan University, and is an editor of the journal *Historical Materialism*.

Patrick Bond is a political economist, currently professor at University of KwaZulu Natal School of Development Studies. He has pursued longstanding research interests and NGO work in urban communities and with global justice movements in several countries. He is author of numerous books including *Elite Transition: From Apartheid to Neoliberalism in South Africa* (Pluto Press, 2000) and *Talk Left, Walk Right: South Africa's Frustrated Global Reforms* (Merlin Press, 2004).

Alejandro Colás teaches international relations at the School of Politics and Sociology, Birkbeck College. He is author of *International Civil Society and Social Movements* (Polity, 2002) and editor with Richard Saull of *The War on Terrorism and American 'Empire' After the End of the Cold War* (Routledge, 2005).

Neil Davidson works as a civil servant. He is secretary of the Edinburgh Central Branch of the Public and Commercial Services Union and chair of Livingston Branch of the Scottish Socialist Party. Neil is a visiting fellow of the Department of Sociology and Geography at the University of Strathclyde and a member of the Editorial Board of *International Socialism*. He is the author of two books, *The Origins of Scottish Nationhood* (Pluto Press, 2000) and *Discovering the Scottish Revolution, 1692–1746* (Pluto Press, 2003), for which he was awarded the Isaac and Tamara Deutscher Memorial Prize. Most recently, he has edited *Alasdair MacIntyre's Engagement with Marxism: Essays and Articles, 1953–1974* (Brill, 2006).

Ashwin Desai works as a researcher at the Centre for Civil Society at the University of KwaZulu Natal and as a journalist and lecturer. He is also a community activist. His books include *We are the Poors* (Monthly Review Press, 2002) and *South Africa: Still Revolting* (Impact Africa Publishing, 2000).

Bill Dunn teaches international studies at the University of Sydney. He is the author of *Global Restructuring and the Power of Labour* (Palgrave, 2004).

Michael Hanagan teaches history at Vassar College in Poughkeepsie, New York. He is the author of several books on labour history and has also co-edited a number of books, most recently, *Expanding Rights, Reconfiguring States* (Rowman & Littlefield, 1999) and *Challenging Authority: The Historical Study of Contentious Politics* (University of Minnesota Press, 1998). He is currently collaborating on a world history textbook and on a comparative study of the welfare state in England, France and the United States.

Andrew Herod is Professor of Geography and Adjunct Professor of International Affairs at the University of Georgia, Athens, Ga., USA. He is author of *Labor Geographies: Workers and the Landscapes of Capitalism* (Guilford, 2001), editor of *Organizing the Landscape: Geographical Perspectives on Labor Unionism* (University of Minnesota Press, 1998) and co-editor of *Geographies of Power: Placing Scale* (Blackwell, 2002) and *An Unruly World? Globalization, Governance and Geography* (Routledge, 1998). He writes frequently on issues of labour and globalisation.

Michael Löwy was born in Brazil in 1938 and has lived in Paris since 1969. He is emeritus research director at the CNRS (National Centre for Scientific Research). His most recent book in English is *The Theory of Revolution in the Young Marx* (Brill, 2003; published in the United States by Haymarket Books).

Kamran Matin is a D.Phil. candidate in international relations at the University of Sussex, UK. His doctoral thesis is on the Iranian revolution of 1979. His research interests include theories of revolution, Marxist theories of international relations and Islamic politics.

Hugo Radice is senior lecturer in international political economy and head of the School of Politics and International Studies at the University of Leeds. His principal research interests are in international and comparative political economy, transnational corporations and foreign investment, East-Central Europe, Marxism and management of organisations.

Neil Smith teaches at the Graduate Center of the City University of New York where he also directs the Center for Place, Culture and Politics. Among his books are *Uneven Development: Nature, Capital and the Production of Space* (Blackwell, 1984) and most recently *The Endgame of Globalization* (Routledge, 2005). His book *American Empire: Roosevelt's Geographer and the Prelude to Globalization* (University of California Press, 2003) won the Los Angeles Times Book Prize for biography. He works on the broad connections between space, politics, social theory and history.

Hillel Ticktin is emeritus professor of Marxist studies at the University of Glasgow, editor of *Critique, Journal of Socialist Theory* and has written on Trotsky, Marxist political economy and the nature of the former USSR and its successors.

Suzi Weissman is professor and chair of politics at Saint Mary's College of California. She is an award-winning broadcast journalist and sits on the editorial boards of *Critique* and *Against the Current*. She is the author of *Victor Serge: The Course is Set on Hope* (Verso, 2001) and edited *Victor Serge: Russia Twenty Years After* (Humanities, 1996) and *The Ideas of Victor Serge* (Merlin Press, 1997), as well as many articles on the Soviet Union and Russia. Her emphasis is on working-class and left dissent. She is on the (US) National Workers' Rights Board, which is composed of 50–75 national leaders who intervene with employers and the public to help resolve situations that threaten workers' rights.

Index

Compiled by Sue Carlton

Printed and bound by CPI Group (UK) Ltd, Croydon, CR0 4YY

04/11/2024

14585933-0003